MULTILATERAL REGULATION OF INVESTMENT

# MULTILATERAL REGULATION OF INVESTMENT

*Edited by*

E.C. Nieuwenhuys
and
M.M.T.A. Brus

*with contributions from:*

M.M.T.A. Brus
E.V.K. FitzGerald
Chen Huiping
M. Koulen
P. Malanczuk
E.C. Nieuwenhuys
N.J. Schrijver
M.W. Sikkel
S. Zia-Zarifi

KLUWER LAW INTERNATIONAL
THE HAGUE / LONDON / BOSTON

A C.I.P. Catalogue record for this book is available from the Library of Congress

ISBN 90-411-9844-X

Published by Kluwer Law International,
P.O. Box 85889, 2508 CN The Hague, The Netherlands.

Sold and distributed in North, Central and South America
by Kluwer Law International,
101 Philip Drive, Norwell, MA 02061, U.S.A.
kluwerlaw@wkap.com

In all other countries, sold and distributed
by Kluwer Law International, Distribution Centre,
P.O. Box 322, 3300 AH Dordrecht, The Netherlands.

Lay-out: Anne-Marie Krens, Tekstbeeld – Oegstgeest

*Printed on acid-free paper*

All Rights Reserved
© 2001 E.M. Meijers Institute and Kluwer Law International
Kluwer Law International incorporates the publishing programmes of
Graham & Trotman Ltd, Kluwer Law and Taxation Publishers,
and Martinus Nijhoff Publishers.

No part of the material protected by this copyright notice may be reproduced or
utilized in any form or by any means, electronic or mechanical,
including photocopying, recording or by any information storage and
retrieval system, without written permission from the copyright owner.

Printed in the Netherlands.

# Contents

PREFACE
*C.J.J.M. Stolker* ............................................................................ VII

1 Multilateral Regulation of Investment. Legal, Political and
   Economic Aspects
   *E.C. Nieuwenhuys & M.M.T.A. Brus* ............................................. 1

2 A Multilateral Investment Agreement from a North-South
   Perspective
   *N.J. Schrijver* ............................................................................ 17

3 Developing Countries and Multilateral Investment Negotiations
   *E.V.K. FitzGerald* ...................................................................... 35

4 Comments on the MAI's General Principles for the Treatment of
   Foreign Investors and Their Investments. A Chinese Scholar's
   Perspective
   *Chen Huiping* ............................................................................ 67

5 A Liberal Multilateral Investment System, Transnational Enterprises,
   Home and Host Countries. Some Observations
   *E.C. Nieuwenhuys* ...................................................................... 89

6 Protection Without Protectionism. Linking a Multilateral
   Investment Treaty and Human Rights
   *S. Zia-Zarifi* ............................................................................ 101

7 State-to-State and Investor-to-State Dispute Settlement in the
   OECD Draft Multilateral Investment Agreement
   *P. Malanczuk* .......................................................................... 137

8 How to Establish a Multilateral Framework for Investment?
   *M.W. Sikkel* ............................................................................ 161

9 Foreign Investment in the WTO
   *M. Koulen* .............................................................................. 181

| | |
|---|---|
| APPENDIX: THE MAI NEGOTIATING TEXT (EXCERPTS) | 205 |
| ABOUT THE AUTHORS | 235 |
| INDEX | 239 |

# Preface

The Faculty of Law of Leiden University has a long-standing tradition of research in the field of public international law. Following this tradition, in April 1999 the E.M. Meijers Institute of Legal Studies, the research centre of the Faculty of Law, organized a one-day symposium on the OECD attempt to conclude a Multilateral Agreement on Investment (MAI).

Authors in various disciplines, academics as well as practitioners, have examined important questions related to the efforts to formulate a general convention on multilateral investment. The OECD draft Agreement formed the starting point for their analysis. However, as it had become clear in 1999 that the OECD attempt had failed, the scope expanded to include general aspects of a global regulatory framework on investment. The presentations in the symposium constitute the basis for the articles in this volume. Most authors and participants in the discussion supported the idea that a multilateral agreement in this area is needed. Consensus about the contents of such agreement among the various groups of states would, however, require intense further negotiations. In particular the position of developing countries would deserve much more attention.

Authors in this volume include academics working within the context of a collaborative framework established by several law faculties in the Netherlands under the title *Global Governance and the Rule of Law in International Society.* Currently the Erasmus University Rotterdam, the University of Amsterdam, the Free University of Amsterdam, the University of Groningen and Leiden University participate in this framework, which is sponsored by the Netherlands Organization for Scientific Research (NWO).

We take pleasure in introducing this volume as it contributes to our aim of enhancing inter-faculty cooperation in legal research and, more importantly, as it will make a valuable contribution to the international debate on a multilateral investment agreement.

*C.J.J.M. Stolker*
E.M. Meijers Institute of Legal Studies, Director

# 1 | Multilateral Regulation of Investment Legal, Political and Economic Aspects

E.C. Nieuwenhuys & M.M.T.A. Brus[*]

1   INTRODUCTION

The world order is changing rapidly. The collapse of the centrally planned economies in Eastern Europe and the former USSR has led to the incorporation of almost all national economies into the world economy. It seems that a liberal world market is emerging with relatively few restrictions resting on its participants. International economic cooperation has increased, financial markets are being deregulated, trade barriers reduced and international capital flows liberalized. This economic globalization has led to considerable economic growth at the macroeconomic level, but not yet to real social development. The many plans as developed, for instance, at the Copenhagen summit of 1995 on worldwide social development have not been implemented in practice.[1] The Human Development Report 2000 of the UN Development Programme (UNDP) contains a wealth of statistical material indicating that despite economic growth the gap between rich and poor, both within and between countries, has increased.[2] More people live in absolute poverty; a large part of the world population is still deprived of work, labour standards, education, health and basic standard of living.

There is much debate on the social aspects of the global economy; on globalization with a human face. Particular attention in this debate is devoted to the role of transnational enterprises, as they have become prominent actors on the international scene alongside states and international governmental organizations. The traditional power of states to protect and realize social and economic rights has diminished as a result of globalization, deregulation and privatization; the economic power and influence of transnational enterprises has substantially increased.[3] The investments made by these enterprises can enrich the social and economic development of many countries and contribute to the improvement of the quality of life of people everywhere. However, it

---

- Eva Nieuwenhuys is Lecturer, Faculty of Law, Department of Metajuridica, Leiden University; Marcel Brus is Senior Lecturer in public international law, Faculty of Law, Department of Public International Law, Leiden University.
1   Copenhagen Declaration of the World Summit on Social Development, UN Doc. A/Conf.166/9, 19 April 1995.
2   UNDP, *Human Development Report* (2000).
3   M. Sassoli, 'The impact of Globalisation on Human Rights', *ICJ Review* 1999 no. 61, pp. 67-82.

seems that without a clear global agreement on the conditions of investing, in particular in developing countries, it is difficult to find a fair balance between the interests of the investors on the one hand, and of the states and the people of the states, in which these investments are made, on the other. Widely diverging views exist about the need and possible contents of a global agreement on the conditions of investment, and international agreement among states on such conditions of investment is still far off. So far, conditions on investment are the subject of a wide array of national legislation, bilateral, regional, sectoral and multilateral rules, and non-binding international, sectoral, national or corporate codes of conduct. There is no comprehensive global convention or international organization in the field of investment that can be compared with, for example, the World Trade Organization (WTO) or the International Monetary Fund (IMF). Nevertheless, developing standards for international investment is a subject of discussion in many international social and economic fora.

For instance, the UNDP argues in its 1999 Human Development Report that international investment should not only stimulate economic growth but also play a role in improving respect for human rights, the environment and sustainable development.[4] From this point of view, transnational enterprises have a social responsibility next to their profit-making responsibilities and should be subjected to a binding international code of conduct.[5] Within the WTO opinions differ. On the one hand it is argued that conditions of investment should only be discussed in the context of possible implications for international trade, whereas on the other hand it is argued that the WTO should discuss investment in the wider context of sustainable development. Within UNCTAD there are pleas for a strong international regulatory framework for trade and investment in order to achieve economic growth and development. Within the Organization for Economic Cooperation and Development (OECD) an attempt was undertaken to negotiate a Multilateral Agreement on Investment (MAI). Negotiations on this Agreement started in 1995 but were unsuccessfully terminated in 1998.[6] The objective of the negotiations was to create an international investment agreement that would liberalize and protect investment and investors and thereby stimulate international investment and international economic growth.

At the time the negotiations in the OECD reached the point that it was expected they would be concluded by the end of 1998, the editors of this book decided to organize on 1 April 1999 a one-day symposium devoted to the pros

---

4 See, e.g., A. Sen, *Development as Freedom* (1999), stating that respect for human rights is not a result of economic development, but a condition for it.
5 Many transnational enterprises have adopted non-binding corporate codes of conduct, but these are regarded by many as inadequate and incapable of replacing legislation. See, e.g., B. Barber, *Jihad versus Mc World* (1996).
6 Draft text available at <www.oecd.org/daf/investment/fdi/mai/negtext.htm>.

and cons of the MAI. Some serious doubts had been raised about the assumptions underlying the MAI and the contents of the proposed rules, as well as the one-sidedness of the forum of rich industrialized states in which the negotiations took place. The fact that the negotiations were terminated in 1998 led to a somewhat different focus of the symposium. Rather than discussing the MAI itself, the objective became discussing relevant questions related to the development of a multilateral instrument on investment and lessons that could be learned from the attempt undertaken by the OECD. Most of the contributors to this volume presented a paper on a particular aspect of the debate; these papers formed the basis of the articles as presented here. The articles by Chen and Nieuwenhuys were added at a later stage.

There are many questions that have to be answered in the context of multilateral regulation of international investment. The objective of this book is to investigate under what conditions an international investment agreement could make a positive contribution towards the aims and needs of both the investor and of the economies in which the investments are made. Many questions need to be answered before conclusions can be drawn, if at all. Which forum is most appropriate for negotiations on such an agreement? Who should be involved? Is a multilateral agreement desirable, or would it be better to continue on the basis of the current system of national, bilateral and regional regulation? How are investment and trade linked? Is it desirable that international trade be restricted in order to protect investments that stimulate sustainable development? Should an investment agreement focus on economic growth or on the redistribution of capital, knowledge, decision-making power, growth and employment? What should be its scope: should it aim primarily at the treatment of transnational enterprises, or should it, for instance, also cover the protection of human rights and the environment? How should one define investment? Does it only cover direct investment or portfolio investment as well? Should developing countries be protected, and if so, how? Is a uniform liberal approach or a flexible and differentiated approach to be preferred? How should disputes be settled and which rights should be protected in such dispute settlement mechanism?

The above are some of the questions, which are discussed by the contributors. The editors have invited scholars and practitioners with a background in international law, politics and economics to provide different perspectives on the desirability and contents of multilateral regulation of international investment. Although they may differ on many points, they are more or less in agreement about the fact that we should not be disappointed that the OECD MAI project was abandoned. A multilateral regulation of investment will have to be acceptable to large sections of the world community before it can become successful. This was clearly not the case with the OECD project. However, they vary in opinion on what would be the best way to improve on the work on the MAI and what the chances are of reaching agreement on a multilateral agreement on investment in the foreseeable future.

## 2   OUTLINE OF THIS BOOK

One of the fundamental questions in the debate on multilateral regulation of investment is how to find a balance between the needs and interests of developing countries and those of the wealthy industrialized states and their investors, as well as between their respective responsibilities. The flow of foreign investment between industrialized states has not been very contentious in past decades; most of the questions concerning foreign investment were related to the treatment and protection of investments made in developing countries. In this latter context it can be observed that the perceptions on the role of foreign direct investment in promoting the economic and social progress of developing countries have varied considerably in the post-1945 period, and as a consequence, so have international attempts to arrive at international regulation of foreign investment. *Schrijver* in Chapter 2 provides an overview and assessment of these attempts from an international law perspective, against the background of the international investment climate that varied from very friendly to very hostile and shifted from belief in the role of foreign direct investment to suspicion as to the role of multinational enterprises and their impact on the policies of national states. As a result of this, attempts remained unsuccessful, except in some limited fields, such as procedures for international settlement of investment disputes (ICSID) and multilateral investment guarantee (MIGA) facilities.

Absent agreement on a comprehensive multilateral investment protection convention, bilateral investment treaties (BITs) came to serve as a major vehicle for the protection of foreign investment interests. Next to these BITs, some multilateral investment treaties (MITs) on a regional and interregional level have been concluded. All these treaties cover only a few aspects of investment regulation, however. They mainly deal with investment promotion and protection and dispute settlement and contain mainly rules for state behaviour. From Schrijver's analysis it becomes clear that these BITs and MITs are too one-sided in their focus on state behaviour to serve the purpose of providing a regulatory framework for international investment. The responsibilities of the foreign investors are disregarded, as is the increasingly important role of international institutions such as the ILO, OECD, UN, NAFTA or EU.

In view of the limitations of the available instruments and in view of the interests at stake, there can be little doubt that it would be relevant to include the main rules of modern international investment law in a global multilateral investment convention. Inspiration and building blocks for such a convention could be found in, for example, the 1972 Guidelines for International Investment from the International Chamber of Commerce (ICC), the principles and rules of international investment law reflected in bilateral and multilateral investment treaties, the arbitral awards of various tribunals and soft law instruments such as the UN resolutions on permanent sovereignty, the Draft UN Code of Conduct on Transnational Enterprises and the 1992 World Bank

Guidelines on the Treatment of Foreign Investment. Ideally, a global multilateral investment convention should address in a balanced manner the rights, duties and responsibilities of the three key parties concerned: foreign investor, host state and home state. It should pursue an integrated approach in which foreign property rights are protected and foreign investors are accorded fair and equitable treatment. At the same time economic and social development should be promoted, the environment protected and respect for other universal values, including respect for core labour standards and human rights, promoted. The special needs and interests of developing countries should be recognized and addressed, as should their right to determine their own social and economic policies.

The MAI did not meet the above-mentioned standards and Schrijver gives a number of reasons why we should not shed tears over the failure of the MAI. On the other hand, he warns against using the MAI as the scapegoat of globalization and against according too much weight to the often equally one-sided opinions of NGOs. Any attempt towards a multilateral investment convention that does not balance rights and duties of foreign investors and of host states and home states is bound to fail.

This introduction to the international legal aspects of the development of an international regulatory framework for investment, in which particular attention is given to North-South issues, is followed by an article that focuses on these issues from a perspective of development economics. *FitzGerald* in Chapter 3 discusses the questions and dilemmas that are related to the economic position of developing countries. There is no doubt that a multilateral framework for investment can be of great advantage to developing countries, in particular to the smaller, more vulnerable countries, which are not in a strong negotiating position. Developing countries are highly dependent on foreign investment to provide them with technology and management as well as financial resources; however, domestic investment and expatriate investment (return of resources that left due to capital flight) are of importance as well. It is in the interest of developing countries to establish a favourable climate for investment and to adjust their economies to the discipline of world markets. Accession to an international regulatory framework would encourage the development of domestic law, institutions and regulation and thereby boost the confidence of foreign, domestic and expatriate investors; it would increase transparency about which international standards apply from which a state cannot easily withdraw.

However, FitzGerald clearly indicates that an international investment framework should take the specific circumstances of developing countries into account, and, within this group, the differences between groups of countries, such as between small and large, low-income and middle-income countries and the corresponding negotiation asymmetries. Beyond the core requirements in an international regulatory framework, in particular asset protection, national treatment, and dispute settlement, the framework should allow for exceptions to developing countries to the minimum extent necessary for realizing their development objectives. Restrictions on foreign investment, for example, through performance requirements, should be limited and be made consistent with the core obligations of the international regulatory framework. FitzGerald discusses labour and environmental standards and the management of capital flows; issues in which the particular situation of developing countries should be taken into account. Suggestions are made on how to deal with this in a multilateral investment agreement.

From his analysis it becomes clear that, other than was the case with the MAI, the position of developing countries and the possible exceptions from the general standards laid down in a future agreement, will have to be addressed in closer detail. Henceforth, more negotiations will have to be held, in which the developing countries will be able to participate fully. The issue in this debate is not the lowering of international standards to accommodate the interests of developing countries, but the raising of domestic standards. This debate is complicated by the fact that there is no symmetry in negotiating positions. Negotiations cannot be conducted on the basis of reciprocity. FitzGerald explores how reciprocal concessions might be made to developing countries in exchange for market access by foreign investors from developed countries. A logical form of reciprocity in international investment negotiations would be for industrial countries to ensure that profits taxes are levied on and paid by international firms in such a way, that the developing countries where they operate can obtain a fair share of the return on investment in the form of fiscal revenue and invest this in wider development objectives. In addition, international agreement could prevent the damaging competition between host countries on tax incentives. However, the likelihood of an agreement being reached on a comprehensive system of multilateral tax administration is low. The resolution of double taxation problems will require a major effort from aid donors. Developing countries need help to strengthen their own administrative systems in order to make double taxation arrangements work. This help includes not only technical assistance and material resources to enhance their own tax administrations, but also the sharing of information and above all the willingness to sign double taxation agreements with developing countries.

Whereas FitzGerald develops his argument on the basis of acceptance of some core obligations into a multilateral regulatory framework for investment as indicated above, *Chen* in Chapter 4 focuses on the contents of some of these core obligations as incorporated in the draft MAI and their consequences for developing countries. She argues that the standard of treatment of foreign investors and their investments provided for in the draft MAI is the highest standard so far among existing international frameworks for foreign investment, and that it represents the treatment of foreign investors and their investments, which is preferred by developed countries. For developing countries, however, this standard of treatment will prejudice their state sovereignty and will have a negative impact on their national economic development.

In the first part she discusses broad and narrow definitions of the general standards of treatment: national treatment, most-favoured-nation treatment and non-discriminatory treatment. This is followed by an analysis of the implications of these standards as included in the draft MAI, as compared to the wording of these standards in other international investment agreements. She gives ten reasons why the MAI sets standards that are too high to be acceptable to developing countries. The fact that very high standards were to be set would have required the draft MAI to allow various exceptions and restrictions to these standards. However, compared to the exceptions and restrictions in other international investment agreements, their scope is more limited.

Chen continues by analyzing the impact of the standards of national treatment and most-favoured-nation treatment on liberalization of international investment. She argues strongly against the proposed standards, as they would lead to a degree of international investment liberalization that would not be acceptable to developing countries. It would require them to almost completely open up their economies to foreign investors and refrain from protecting their national economy and national investors and from adopting national laws and policies on foreign investment. These points are illustrated in the final part of the article where the rather restrictive foreign investment policies of China are discussed.

It is interesting to compare the approach of FitzGerald to the one taken by Chen. She clearly reflects the opinion of a scholar from a large developing country (China) that is to a lesser degree dependent on foreign investment for its economic development and that has the bargaining power to pose restrictions on foreign investment, and challenges the general principles of treatment of foreign investment as incorporated in the MAI. FitzGerald accepts the standards of national treatment and most-favoured-nation treatment, although not necessarily in the interpretation and form given to them in the draft MAI, as a precondition for establishing a favourable investment climate, in particular in the more vulnerable developing countries. He tries to find methods to strengthen the domestic economies by suggesting exceptions that take into account the unequal positions of the states involved. Where Chen is concerned about the loss of economic sovereignty, FitzGerald states that the loss of sovereignty is not the relevant issue, but whether the economic gains exceed the economic values of the policies precluded by acceding to a multilateral investment agreement.

Like Chen, *Nieuwenhuys* in Chapter 5 takes a very critical position towards the MAI and the values that it represents. She argues that upgrading the prosperity of the host countries would require a more flexible instrument.

The draft MAI was property-protection oriented and incorporated general principles of treatment that would grant transnational enterprises entry to as many sectors as possible in as many countries as possible, subject to the least possible number of conditions. The concept of investment was broadly defined to include portfolio investments and direct investments in the form of foreign capital or in the form of tangible and intangible assets. The liberal provisions on admission and establishment would have given transnational enterprises the right to be admitted to countries without prior approval by a public body authorized to grant such approval. The transnational enterprises would have been given the right to invest in all sectors of the economy, whether or not in the form of a legal person established in accordance with the law of the host country. According to the principle of equitable and non-discriminatory treatment, transnational enterprises would be entitled to be treated the same as national enterprises and to be treated the same as enterprises from the most-favoured nations. Furthermore, in terms of the principle of non-discrimination and of freedom from performance requirements, the entry of a transnational enterprise could not be made dependent on meeting special requirements. The draft MAI did not contain binding social clauses or clauses on environmental protection. Transnational enterprises would be mostly given rights, whereas the host states would have to subject themselves to deregulation and privatization. In her view it is obvious that the MAI would have been mainly in the interests of transnational enterprises.

A multilateral regulatory framework for investment based on these premises would deprive the middle and low-income countries of the possibilities of protecting their emerging economies from the adverse effects of too rapid an entry into the international market. It would furthermore deprive them of the opportunity of utilizing the investments of transnational enterprises to increase their production capacity and their access to the global market. Her conclusions in this respect are in line with Chen's conclusions. Nieuwenhuys suggests that a flexible instrument would be needed, allowing temporary closure of certain sectors to foreign investment and performance requirements on foreign investment in order to ensure a positive contribution to socio-economic development of the host state.

So far the contributors to this volume focused on general features of a multilateral regulatory framework of investment. Two more closely defined topics are dealt with in Chapters 6 and 7. These are the linkage of such a framework to the protection of human rights and the mechanisms for dispute settlement. The first topic has attracted much attention in the public debate on the MAI and on investment in developing countries in general, as has for example the debate on the incorporation of minimum environmental safeguards. The latter aspect, however, is not discussed in this book, although the article by Zia Zarifi on the issue of human rights could serve as a useful background for considering the environmental issues involved.

In Chapter 6 *Zia-Zarifi* explores if and how far an investment agreement should incorporate clauses on human rights. His point of departure is the view that the basic point of economic policy as well as of promoting respect for human rights is to form a better society. This means that both economic policy and human rights are significant to the polity, and one set of concerns does not inherently preempt the other. However, to be able to address human rights issues in a predominantly economic context, or economic issues in a human rights context, it is necessary to link these fields explicitly. If a given measure is called for, it has to be clear whether human rights bodies or trade bodies should interpret if this measure is based on international human rights obligations or on hidden protectionism. Furthermore, it has to be clear which human rights intersect most strongly with economic policies and should be the subject of linkage. Zia-Zarifi identifies three categories of rights and acts that are the most likely candidates for linkage: social rights, labour rights and internationally recognized prohibited acts (such as war crimes, genocide and torture).

In order to analyze the broad topic of linking investment to human rights, Zia-Zarifi adopts a schematic approach which divides the reasons for (not) linking investment and human rights into four categories: conceptual, instrumental, political and institutional reasons. All four categories are addressed separately. At the conceptual level, he concludes that explicit incorporation of human rights concerns in an investment treaty would further clarify and support the argument that international investment is beneficial to the world population. At the instrumental level it is argued that an international investment agreement that incorporates human rights in a positive manner and avoids prohibiting affirmative action on, for instance, historically discriminatory employment practices, would be in line with the OECD's aims to encourage social progress. The desire of states to attract foreign investment could be made instrumental in addressing their human rights obligations. At the political level the issue is how democratic governments can attract sufficient political support for subscribing to an international investment agreement. They have to reconcile the interests of various kinds of interest groups, such as trade unions, human rights or environmental NGOs, and the business community. The failure to attract sufficient domestic support for the MAI, as analyzed in more detail in Chapter 8 by Sikkel, was a major reason for the termination of negotiations in 1998. In Zia-Zarifi's view, any willingness on the side of the international business community to accept greater social responsibilities would reflect their degree of political maturity. Finally, at the institutional level it is argued that strong economic institutions like the WTO, IMF and World Bank should play a role in promoting human rights and social and environmental values, and that they should adopt an attitude that would allow the inclusion of these issues in their work. Although there will be much opposition from NGOs that do not have faith in these institutions, as well as from the economists that dominate them, it would, in Zia-Zarifi's view, not be a sign of weakness, but rather of strength and a confirmation of their dominant role in today's world.

In the final part of his article, the four categories or levels of analysis are used to show in more detail how a multilateral investment agreement and human rights can be linked. Firstly, the objective of and commitment to protection and promotion of human rights should be clearly indicated in the agreement and should also realistically address the asymmetries between countries in their abilities to meet these objectives. Secondly, the substantive provisions in a multilateral investment agreement must reflect this general objective and commitment. This will require a clear understanding of the scope of such an agreement. The definitions of investment and expropriation are of great importance in this respect, as well as the provisions on non-discrimination and on settlement of disputes. What should be avoided is, that the provisions on these issues would unduly restrict the development and implementation of human rights policies, or lead to a race to the bottom in the competition for foreign investment. Thirdly, the political aspects of building support for an investment agreement are discussed. Transparency with regard to proposals and discussion, including, for instance, meetings with human rights NGOs and academics, may help to avoid the mistakes made by the OECD on the MAI. Fourthly, it is important to provide for institutional structures and expertise in human rights matters, for example, in collaboration with the ECOSOC or the ILO, within a multilateral investment framework. To create an internal watchdog mechanism seems of crucial importance; the World Bank's Inspection Panel can be regarded as an example. Zia-Zarifi admits that linking human rights and international investment would complicate international negotiations on a future multilateral agreement. However, negotiations that do not incorporate these genuine concerns would most probably lead to failure.

NGOs made human rights and social and environmental issues into focal points in their criticism of the draft MAI. Surprisingly, they also focused on the dispute settlement paragraphs in the draft MAI and claimed that foreign investors would be given special privileges to challenge host states, and that, following the outcome of the Ethyl Case under NAFTA,[7] governments would be curtailed in their power to adopt legislation in the public interest. In Chapter 7 *Malanczuk* describes the dispute settlement procedures as proposed in the draft MAI and compares them to the provisions and practices under bilateral and international investment agreements. The dispute settlement provisions provide for state-to-state procedures as well as investor-to-state procedures. This approach is well known from earlier agreements and reflects, from a technical point of view, the general trend in these agreements. The main difference is that the scope of the draft MAI is much broader than that of existing agreements. The broad definition of investors and investment, the unqualified right of entry, the obligation on host states to provide for transparency with regard to laws, regulations and decisions, and the restrictions on performance requirements are all examples that were already discussed in the preceding Chapters. This means that although the dispute settlement procedures may be more or less similar to established practice, this would not be the case for the scope of application. Malanczuk therefore concludes

---

7   This case is referred to by Zia Zarifi, Malanczuk and Sikkel in their articles.

that the criticism of the dispute settlement provisions in the MAI as such was to a large extent based on misunderstandings. Finally, he points to the fact that if further negotiations on a multilateral investment agreement would be conducted within the WTO, it would require a thorough discussion on the role of the home state in the settlement of disputes, as the WTO does not allow for non-state actor involvement. Currently, the state-to-state dispute settlement mechanisms are too dependent on diplomatic and political considerations to be regarded as mechanisms that would provide sufficient guarantees to foreign investors.

Was the failure of the MAI due to clashing ideologies or was it the result of structural weaknesses built into the negotiation process? In Chapter 8 *Sikkel* analyzes reasons that have led to its failure. Of course, the existence of an ideological aspect cannot be denied. The opposition of many NGOs reflects the resistance against the ideologies of liberalization of the global economy and the role of multilateral enterprises therein. On the other hand, there were also many problems at the political level that weakened the support from some of the most important governments, notably France and the United States; criticism from NGOs as well as from the business community made the MAI into a politically unattractive issue in domestic politics. Based on his analysis of the reasons for the MAI's failure, Sikkel suggests some lessons that can be learned from this and how they can be taken into account in future negotiations.

Sikkel recalls how the negotiations started and how they were conducted during the first few years. A 1991 OECD decision to study the advantages and feasibility of a so-called 'wider investment instrument', was followed by six years of study and technical negotiations, which showed remarkable progress but went almost unnoticed. However, in early 1996 local groups in Canada and the United States, who had been active in the debate about NAFTA, began to take note of the MAI negotiations, which was soon followed by an international NGO campaign against the MAI. In little over a year the character of the negotiations changed from technical and unnoticed by the outside world to highly visible and politicized. A direct dialogue between NGOs and the MAI Negotiating Group became inevitable, particularly when on 27 October 1997 the NGOs, representing a wide range of interests and a varied intensity of opposition to the MAI, managed to agree on a joint position. The Chairman of the Negotiating Group in March made a final attempt to bridge the gap by proposing packages of compromise texts, including provisions on labour and environment, but he did not succeed. The Europeans saw too many NAFTA-inspired texts, and the Americans were against making the 'not-lowering-standards clause' binding. In addition, as a result of including, for instance, provisions on labour and the environment, and the proposal to annex (and update) the Guidelines for Multinational Enterprises to the MAI, the business community, mostly in the United States, started to change its perception of the MAI. It changed from something that, at least in theory and perhaps in the longer term also in practice, would be of value to them into something that in the short term would be more of a liability. The resulting erosion of support for the MAI was certainly noted by politicians. On 14 October 1998 Prime Minister Jospin announced that France had decided to withdraw from the negotiations, leaving the other negotiators no other option but to end the negotiations.

The lesson that can be learned from the failure of the MAI is that any organization interested in globalization in general and in investment rules in particular should take the concerns of different groups very seriously if it hopes to have those rules approved by parliaments and supported by society in general. Since different concerns have to be addressed, expertise has to be drawn from different quarters. Both at the national and at the international level experts in the field of investment and finance, development, environment, labour standards, human rights and any other field considered relevant by interested groups should be consulted. Not only government experts but also academics and NGOs could provide valuable input.[8] In the national administrations all interested ministries or departments should be involved in the development of national positions. At the international level the involvement of both developing and developed countries must be ensured. NGOs have become important players and transparency in international negotiations is a must. To establish a future multilateral framework on investment, a start could be to undertake a new feasibility study. However, unlike in 1991, that study should not only address technical issues but also the politically sensitive issues, such as the relationship between investment protection and the right to regulate, the relationship between investment and labour standards and protection of the environment, the position of developing countries and the balance of rights and duties of investors. Whether a new feasibility study, as suggested by Sikkel, would be needed can be questioned. Much work has already been done. The work of the WTO Working Group on the Relationship of Trade and Investment, as discussed in the next Chapter, is a point in case.

None of the contributors suggest that the international debate on multilateral regulation of investment should be abandoned. On the contrary, most suggest that such regulation would be useful, but they are not very optimistic about the chances of success in the near future. One important question, if negotiations would be resumed, is what would constitute the proper forum for this. To provide at least a partial answer, *Koulen* in Chapter 9 discusses the WTO as a possible forum. The WTO has become the leading forum in international trade matters and already deals with questions of investment regulations in so far as they are relevant to the international trade regime. Some international agreements that include investment-related issues are Annexed to the WTO Agreement; for example, the General Agreement on Trade in

---

8   On the influence of NGOs on international economic institutions see, e.g., R. O'Brien, A. Goetz, J. Scholte and M. Williams, *Contesting Global Governance* (2000).

Services (GATS), the Agreement on Trade Related Aspects of Intellectual Property Rights (TRIPS) and the Agreement on Trade Related Investment Measures (TRIMS).

Besides discussing these existing arrangements, Koulen deals with the establishment and work of the WTO Working Group on the Relationship of Trade and Investment. It will not come as a surprise that within the WTO a variety of opinions exist with regard to the desirability of the development of multilateral rules on investment within the WTO. Proponents, for example, point at the increasing importance of foreign investment in the process of global economic integration and the growing complementarity of trade and investment, the changing geographic pattern of foreign direct investment flows, the increasing competition among governments to attract foreign investment, and the need to address foreign investment issues in a global forum in order to avoid a confrontation along North-South lines. Arguments advanced by opponents to discussions on investment in the WTO are that in comparison to the bilateral and regional investment agreements a multilateral instrument would reduce flexibility in regulating investment in accordance with national development priorities. Furthermore, in their view, there is no evidence that multilateral regulation would lead to an increase in foreign investment.

In the second half of 1999, interesting developments took place during the preparations for the third WTO Ministerial Meeting (Seattle, 30 November to 3 December 1999). Concrete proposals to launch negotiations on investment were submitted. These proposals were quite different from the failed MAI in the sense that the scope would be much more limited, for example by only including rules on foreign direct investment. They took account of the various concerns that had been raised in the WTO Working Group. Nevertheless, opposition against these negotiations remained strong as well, and included the United States. As the WTO Members could not reach agreement at the Seattle Ministerial Meeting, the debate remained inconclusive. However, the Working Group will continue its work, unaffected by the outcome of the Seattle meeting. Moreover, investment-related issues will remain on the agenda of the WTO as part of the further development of the GATS and the TRIMS Agreement.

Consensus within the WTO on regulation of investment is still far off. However, Koulen observes the quite remarkable fact that a substantial number of WTO Members at different levels of economic development have expressed support for starting negotiations on this topic. Many problems and controversies still have to be solved. Nevertheless, Koulen's observation that a WTO multilateral framework on investment will require more than the consolidation of provisions typically contained in bilateral and regional investment agreements - a point that is of course underlined by the failure of the MAI - is of importance.

3   CONCLUSION

A multilateral investment agreement could contribute to an increase in worldwide prosperity. However, the conditions under which foreign investments may be made must be suited to this end. Still, no agreement can be reached in international fora about the question what such suitable conditions for foreign investment are. The contributors to this volume also vary in opinion about what would be the best way to improve on the work of the MAI and under what circumstances a multilateral agreement on investment could be reached in the foreseeable future. They also have diverging views about the way in which a multilateral investment agreement should address the rights, duties and responsibilities of developing countries on the one hand, and of wealthy, industrialized states and their investors on the other. However, despite these diverging views, some conclusions may still be drawn.

Most of the authors think that the conclusion of a multilateral investment agreement would be desirable and that the international debate on multilateral regulation of investment should continue. Transparency with regard to this debate is required as well as dialogues with NGOs, academics and the business community, according to *Zia-Zarifi* and *Sikkel*. Furthermore, like most of the other authors, they think that developing countries should be involved in the negotiations. Negotiations should take place in a worldwide forum, but which forum is the most suitable is a question that remains unanswered, although *Malanczuk* and *Koulen* both enter into the pros and cons of the WTO as a forum for negotiations.

Most authors are likewise of the opinion that the special needs and interests of developing countries have been insufficiently recognized in the MAI. A future multilateral investment agreement should offer more protection to developing countries and allow these countries to make exceptions to the obligations arising from the agreement for the sake of their social and economic development. Again, however, opinions differ about the question to what extent exceptions should be allowed. *Schrijver* argues that developing countries have the right to determine their own social and economic policies. *Chen* and *Nieuwenhuys* also emphasize this point. *Chen* argues that the draft MAI provided a standard of treatment of foreign investors and their investments that was much too high and that developing countries must be allowed to apply various exceptions and restrictions to these standards. *Nieuwenhuys* argues that flexibility is required and that developing countries must be allowed to close off certain sectors to foreign investment and to set performance requirements for foreign investment. On the other hand, *FitzGerald* is of the opinion that the framework for investment should only allow for exceptions for developing countries to the minimum extent necessary for realizing their development objectives. He argues that it would be in the interest of developing countries to establish an investment-friendly climate. When developing countries commit themselves to treat investors fairly and equitably, this will enhance investors' confidence and attract foreign capital as well as domestic investment and expatriate investment. As opposed to *Chen*, he therefore does not object to a multilateral investment agreement obliging countries to extend national and most-favoured-nation treatment to foreign investors, as long as circumstances are the same.

That the MAI was too one-sided in scope is a conviction that is shared by a number of authors. *Schrijver, Nieuwenhuys* and *Zia-Zarifi* all stress that a future multilateral investment agreement should focus on state behaviour as well as on the responsibilities of foreign investors. Foreign property rights should be protected and foreign investors should be accorded fair and equitable treatment. At the same time, foreign investors have to protect the environment and respect core labour standards and human rights.

Finally, a number of authors also indicate that it would be preferable if a future investment agreement would define the concept of investment in such a way that it would only include direct investment and not, as was the case in the MAI, portfolio investment as well. As a point in case, *Malanczuk* points out that due to the broad definition of the concepts of investor and investment the MAI protected more rights under its dispute settlement procedure than do the provisions of other bilateral and international investment agreements.

# 2 | A Multilateral Investment Agreement from a North-South Perspective

*N.J. Schrijver*[*]

## 1 INTRODUCTION

This article assesses developments in international investment law from a North-South perspective. In section 2 it first discusses changing perceptions on the role of foreign direct investment in promoting the economic and social progress of developing countries. The article in section 3 then reviews various attempts during the post-1945 period to arrive at multilateral investment agreements and describes how true success could only be achieved in some areas, such as procedures for international settlement of investment disputes and multilateral investment guarantee facilities. Section 4 discusses the various levels of current international investment regulation, most notably through bilateral investment treaties, and observes that a patchwork of agreements, codes and guidelines is currently in place. Therefore, the relevance of a new attempt to arrive at a multilateral investment convention is the topic of section 5, which includes a discussion *in abstracto* of the most salient features of such a convention. By putting these features to the test in reviewing, in section 6, the recent project by the Organization for Economic Cooperation and Development (OECD) for a Multilateral Agreement on Investment (MAI),[1] some insight may be gained into why this effort failed and whether or not this should be deplored.

## 2 CHANGING PERCEPTIONS ON THE ROLE OF FOREIGN DIRECT INVESTMENT IN PURSUING DEVELOPMENT: THE SWING OF THE PENDULUM

Over time a challenging interplay may be noted between perceptions on development policies and regulation of foreign direct investment. Obviously, the current climate is rather conducive to foreign investment, seeking as it does to liberalize the world economy and to agree on legal arrangements,

---

- Nico Schrijver is Professor of International Law, Faculty of Law and Institute for Environmental Studies, *Vrije Universiteit* Amsterdam, and the Institute of Social Studies, The Hague. He gratefully acknowledges useful comments on an earlier draft by Paul Peters (formerly with Royal Dutch/Shell Group) and Esther Kentin (Ph.D. candidate, *VU*) as well as the two editors of this volume.
1 Draft text available at <www.oecd.org/daf/investment/fdi/mai/negtext.htm>.

which reduce risk and enhance trust in foreign investment. Many countries view foreign direct investment as vehicles for progress, including even the Socialist Republic of Vietnam and the People's Republic of China, and only few seek to curtail foreign investment. Nevertheless, one should not forget that there have been times when this was not the case and undoubtedly, sooner or later, the pendulum will swing into the other way again.[2]

The 1944 Bretton Woods order sought to stimulate freedom of international investment, next to freedom of trade and freedom of international payments.[3] Early efforts to regulate foreign investment were met with considerable hostility, as was exemplified by the aborted Havana Charter for Trade and Employment, the constitution for an International Trade Organisation.[4] Indeed, throughout the 1950s the prevailing development doctrine was very much influenced by traditional neo-classical and growth theories, among others that by Rostow.[5] These theories put heavy emphasis on foreign direct investment and economic development as such. Foreign private investment was perceived as the main instrument to provide for resources that were scarce locally, notably foreign capital, entrepreneurship, technology, human skills and access to international markets. It was thought that in certain sectors, industrial development spurred on by foreign investment more or less automatically would have 'spin-off' and 'spill-over' effects into national development in terms of GDP growth rates and that the resulting benefits would 'trickle down' to the local population. International public aid and technical assistance could assist less-developed countries in preparing their infrastructure for such a take-off with foreign direct investment.[6] The World Bank's International Finance Corporation (IFC),[7] established in 1956, and the United Nations Special Fund (1958),[8] were created in support of such policies. However, during the second half of the 1950s new theories came to the fore, which allocated a larger role to local industry and which emphasized the asymmetrical relations between developed and developing countries. To a certain extent this was already reflected in the 1955 revision of Article XVIII of the General Agreement on Tariffs and Trade (GATT) dealing with "Governmental Assistance to Economic Development". Countries in the early stages of their development were entitled to maintain existing tariff protection or even to introduce new ones should

---

2   See C. Oman and G. Wignaraja, *The Postwar Evolution of Development Thinking* (1991); P. Muchlinski, *Multinational Enterprises and the Law* (1995), pp. 3-15.
3   See Art. I (ii) of the Articles of Agreement of the IBRD: "The purposes of the Bank are: ... To promote private foreign investment by means of guarantees or participating in loans and other investments made by private investors". Text in 2 UNTS, p. 134.
4   Art. 12, entitled 'International Investment for Economic Development and Reconstruction'. See also C. Wilcox, *A Charter for World Trade* (1949).
5   Elaborated in W. Rostow, *The Stages of Economic Growth, a Non-Communist Manifesto* (1960).
6   See, for an analysis of some pros and cons of private foreign investment for development, M. Todaro, *Economic Development* (2000), 7th edn., pp. 582-590.
7   Text in 264 UNTS, p. 117 and 439 UNTS, p. 318.
8   See GA Res. 1240 (XIII).

this be necessary to protect their 'infant industries'. The United Nations Conference on Trade and Development (UNCTAD), which convened for the first time in 1964, built on these concepts and sought to enhance the developing countries' position in international trade through a variety of international policy instruments such as commodity agreements and preferential trade regimes.[9] Furthermore, in 1966, the UN Industrial Development Organization (UNIDO) was established, vested with the specific responsibility to stimulate local industrial development.[10]

During the late 1960s, also as a result of the positive outcome of the GATT Kennedy Round, the international political climate became more conducive to international business and belief in the role of foreign direct investment was enhanced once more. Multinational corporations expanded their activities in developing countries considerably. However, things were to change relatively soon. The West was confronted with an economic crisis, reflected in high inflation and rising unemployment and exacerbated by a major budget deficit of the United States resulting from the costly war fought in Vietnam. In various parts of the world political and economic nationalism increased and socialist policies multiplied, culminating in a wave of nationalizations.[11] Around the same time, Arab oil-exporting countries launched a cartel policy, typified by production limitation and considerable rises in oil prices. Widespread suspicion arose as to the role of multinational corporations and their impact on the policies of states. Furthermore, governments and trade unions began to question more vigorously the actual effects of foreign investment on employment, income distribution and social progress as well as their effect on international relations. These developments combined to result in an increasingly hostile climate for foreign investment. At various international policy levels codes of conduct on multinational enterprises were negotiated.[12] In the context of the OECD, Guidelines for Multinational Enterprises were adopted in 1976.[13] In 1977, the ILO adopted a Tripartite Declaration of Principles Concerning Multinational Enterprises and Social Policy.[14] Furthermore, as part of the scheme for a 'New International Economic Order',[15] the UNGA instituted a

---

9  See 'General and Special Principles Recommended by UNCTAD I to Govern International Trade Relations and Trade Policies Conducive to Development', *Proceedings of the United Nations Conference on Trade and Development, Vol. I: Final Act and Report* (1964).
10 GA Res. 2152 (XXI).
11 See A. Akinsanya, *The Expropriation of Multinational Property in the Third World* (1980).
12 See N. Horn (ed.), *Legal Problems of Codes of Conduct for Multinational Enterprises* (1980).
13 Text in 15 ILM (1976), p. 967. Review published in 18 ILM (1979), p. 986.
14 Text in 17 ILM (1978), p. 422.
15 See the NIEO Declaration and Action Programme as contained in GA Res. 3201 (S-VI), para. 4, sub g and GA Res. 3202 (S-VI), Ch. X, 1 May 1974. See also the Charter of Economic Rights and Duties, of which Art. 2.2 reads: "Each State has the right: a. To regulate and exercise authority over foreign investment within its national jurisdiction in accordance with its laws and regulations and in conformity with its national objectives and priorities. No State shall be compelled to grant preferential treatment to foreign investment; b. To regulate

UN Commission on Transnational Corporations, which had, as one of its main tasks, to draw up a Code of Conduct. For many years the Commission devoted much time and energy to this cumbersome task and at various moments in time a compromise was almost within reach. Yet, during the 1980s the swing gradually returned to policies of liberalization and private sector development, which were perceived as being at odds with UN efforts to regulate foreign investment. Hence, the momentum for such a universal code of conduct on transnational corporations faded. Expropriations became rare.[16] During the 1980s and early 1990s, notions of liberalization and privatization came to dominate the debate and a shift in emphasis can be noted from strict regulation in earlier periods, to liberalizing government policies in later ones.[17] However, it must be noted that in recent years the mood is changing somewhat. While most countries still seek to maintain a favourable climate for foreign investment, there is now once again increased attention for the role of the state in creating a so-called 'enabling environment'. The 1997 World Development Report by the World Bank on *The Role of the State in a Changing World* is a clear reflection of the current wisdom: it is argued that "the state is central to economic and social development, not as a direct provider of growth but as a partner, catalyst, and facilitator".[18]

---

and supervise the activities of transnational corporations within its national jurisdiction and take measures to ensure that such activities comply with its laws, regulations and conform with its economic and social policies. Transnational corporations shall not intervene in the internal affairs of a host State. Every State should, with full regard for its sovereign rights, co-operate with other States in the exercise of the right set forth in this subparagraph; c. To nationalize, expropriate or transfer ownership of property, in which cases appropriate compensation should be paid, taking into account its relevant laws and regulations and all circumstances that a State considers pertinent. In any case where the question of compensation gives rise to a controversy, it shall be settled under the domestic law of the nationalizing State and by its tribunals, unless it is freely and mutually agreed by all States concerned that other peaceful means be sought on the basis of the sovereign equality of States and in accordance with the principle of free choice of means." This Article was one of the major bones of contention between the Group of 77 and the OECD countries and a major reason why the latter could not vote in favour of the CERDS, as contained in GA Res. 3281 (XXIX), 12 December 1974. For an analysis see R. Meagher, *An International Redistribution of Wealth and Power: A Study of the Charter of Economic Rights and Duties of States* (1979).

16  M. Minor, 'The Demise of Expropriation as an Instrument of Developing Countries' Policy', 25 *Journal of International Business Studies* (1994), p. 177.
17  See T. Brewer and S. Young, 'The Multilateral Agenda for Foreign Direct Investment: Problems, Principles and Priorities at the OECD and the WTO', in 18 *World Competition* (1995), no. 4, p. 67.
18  J. Wolfensohn, 'Foreword to the State in a Changing World', *World Development Report 1997*.

## 3   A SORRY FATE: EFFORTS TO AGREE ON A MULTILATERAL INVESTMENT AGREEMENT

During the post-1945 period various efforts were made to progressively develop and codify international investment law.[19] The 1948 Havana Charter for an International Trade Organisation (ITO) included an extensive article on regulation of foreign investment. Among other things, it recognized that a state, insofar as other agreements would permit, had the right to install appropriate safeguards: to ensure that foreign investment was not used to interfere in its internal affairs or national policies; to determine whether, to what extent and upon what terms it would allow future foreign investment; and to prescribe and give effect on just terms to requirements as to the ownership of existing and future investments and to other reasonable requirements with respect to such investments.[20] However, such regulatory powers of the host state raised considerable protest in Western business circles and were among the main reasons why the whole ITO project was aborted only a few years after the conclusion of the Havana Charter. Nonetheless, to a certain extent this project of protecting the rights of host states was given a follow-up through UN resolutions on permanent sovereignty over natural resources.[21] Two main concerns served as a *leitmotif*. First, during the decolonization process newly independent states sought to develop new principles and rules of international law in order to assert and strengthen their social and economic development. Second, these resolutions were also meant to underscore in economic terms the rights of all colonial peoples to reserve future benefits from resource exploitation upon independence. More in particular, it was claimed that 'inequitable' legal arrangements from the past had to be altered or even annulled, because they were in conflict with the very concept of 'permanent' sovereignty of peoples over their natural resources. This development culminated in the 1962 Declaration on Permanent Sovereignty over Natural Resources, which affirms the right of states to regulate foreign investment according to their own objectives and development plans.[22] The Declaration emphasizes that the use of natural resources as well as the import of foreign capital required for these purposes should be in conformity with the rules and conditions which "the peoples and nations freely consider to be necessary or desirable with regard to the authorization, restriction or prohibition of such activities". However, and here the balance with Western countries was found, it also specifies that once a state authorizes the admission of foreign capital, the investment shall be governed by the terms of the authorization, national

---

19   See M. Sornarajah, *The International Law on Foreign Investment* (1994); P. Muchlinski, *supra* note 2, Ch. 16.
20   See Art. 12 of the Havana Charter, 1948.
21   See N. Schrijver, *Sovereignty over Natural Resources: Balancing Rights and Duties* (1997), Part I.
22   GA Res. 1803 (XVII), 14 December 1962, adopted by 87 to 2 votes, with 12 abstentions.

legislation and international law, and that agreements freely entered into shall be observed in good faith.[23] Yet, formally the Declaration is merely a non-binding resolution of a political organ of the United Nations. Nonetheless, it was and is widely perceived as expressing the *communis opinio* in the field, also in view of its balanced wording and wide acceptance.

From quite another angle, Western countries made various attempts to draft an international investment code and to cast it in the form of a multilateral convention.[24] In 1959 a committee led by Dr. Abs, Director General of the *Deutsche Bundesbank*, and Lord Shawcross from the United Kingdom, published a Draft Convention on Investments Abroad, commonly known as the Abs-Shawcross Convention. It aimed to set a minimum standard for the protection of property abroad and the treatment of foreign investment. The Draft Convention covered such issues as the observance of agreements, the requirement that expropriation must lawfully include the public interest condition, due process of law, non-discrimination and compensation, as well as dispute settlement through inter-state and investor-to-state arbitration or through the International Court of Justice. However, at the time there proved to be little interest among capital-importing countries for laying down substantive rules of the international law of foreign investment in a binding instrument. A more limited project resulted in the OECD Codes on the Liberalization of Current Invisible Operations and on the Liberalization of Capital Movements. Soon after, the Organization for Economic Cooperation and Development undertook two consecutive attempts to draft a multilateral convention on foreign investment. In 1962 a first version of a Draft Convention on the Protection of Foreign-Owned Property was published,[25] and in 1967 a revised version with a commentary and notes followed.[26] These built on the Abs-Shawcross Draft, but their provisions were couched in somewhat less clear-cut terms. Moreover, it was provided that "no State is bound – unless it is agreed otherwise – to admit aliens into, or permit the acquisition of property by aliens in, its territory". Obviously, this was done in an attempt to seek acceptance beyond OECD membership. Yet, the topic was already too politicized and especially among capital-importing countries there was little appetite for participation, given the background of this Draft Convention.

In the meantime, a more limited project had been undertaken in the context of the International Bank for Reconstruction and Development, commonly known as the World Bank. It proved to be successful. In 1965 the Convention on the Settlement of Investment Disputes between States and Nationals of

---

23 See paras. 3 and 8 of the 1962 Declaration. See also GA Res. 2158 (XXI) of 25 November 1966 on Permanent Sovereignty over Natural Resources.
24 See G. Schwarzenberger, *Foreign Investments and International Law* (1969), Part 2.
25 Text reproduced in 1-2 ILM (1962-3), p. 241.
26 Text in 7 ILM (1968), p. 117. See also G. Schwarzenberger, 'Some Aspects of The O.E.C.D. Draft Convention of 1967 on the Protection of Foreign Property', in M. Blegvald et al., *Liber Amicorum in Honour of Professor Alf Ross* (1969), pp. 447-457.

Other States (ICSID) was adopted.[27] It provided for procedures and facilities for conciliation and arbitration of investment disputes and aimed to attain a "careful balance between the interests of investors and those of the host States". In doing so, it was hoped that the Convention would provide "additional inducement" and would stimulate "a larger flow of private international investment" into countries in need of foreign capital. ICSID itself does not act as conciliator or arbitrator, but only provides the necessary procedural facilities and keeps a list of qualified persons from which the parties to a dispute are able to choose conciliators or arbitrators. Procedures under the auspices of ICSID must conform to three main criteria:

a) Both parties must have consented to have recourse to ICSID but once consent is given it cannot be withdrawn unilaterally;
b) One party has to be a Contracting State and the other a national of another Contracting State;
c) Procedures must involve a legal dispute arising out of an investment.

ICSID does not merely provide for procedures by investors against their host states, but also for procedures instituted by host states against foreign investors. The Convention affirms that the primary competence for legislating in respect of foreign investors and for settling investment disputes between host states and foreign investors lies with the authorities of the host state. The host state may require exhaustion of local remedies prior to arbitration, but only a few host states have availed themselves of this possibility.[28] In the case of arbitration, the applicable law is the law of the Contracting State *and* such rules of international law as may be applicable.[29] Although throughout its existence relatively few proceedings have been conducted under the auspices of ICSID (recently their number has somewhat increased), hundreds of investment contracts, bilateral investment treaties and national laws contain provisions for the submission of disputes to ICSID. Such treaty clauses are instrumental in generating trust and are interpreted to meet the requirement of a party's consent to the jurisdiction of ICSID in advance.[30]

Next to these draft property protection conventions and procedures for the international settlement of investment disputes, the establishment of an international insurance facility had been on the agenda since the early 1960s. Earlier efforts towards this end by the OECD and the World Bank and later UNCTAD and the European Community failed. At the national level various schemes have been established, including the US Overseas Private Investment Corporation (OPIC) and the Netherlands' Credit Corporation (NCM). Also, in 1981, one agency was established on a regional basis, namely the Multinational

---

27 Text in 4 ILM (1965), p. 532.
28 See Art. 26 of ICSID.
29 Art. 42, para. 1 of ICSID.
30 See A. Broches, *Selected Essays. World Bank, ICSID, and Other Subjects of Public and Private International Law* (1995), Part III.

Arab Guarantee Agency.[31] In 1985, at last, following a proposal of the Board of Governors of the World Bank, a Convention Establishing the Multilateral Investment Guarantee Agency (MIGA Convention) was adopted.[32] MIGA's main purpose is to issue guarantees to investors against non-commercial risks, in particular those related to investments in developing countries. MIGA is designed to operate on a self-sustaining basis.[33] The MIGA Convention aims to encourage the flow of investments for productive purposes to developing countries and does not encroach on the national economic jurisdiction of the host state. For example, it leaves control over admission and regulation of foreign investment with the host country. The Convention merely provides that, in guaranteeing an investment, MIGA "shall satisfy itself as to ... the investment conditions in the host country, including the availability of fair and equitable treatment and legal protection for the investment".[34] In the case that MIGA considers that fair treatment and legal protection is not adequately assured under the domestic law of the host country or under an investment treaty, it may conclude an agreement with the host country, or make other arrangements for fair treatment to be extended to the investment in question. MIGA's responsibilities also include improving the general investment conditions in developing countries. This may entail, but formally only at the request of the government of a Member State, advice on such matters as the drafting of investment codes and reviewing investment incentive programmes.

After a French initiative, a working group of the World Bank institutions led by the World Bank's Vice-President and General Counsel Ibrahim Shihata, formulated 'Guidelines on the Treatment of Foreign Direct Investment'.[35] These guidelines set out a general framework for the treatment of foreign investment by host states. However, they only establish rules of behaviour for host states and mainly from the perspective of the interests of the foreign investor with a view to promoting foreign investment. Hence, they do not include rules for proper behaviour on the part of foreign investors nor of their home states. Moreover, they address *bona fide* foreign investments only and

---

31 Organization of the Islamic Conference, *Treaty on Promotion, Protection and Guarantee of Investments among Member States* (1981), in force 1988. Text in H. Moinuddin, *The Charter of the Islamic Conference and Legal Framework of Economic Co-operation among its Member States* (1987), p. 197. The treaty is basically a multilateral investment protection and promotion treaty. In Art. 10 the host state provides guarantees against deprivation of ownership; in Art. 15 an additional guarantee through insurance is provided, for which a separate agency was to be established. See also S. El Nagger (ed.), *Investment Policies in the Arab Countries* (1980).
32 Text in 24 ILM (1985), p. 1605.
33 See I. Shihata, *Multilateral Investment Guarantee Agency: Origins, Policies and Basic Documents* (1988).
34 Art. 12 (d) of the MIGA Convention.
35 For an account see I. Shihata, *Legal Treatment of Foreign Investment. The World Bank Guidelines* (1993).

do not deal with such sensitive issues as disclosure of information, restrictive business practices, the avoidance of corrupt practices and non-interference in domestic affairs. The joint Development Committee of the World Bank and the IMF decided to "call the attention" of member countries to these guidelines as "useful parameters in the admission and treatment of private foreign investment in their territories, without prejudice to the binding rules of international law at this stage of its development".[36]

## 4   ON BITS AND MITS: A POLICY OF 'LET A HUNDRED FLOWERS BLOSSOM'?

In the absence of agreement on a comprehensive multilateral investment protection convention, bilateral investment treaties (BITs) have come to serve as major vehicles for the promotion and protection of foreign investment. These treaties take root in the former Friendship, Commerce and Navigation (FCN) Treaties that for a long period served as one of the common instruments of traditional diplomacy. In addition to their 'friendship' function, the FCN treaties used to cover a broad range of topics relating to: the rights of the nationals of each party and the protection of their property abroad; trade, including such issues as national treatment and most-favoured-nation treatment; and navigation and consular jurisdiction. After 1960, as a result of the conclusion of multilateral trade instruments such as General Agreement on Tariffs and Trade (GATT) and of special bilateral trade treaties, the relevance of FCN treaties rapidly decreased. However, soon capital-exporting states, in particular Germany and France, began negotiating bilateral treaties focusing exclusively on the promotion and protection of foreign investment. The number of bilateral investment treaties grew rapidly, and currently more than 1,700 have been concluded, involving nearly all states, including over a hundred developing countries. Most BITs are treaties between industrialized and developing countries, or between industrialized and formerly communist countries. But it is interesting to note that in recent decades a growing number of BITs have been concluded between developing countries or between (formerly) communist and developing countries.

The main objectives of these treaties are: the promotion of foreign investment; the protection of acquired rights; minimization of loss and risk in the case of expropriation; and dispute settlement. Most BITs include rules on: fair treatment to foreign investors; most-favoured-nation treatment and national treatment; repatriation of capital, profits and other assets; the conditions applying to expropriation and nationalization, including compensation stand-

---

36   Text of the Statement by the Development Committee as well as of the Guidelines in 31 *ILM* (1992), pp. 1366-1384.

ards, and to loss or damage due to war and revolution; due process of law; and dispute settlement through international arbitration.[37]

The legal merits of these BITs have often been a source of controversy and, perhaps more in the past than currently, have given rise to divergent opinions.[38] It is now more commonly understood that while the BITs may not in themselves be able to reflect or generate customary international law including an *opinio iuris communis*, they can certainly clarify and consolidate widely accepted principles of international investment law as well as identify new trends.[39] A notable example of the latter is the decreasing reluctance to resort to international arbitration without prior exhaustion of local remedies.[40]

Next to these BITs, some multilateral investment treaties have been concluded on a regional or interregional level. The first one to mention here is the Agreement on Arab Investment of 1973, which deals with inter-Arab investments. The Inter-Arab Investment Protection Treaty of 1980 subsequently replaced it.[41] While it is recognized that it is part of the sovereignty of individual Arab States to determine the procedure, terms and limits which control Arab investment, it grants a right of establishment to each other's enterprises and provides for an Arab Investment Court which has jurisdiction to settle any dispute between States Parties or between Arab investors and Arab host states. A similar regional treaty is the Maghreb Union Treaty on promotion and protection of investments, signed on 23 July 1990. In a similar vein, the ASEAN Investment Agreement (1987) provides for the right of host states to govern foreign investment as well as for the opportunity of resorting to national or international arbitration.[42] Reference can also be made to Chapter XI on investment of the North American Free Trade Agreement (NAFTA, 1992) and the very similar and equally extensive investment promotion and protection provisions of the Energy Charter Treaty (1994).[43] Furthermore, the Lomé Conventions (now called the Convention of Cotounou, 23 June 2000) between the European Community and (by now) 71 developing countries in Africa, the Caribbean and the Pacific also contain investment promotion and protection provisions and call on the parties to provide for 'fair and equitable

---

37  R. Dolzer and M. Stevens, *Bilateral Investment Treaties* (1995).
38  See for some critical views the articles by S. Chowdhury, in K. Hossain and S. Chowdhury (eds.), *Permanent Sovereignty over Natural Resources in International Law: Principle and Practice* (1984) and Sornarajah, *supra* note 19, p. 276.
39  See Schrijver, *supra* note 21, pp. 191-193. For a different view, A. Guzman, 'Why Developing Countries Sign Treaties that Hurt Them: Explaining the Popularity of bits', in 38 *Virginia Journal of International Law* (1998), no. 4, p. 643 and p. 682.
40  See P. Peters, 'Exhaustion of Local Remedies: Ignored in Most Bilateral Investment Treaties', in 44 *NILR* (1997), pp. 233-243; and the non-application of Art. 26 of the ICSID Convention (see above in section 3).
41  Arab League, *The Unified Agreement for the Investment of Arab Capital in the Arab Countries* (1980), in force 19 May 1987.
42  Text in 27 *ILM* (1988), p. 612.
43  Texts in 32 *ILM* (1993), p. 289 and 34 *ILM* (1995), p. 360, respectively.

treatment' to private investors. Though their terms and standards may vary somewhat, all these regional and interregional treaties seek to guarantee to investors of other Contracting Parties a fair and equitable treatment and protection and security.

## 5    THE CASE FOR A MULTILATERAL INVESTMENT CONVENTION AND ITS SALIENT FEATURES

Almost all countries, including nearly all developing and formerly communist countries, nowadays take part, in one way or another, in multilateral efforts to promote and regulate foreign investment. The days of simply equating developing countries with capital-importing, and industrialized countries with capital-exporting countries are over. Moreover, it is sometimes even unclear which state is the relevant home state of a foreign investor.

Most of the instruments referred to in the previous section cover only a few aspects of investment regulation and deal mainly with investment promotion and protection. This is increasingly perceived as being too one-sided. In addition, they are either addressed to the host country or to the investor. The bilateral and multilateral investment treaties have been concluded between states and contain rules for state behaviour, but it goes without saying that the subject matter is also very much a matter of concern to foreign investors. To a limited extent, multinational enterprises, as foreign investors, are addressed in codes of conduct of the ILO and OECD. International institutions also increasingly come into play: for example, a State or transnational corporation may nowadays be called to account in an international organization such as the ILO, OECD, UN, NAFTA or EU. Yet, most of the responsibilities of foreign investors as well as the role of international institutions are disregarded in BITs and MITs, in particular environmental and social responsibilities.

In view of these limitations of the available instruments and in view of the interests at stake, there can be little doubt that it would be of relevance to include the main rules of modern international investment law in a global multilateral investment convention. The overall objective of such a convention should be to enhance trust and reduce risk, both for foreign investors and for host states, by providing for fair and equitable treatment of foreign investors, by respecting the sovereignty of host states and by genuinely contributing to the sustainable development of the host country and the well-being of its population. Hence, it should ideally address in a balanced manner the rights, duties and responsibilities of the three key parties concerned: foreign investor, host government and home government. The nearly forgotten 1972 Guidelines for International Investment of the International Chamber of Commerce (ICC) could serve as a source of inspiration for such an approach.[44] They address the parties concerned and include rights and responsibilities. In addition, a wide variety of other building blocks can also be found. First of all, these are the principles and rules of international investment law reflected in bilateral and multilateral investment treaties. Second are the arbitral awards of various tribunals, including ICSID-sponsored tribunals and the Iran-US Claims Tribunal. Thirdly, useful reference material can also be found in 'soft law' instruments such as UN resolutions related to permanent sovereignty, the Draft UN Code of Conduct on Transnational Corporations and the 1992 World Bank Guidelines on the Treatment of Foreign Investment.

If such a project for multilateral investment regulation is to have any added value, it must pursue an integrated approach. Without even for a moment belittling the need to protect foreign investment and foreign investors and accord them fair and equitable treatment, it is equally essential to now move beyond the property-protection type of investment promotion and protection conventions and to perceive foreign investment as an integrated part of international efforts towards sustainable development in the sense of promoting economic and social development, while at the same time protecting the environment and respecting other universal values such as labour standards and human rights. As in various other fields of international economic law, the special needs and interests of poor and needy countries should be recognized and addressed. While it is important to assist them in preparing their infrastructure and establishing a climate conducive to foreign investment, it is equally important to recognize and respect their right to determine their own social and economic policies.

In sum, a multilateral investment treaty should contribute to reducing risk and suspicion and should enhance trust in foreign investment by providing, in unambiguous terms, for: observance of investment agreements, be they state-to-state or investor-to-state; respect for the sovereignty of the host state to regulate foreign investment within the limits of international law, while recognizing the special needs and interests of needy developing countries; an integrated approach, seeking to promote and protect foreign investment as well as promoting their genuine contribution to the achievement of public policy goals in the fields of development, employment, environmental conservation and respect for human rights; a balance between rights and duties of all relevant actors, most notably the foreign investor and the host state; and, a right to resolve differences, perhaps first through local remedies, but ultimately through international dispute settlement procedures.[45]

---

44 International Chamber of Commerce, Paris, 1973, publ. no. 272. The text can also be found in P. Kunig, N. Lau and W. Meng (eds), *International Economic Law: Basic Documents* (1989), pp. 589-598.
45 For an overview and analysis P. Peters, 'Dispute Settlement Arrangements in Investment Treaties', in 22 NYIL (1991), pp. 91-161.

## 6     DOES THE MAI STAND THE TEST?

In 1995, the OECD Council decided to embark on a new attempt to articulate principles and rules for the promotion and protection of foreign investment in a multilateral treaty. The OECD aimed at completion of negotiations within a few years. The treaty would be open for signature to both its 29 Member States and to developing and formerly communist countries. It was to contain "high-standard, state-of-the-art provisions for liberalization, investment protection and dispute settlement and provide for a satisfactory balance of commitments". After three years of preparatory work, an extensive draft treaty was published on 24 April 1998, consisting of twelve Sections, with an additional commentary of approximately 75 pages. Obviously, the core of this draft built on the extensive body of bilateral investment treaties, as well as on the investment Chapters of NAFTA and the Energy Charter Treaty. In the autumn of 1998 the MAI negotiations reached a deadlock. Although there was agreement on "a period of assessment and further consultation between the negotiating Parties and with (sic!) the interested parts of their societies",[46] few believe that the MAI could get afloat again.[47]

What could be the systematic reasons for this failure? First of all, the forum of the MAI negotiations raises major questions and concerns. The OECD, as a homogeneous group of countries from which approximately 90% of foreign investment flows originate, of course has the right to draft a MAI applicable to investment relations among OECD member countries. It has, however, frequently expressed the hope that upon adoption the MAI would emerge as a global investment treaty. Thus, the Preamble states that the MAI aims to establish "a broad multilateral framework for international investment with high standards for the liberalization of investment regimes and investment protection and with effective dispute settlement procedures". Third (i.e., non-OECD) countries would be able to accede to the MAI, but only after its conclusion by the OECD countries. Of course, third countries would not be compelled to accede to the MAI. Yet, especially small and medium-sized developing countries might have feared that not joining the OECD's MAI would (further) marginalize their foreign investment chances. This raises the question whether the World Trade Organization or the World Bank as worldwide bodies would not have been a more appropriate forum for negotiating a truly multilateral investment agreement. After all, as set out above, the World Bank has done extensive work in this field, through ICSID, IFC, MIGA and the 1992 Guidelines on the Treatment of Foreign Investment (which seem to have been set aside remarkably soon by the OECD countries). Furthermore, the World Trade Organization, during its first Ministerial Meeting in Singapore in December 1996, decided to establish a working group on the relationship between Trade and

---

46   See OECD Ministerial Declaration, 28 April 1998.
47   See 'The Sinking of the mai', *The Economist*, 14 March 1998, p. 85.

Investment, which was not illogical in view of the Uruguay Round Agreement on Trade Related Investment Measures and its General Agreement on Trade in Services (GATS).[48] However, especially the US insisted on the OECD as the most appropriate forum for negotiating a MAI.

Substantively, the draft as it stood in April 1998 raises many questions.[49] First of all, one may wonder whether the whole undertaking is not too ambitious in the sense that the MAI addresses both foreign direct investment and portfolio investment, which so far used to be beyond the scope of most investment agreements. Second, the coverage of the MAI is more extensive than of most BITs since it purports to provide not only guarantees for investment itself (post-entry stage), but also for making the investment (the pre-entry stage).

Third, as to the actors involved, there may indeed still be reason to view governments and investors as the primary actors in international investment regimes. However, unlike the OECD and ILO Codes of Conduct for Multinational Enterprises in the 1970s, there is virtually nothing in the draft MAI referring to trade unions or consumer and environmental organizations, despite the fact that the text in various Sections and in varying drafts touches on employment, labour and environmental issues.[50] This is one of the reasons why the MAI provoked such fierce opposition from non-governmental organizations, which fear an ecological, social and cultural 'race to the bottom'.[51] As in the case of the developing countries, here too it is 'for them, but without them'.[52] There is not a single reference to the role other international institutions, such as the ILO or the UN, might play in standard-setting, implementation and supervision in areas within their respective competences.

Fourth, there can be little doubt that the draft MAI reflects a clear bias in favour of foreign investors' rights, articulating as it does the rights of foreign investors, including a right of establishment, while not even once mentioning the word 'sovereignty'. On the other hand, it is surprising that the MAI fails

---

48 See WTO Singapore Ministerial Declaration, 13 December 1996, 36 *ILM* (1997), p. 218, para. 20. See also E. Graham, *Foreign Direct Investment in the New Multilateral Trade Agenda* (1996), Occasional Paper WTO Series, no. 4.
49 See the excellent article by A. Böhmer, 'The Struggle for a Multilateral Agreement on Investment – an Assessment of the Negotiating Process in the OECD', 41 *German Yearbook of International Law* (1998), pp. 267-298; see also 'Proceedings of the Symposium on The International Regulation of Foreign Direct Investment: Obstacles and Evolution', 31 *Cornell International Law Journal* (1998), no. 3, pp. 455-728.
50 See I. McDonald, 'The Multilateral Agreement on Investment: Heyday or MAI-day for Ecologically Sustainable Development?', 22 *Melbourne University Law Review* (1999), no. 3, pp. 617-56.
51 Several newspapers, including the International Herald Tribune of 17 February 1998, featured a page-size protest advertisement by various NGOs against the MAI.
52 A few developing countries were involved in the MAI consultations. Mexico and South Korea are members of the OECD, while a group of nine countries had been invited as observers. These included: Argentina, Brazil, Chile, Estonia, Hong Kong, China, Latvia, Lithuania and the Slovak Republic.

to include a standard clause of international investment law as reflected in BITs and MITs, namely the *pacta sunt servanda* rule with regard to the commitments of the host country to the investor.

Fifth, parts of the draft echo contemporary ideologies of privatization and liberalization; one may wonder whether these do not require some closer qualification, now that the role of the state in creating an enabling environment is (once again) being emphasized, as discussed above in section 2.[53] The draft MAI refers just once to objectives such as promoting development, creating employment, improving living standards and conserving the environment. It is clear that liberalization and privatization were meant to be pursued above all else in order to create an investment climate that is transparent and secure.[54]

Sixth, the draft MAI stipulates that foreign investors shall be treated on equal terms with domestic investors (national treatment) or with other foreign investors (most-favoured-nation treatment), whichever is more favourable to the investor. While this implies that host states are not under any obligation to grant foreign investors more favourable treatment than their own nationals, there may be circumstances when the host state wants to extend preferential treatment to its nationals. Obviously, national treatment governs a broad economic and social realm, including consumer protection, tax incentives, labour law, infant industry protection and environmental conservation. Such unqualified anti-discrimination clauses, covering treatment of foreigners as compared with that given to nationals, may not be acceptable to some countries, which want to reserve the option of providing preferential treatment to certain regions and segments of society over others and over foreigners. This may also be the case with respect to developing countries' emphasis on policies and laws on natural resources, transfer of technology, workers' rights, indigenous peoples' rights and social programmes, which may conflict with the MAI's international liberalization programme.[55] Performance requirements that governments may want to impose on investment in the process of seeking to achieve certain economic, social or environmental goals would certainly be at odds with the MAI. Hence, respect for the right of host countries (in particular developing countries) to determine their own development policy and retain certain mechanisms to achieve national priorities in accordance with current international law is a very real concern. Fear of loss of sovereignty is by no means a concern with respect to developing countries only. Western nations, such as France and Canada, are afraid of adverse effects on their

---

53 See also S. Picciotto and R. Mayne (eds), *Regulating International Business. Beyond Liberalization* (1999).
54 *Cf.* H. Tuesselmann, 'The Multilateral Agreement on Investment: The Case for a Multispeed Convergence Approach to Liberalization', 6 *Transnational Corporations* (1997), no. 3, pp. 87-111.
55 See also A. Gasener, 'Development-friendliness Criteria for a Multilateral Investment Agreement', 6 *Transnational Corporations* (1997), no. 3, pp. 135-42.

'cultural sovereignty'. The French government was worried that, under the MAI, American filmmakers would be able to claim the same film promotion subsidies as their French counterparts.[56] Certain Western countries with highly developed social welfare sectors, such as the Scandinavian countries, Canada, Germany and France, have expressed the fear that sovereignty with regard to economic matters would be eroded and that international enterprises would, under the MAI, be able to demand compensation if the minimum wage became substantially higher than when the company first set up its subsidiary.

Seventh, the MAI gives investors rights and protection, including the ability to sue governments. However, as noted above, the MAI imposes no obligations on them to operate in accordance with national and international standards. Hence, investor rights should be better balanced against investor responsibilities, as was the case in the 1972 Guidelines for International Investments of the International Chamber of Commerce, the OECD Guidelines on Multinational Enterprises and the 1990 Draft UN Code of Conduct for Transnational Corporations.

Lastly, the dispute settlement clause internationalizes dispute settlement procedures, in line with current practices reflected in most BITs and MITs, but disregards the position taken by a number of states, which emphasize the applicability of national law[57] and the local remedies rule.[58] The MAI procedure for adjudicating conflicts between a foreign investor and a host country is remarkable. Under the MAI rules on investor-to-state dispute settlement, the primacy of the national judicial process – the 'local remedies rule' – has been replaced by a choice for the investor between:
a) the national judicial process;
b) a procedure previously agreed between the parties to the dispute; and
c) international arbitration, for example, under the rules of the World Bank Centre ICSID, UNCITRAL or the International Chamber of Commerce.

Thus, in joining the MAI, a state would give unconditional permission for a dispute to be subject to international arbitration, thereby allowing its national judicial process to be bypassed and, in principle, this applies also for the pre-establishment stage. Moreover, the applicable law is international law; only in specific situations can the national law of the host state also be applied. On this point, too, the draft MAI constitutes a clear example of limitation of state sovereignty in the interests of investment protection.

---

56  Cf. J. Lang, 'L'Ami, c'est l'ennemi', Le Monde, 10 February 1998.
57  See P. Peters, 'The Semantics of Applicable Law Clauses and the Arbitrator', in M. Sumampouw et al., Law and Reality. Essays in honour of C.C.A. Voskuil (1992), particularly pp. 239 et seq. on the 'Sri Lanka-clause'.
58  See however on the nearly consistent reliance on international arbitration without prior recourse to local remedies in recent BITs, Peters, supra note 40.

## 7  CONCLUSION

While the case for a comprehensive multilateral investment convention is strong, there is not much reason to shed tears over the failure of the OECD project for a Multilateral Agreement on Investment. Apart from the fact that the OECD is no longer the most logical choice of forum for negotiating such a global convention, the draft MAI as it stood by 24 April 1998 may rightly be criticized for granting extensive rights to foreign investors, without imposing duties on them. Stigmatizing the MAI as 'the Charter of Rights and Freedoms of Multinational Enterprises' or as an 'ecological, social and cultural race to the bottom' may be stretching the argument, but such criticism is invited by the OECD's one-sided approach. In addition, the negotiators proved to be out of step with the times by ignoring to a considerable extent concerns relating to cultural identity, employment, labour standards, human rights, consumer protection and environmental conservation. That is not to say that all these issues should be addressed in a substantive way in a MAI, but we should at least be aware of the fact that the environment in which foreign investors operate is also shaped by such concerns. Inspiration towards such an end could have been drawn from documents such as the 1992 Rio Declaration of Principles on Environment and Development, the 1995 Copenhagen Declaration of the World Summit on Social Development and the 1998 ILO Declaration on core labour standards.[59] We should be careful not to use the MAI project as the scapegoat for globalization and caution is necessary when letting NGOs, which are often one-sided and not very democratic, assume the responsibilities of governments. Any attempt towards a multilateral investment convention that does not balance rights and duties of foreign investors and of host states and home states is bound to fail. The same is true for a convention which is merely property-protection oriented rather than aimed at reducing risk and enhancing trust between industrialized and developing countries, foreign investors, their employees and society as a whole.

---

59  Text in 37 *ILM* (1998), p. 1233. Para. 2 of this 1998 ILO Declaration provides that all ILO members, even if they have not ratified the Conventions in question, have an obligation to respect the following fundamental principles: freedom of association and the right to collective bargaining; the elimination of all forms of forced or compulsory labour; the effective abolition of child labour; and the elimination of discrimination in respect of employment and occupation.

# 3 | Developing Countries and Multilateral Investment Negotiations

## E.V.K. FitzGerald[*]

To a large extent, an investment friendly environment is also a development-friendly environment. At the same time it is important to ensure that the development needs and concerns of host developing countries are centrally addressed by any investment agreement so that it is development-friendly as well as investment-friendly in its orientation.[1]

## 1 INTRODUCTION

During the 1990s, the level and nature of international investment flows changed radically, reflecting the process of post-Cold War economic globalization. The agenda of the Uruguay Round did not anticipate the investment dimension of trade issues; and thus they were not properly built into the mandate of the WTO. A US initiative attempted to establish a Multilateral Agreement on Investment (MAI)[2] between OECD countries, which would have been extended to developing countries; but negotiations broke down after disagreement between the EU and USA. The EU itself included investment disciplines in its proposed agenda for the 'Millennium Round' of multilateral trade talks, which were stalled in Seattle at the end of 1999. The eventual outcome will be of particular relevance to developing countries, which rely on inward investment to provide technology and management as well as financial resources, and their interests will require special consideration in any global investment discipline that might be established.

Although no draft text for an MFI exists yet, there is a strong case for attempting to establish its main elements well in advance. The 'development

---

[*] Valpy FitzGerald is Reader in International Economics and Finance at the University of Oxford, and Professorial Fellow of St Anthony's College, Oxford. He is Director of the Finance and Trade Policy Research Centre at Oxford, and Extraordinary Professor of Development Economics at the Institute of Social Studies at The Hague. Research for this article was undertaken with the support of the Department for International Development (DfID) of the UK Government. The opinions in this paper are the author's alone and do not necessarily reflect those of the DfID. I would like to thank Rodrigo Cubero and Alex Lehmann for their valuable contributions to this study and to our previous report on the Multilateral Agreement on Investment (E. FitzGerald, R. Cubero and A. Lehmann, *The Development Implications of the Multilateral Agreement on Investment* (1998)).

1 UNCTAD, *World Investment Report 1998*, p. 75.
2 Draft text available at <www.oecd.org/daf/investment/fdi/mai/negtext.htm>.

interest' could be openly defined from the outset, rather than becoming a subsequent point of contention, as was the case in the MAI negotiations.[3]

The present paper explores three problem areas from the point of view of developing countries. After a brief outline of what an MFI might contain in section 2, the scope for independent national development policies within a global investment discipline is discussed in section 3. In section 4 the compatibility of capital account controls with the core rights of foreign investors is examined, while section 5 takes up the asymmetric nature of investment negotiations between developed and developing countries. The paper concludes with recommendations as to how these three problem areas might be approached, in section 6.

## 2 POOR COUNTRIES AND INTERNATIONAL INVESTMENT RULES

### 2.1 The importance of foreign investment to poor countries

The increasing globalization of capital markets is widely regarded as a unique opportunity for poor economies to accelerate their rate of growth by accessing financial resources and productive technology, and thus to reduce poverty by generating new jobs and providing fiscal resources for human development. Foreign Direct Investment (FDI) flows to developing countries have risen fivefold over the past decade, as Table 1 indicates.

Table 1: Inward flows of Foreign Direct Investment (US$ billion)

|  | 1986-91 | 1993 | 1995 | 1997 |
|---|---|---|---|---|
| Developing Countries, of which: | 29.1 | 72.5 | 105.5 | 148.9 |
| · Africa | 1.7 | 2.1 | 3.9 | 2.9 |
| · Latin America. & Caribbean | 9.5 | 17.2 | 31.9 | 56.1 |
| · Asia | 15.1 | 47.3 | 66.6 | 82.4 |
| · Least Developed Countries | 0.8 | 1.7 | 1.1 | 1.8 |

Source: UNCTAD, supra note 1. 'Africa' excludes North Africa and South Africa; 'Asia' is South, East and South-East Asia.

---

3 The 29 OECD Members launched negotiations in 1995 for a Multilateral Agreement on Investment (MAI), which was originally due to be signed in 1998; but negotiations were suspended in late 1998. One of the key recommendations of our previous report on the MAI (FitzGerald et al., *supra* note *, p. 6) was that were the Paris negotiations to break down, the WTO would be a better forum for negotiations than the OECD - both because of the close technical relationship between trade and investment issues, and because developing countries could be directly represented.

Nonetheless, this increasingly important source of finance requires developing countries to adjust their economies to the 'discipline' of world markets because failure to meet the standards required by foreign investors will be penalized by lower investment and growth as capital resources move elsewhere. These investors include those domestic entrepreneurs who can more easily move their funds abroad – particularly if neighbouring countries have better business conditions. Since the mid-1980s developing countries have, in consequence, embarked on an unprecedented unilateral liberalization of their investment regimes. They have attempted to construct a strong business environment based on market growth, solvent financial systems, working infrastructure, and laws and regulations that are fairly enforced.

Moreover, a significant consequence of the recent volatility in global financial markets has been increased efforts to encourage direct foreign investment as it represents a longer-term commitment to the 'real economy'. The danger is that if the poorest countries – and vulnerable regions within industrializing countries – are unable to compete effectively for investment they will face increasing risks of social stress and declining living standards.

International investment agreements are intended to 'lock in' this liberalization and thereby enhance investor confidence in regulatory environments. The investors in question are not only multinational firms. On the one hand, 'expatriate' capital (that is, the assets of nationals held overseas, whether their owners are resident or not) will be encouraged to return to its 'home' economy by credible investment guarantees. On the other hand, domestic investors will regard foreign investment regulations as a strong indication of the treatment that they themselves will receive. Indeed, as Table 2 shows, in Africa FDI accounts for half of business investment[4] while in Latin America and Asia it represents a quarter and a fifth respectively.

*Table 2: Inward FDI as share of Gross Fixed Capital Formation (GFCF) (percent)*

|  | 1986-91 | 1994 | 1996 | FDI/Businessinvestment |
|---|---|---|---|---|
| Developing Countries, of which: | 3.4 | 7.6 | 8.7 | 22% |
| · Africa | 6.7 | 14.1 | 13.2 | 53% |
| · Latin America & Caribbean | 5.3 | 8.9 | 12.8 | 25% |
| · Asia | 3.6 | 7.9 | 8.3 | 21% |
| · Least Developed Countries | 1.3 | 1.3 | 2.2 | 13% |

Sources and definitions as Table 1.

---

4   Obtained by dividing the 1996 FDI/GFCF ratio by the estimated share of business investment (private less household investment) in total domestic investment using IFC data.

In fact 'foreign' and 'domestic' investment are not completely separate - let alone antagonistic – categories. Indeed there is a strong complementarity between them for at least three reasons. First, foreign firms generally have a strong positive effect on local technology acquisition and skilling, particularly in manufacturing; and on the private sector as a whole when infrastructure provision such as modern telecommunications or banking services are involved. Second, the conditions that attract foreign investment – such as a stable legal environment, supportive government policies, skilled labour and modern infrastructure – also promote domestic investment, which generally accounts for the greater part of capital formation. Third, the widespread history of capital flight in developing countries means that much of 'domestic' capital is in fact non-resident ('expatriate'), and the encouragement of the return of these resources requires that domestic investors be afforded the same standard of guarantees as foreign investors.

This means that for developing countries one of the great advantages of subscribing to international investment rules is the reduction of the uncertainty faced by domestic and expatriate investors in the face of discretionary and changeable government policies. Reduced uncertainty will in turn raise the rate of private investment as a whole, and shift it towards productive longer-term projects, which create employment and generate exports.[5]

## 2.2 International investment agreements

International investment agreements involve much more than the baseline conditions for investment liberalization listed above. Equitable and non-discriminatory treatment of foreign investors is required, as are appropriate conditions for transfer of funds, taxation, performance criteria and corporate practice. Investment protection provisions should also address such issues as expropriation and protection from civil strife. International agreements – such as bilateral investment treaties, double taxation treaties, regional trade agreements and certain WTO provisions – play a key role in building investor confidence by locking in policy commitments over time.[6] In particular, there is a close relationship between trade and investment agreements at the bilateral, regional and multilateral levels.

---

5   This, of course, is why so many poor countries already belong to multilateral arrangements designed to promote private investment. E.g., of 52 African countries: 40 are Parties to the convention establishing the Multilateral Investment Guarantee Agency, MIGA (mostly since mid-1990s); 42 are signatories to the Convention on the Settlement of Investment Disputes between States and Nationals of other States (mostly since late 1960s and 1970s); 26 are Parties to the Convention on the Recognition and Enforcement of Foreign Arbitral Awards (spread over whole 1959-1997 period); and 40 are Members of the World Intellectual Property Organization, WIPO (between 1951 and 1997).
6   WTO, *Annual Report 1996* (1996).

The accelerating trend towards bilateral and regional arrangements for investment regulation[7] thus reflects a move away from national rights to control foreign investment in a discriminatory manner and norms for corporate conduct. By the end of 1997, the total number of treaties had reached 1,513.[8] Such new agreements are usually based on general standards of treatment, coupled with norms on specific matters such as expropriation, compensation and the transfer of funds, and mechanisms for the international settlement of disputes. For developing countries themselves being party to a multilateral investment agreement would have considerable advantages over the existing patchwork of BITs because investors would have a single standard to rely upon which could be well understood and monitored. The confidence of not only foreign but also domestic investors in a multilateral commitment is much greater than a in regional or bilateral one (let alone domestic legislation) precisely because it ensures that the policy regime is unlikely to shift in the future due to the cost of withdrawal from a multilateral treaty. This is why merely replicating investor protection of a high standard in domestic legislation is insufficient to encourage foreign investment in small or weak countries.

Nonetheless, countries wish to retain control over the sectoral or regional allocation of foreign investment. As the UNCTAD points out:

> [F]oreign direct investment is necessary and useful for [poor countries]; it augments their own meagre domestic resources and thereby accelerates their growth, and allows them to obtain higher technology from abroad and improve their production efficiency. At the same time, foreign investment may entail a net outflow of foreign exchange in the course of time, unbalanced sectoral investment and a geographical imbalance in a country's development. Given these possible adverse impacts, the host country needs to take certain safeguards. It should retain the discretion to guide investments into selected sectors and geographical areas and to limit the entry of investment, which is likely to have adverse effects on its balance of payments or its overall development objectives and efforts. The objective of these safeguards should be to ensure a healthy linkage between investment and the domestic economy, and to encourage the dissemination of technology and greater efficiency in domestic industries.[9]

However, one significant weakness in this approach is clearly revealed in this quotation. The justifiable safeguards take the form of government screening of *foreign* investors in order to promote certain sectors or regions, or to protect the balance of payments, or to prevent projects "which are likely to have an

---

7   UNCTAD, *World Investment Report 1996: Investment, Trade and International Policy Arrangements* (1996).
8   See K. Sauvant and V. Aranda, 'The International Legal Framework for Transnational Corporations', in: A. Fatouros (ed.), *Transnational Corporations: Codes of Conduct* (1994) and UNCTAD, *supra* note 1.
9   UNCTAD, *Least Developed Countries Report 1998*, p. 163.

adverse effect ... on its overall development objectives ... ". However these safeguards should also be applied to large *domestic* investors, whose projects are similarly capable of having these negative effects. *If the safeguards were applied in this way, then they would not be discriminatory* and would be fully compatible with the core content of an MFI.

## 2.3 Distinct interests between developing countries

The presumption in international investment agreements between developed countries is that foreign investors are at an initial disadvantage to established domestic firms and regulatory authorities.[10] Specific measures in order to ensure 'national treatment' are thus required. In the case of developing countries - particular small or poor ones - the reverse may be the case. This asymmetry must be the concern of international regulatory regimes.

Smaller countries have special problems in terms of their economic, social and administrative vulnerability to sudden changes in the world economy, or to pressures from more powerful Contracting Parties or even from large multinational corporations (MNCs). Substantial investments in particular sectors such as natural resources (for example: energy, mining), manufacturing (for example: export zones, refineries) or services (for example: banking, tourism) may in fact have strategic implications because of their size relative to the host economy. Similarly, foreign firms may be very large relative to domestic firms, making 'national treatment' an ambiguous concept; and even requiring special protection for small firms.

In contrast, large developing economies are in a stronger bargaining position than small ones with respect to foreign investors due both to their market importance to the investor and to weight in international fora. In many cases these large developing economies have relatively strong administrative structures as well. They have large domestic firms, which can potentially compete effectively with foreign enterprises, while no one foreign investor will gain a monopoly position easily. Finally, the macroeconomic impact of foreign investment is likely to be less than in smaller countries.

In this context 'small' and 'large' does not only relate to population size, as market potential and human capital also relate to income levels. Moreover, a relatively large society may have a weak administration. However, in the long run governance capacity does seem to be related to per capita income. Thus the second dimension would seem to be per capita income, which, when combined with size/strength, would seem to distinguish distinct groups of developing countries from the viewpoint of their interest in an MFI.

---

10 Such as the OECD Codes of Liberalization and Declaration on International Investment, which commit States Parties to liberalize rules and regulations affecting cross-border capital flows and to provide national treatment to foreign-controlled enterprises.

*Figure 1: Negotiating heterogeneity between developing countries*

|  | GDP (US $ trillion at 1997 ppp) | Large/strong | Small/weak |
|---|---|---|---|
| Middle-income countries | 13.0 | | |
| Upper middle-income | 4.4 | Brazil<br>Korea<br>Mexico | Argentina<br>Botswana<br>Chile<br>Malaysia<br>South Africa, etc. |
| Lower middle-income | 8.6 | China<br>Indonesia | Bolivia<br>Colombia<br>Namibia<br>Philippines<br>Swaziland<br>Thailand, etc. |
| Low-income countries | 2.9 | India | Bangladesh<br>Ethiopia<br>Honduras<br>Kenya<br>Mozambique<br>Nicaragua<br>Pakistan<br>Uganda<br>Zimbabwe, etc. |
| Total developing countries | 15.9 | 9.1 | 6.8 |

Figure 1 classifies developing countries by income levels and then by size and thus negotiating strength.[11] The 'large/strong' category contains those developing countries whose GDP exceeds 1% of the world total.[12] Collectively, these six countries account for 25% of world GDP. This fact alone clearly grants them a distinct bargaining position where they can benefit as much from bilateral

---

11  For the listing of countries, see OECD Development Assistance Committee, *Development Cooperation 1997* (1998). Middle-income countries are defined as those developing countries with a per capita GNP of $766-9,385 in 1995; the low-income countries being those with a per capita GNP of less than $765. The low-income countries in the World Bank classification (excluding India) correspond almost exactly with the UNCTAD least-developed group, and thus with the lower right hand cell in Figure 1.

12  This is roughly equivalent to 5% of developing countries' aggregate GDP. Lowering the hurdle to 1% of this total only brings in nine more countries (Argentina, Colombia, Chile, Egypt, Malaysia, Pakistan, Philippines, South Africa and Venezuela) none of which have significant individual negotiating strength.

or regional arrangements as from an MFI because they have sufficient negotiating strength to achieve an advantageous treaty adapted to their own interests. That is not true of the majority of developing countries, who are relatively small or weak even if they have large populations.

Within the 'small/weak' group, it is the middle-income countries that are of most interest to foreign investors as they account for 15% world GDP even after the 'large' countries are excluded. These countries tend to have well-developed business sectors and reasonably efficient administrative systems, and thus are clearly the first candidates for any multilateral investment discipline. Nonetheless, from the development viewpoint, the small poor countries are of most interest and, as has been argued above, it is these countries which could gain most from an MFI.

## 2.4 The core elements of an MFI

Regulatory policy - and commitments made in international agreements - must logically take account of both investors' need for liberal and predictable rules as well as broader national economic development objectives.[13] The main criteria on the basis of which such agreements can be evaluated once definition and coverage are agreed, are: investment liberalization, protection and dispute settlement procedures.[14]

The MFI would be a legally binding agreement that covers a broad range of investments, including portfolio investment, contractual rights and intellectual property. This could mirror the coverage of investment in NAFTA and thus exceed the coverage in most other bilateral and regional agreements. A broad definition of FDI reflects the recognition that comprehensive investment protection covers all assets related to the activities of a foreign affiliate.

Investment protection provisions are of particular importance for developing countries characterized by weak institutions or political and economic instability, as they allow these countries to 'import' conditions of increased certainty, credibility, transparency and stability under a multilateral framework. They also allow developing countries to import the international regulatory 'best practice' and thus strengthen their own domestic institutional capabilities and disciplines.

The wording of the obligations for *national treatment or most-favoured-nation treatment* would mirror similar clauses in other investment agreements. The clause on 'like circumstances' could correspond to NAFTA Article 1102 or GATS Article XVII: the treatment of foreign firms could be materially different from

---

13 International investment treaties are too numerous to summarize here. UNCTAD, *supra* note 7, collates the key features of the main international investment treaties.
14 P. Sauvé, 'A First Look at Investment in the Final Act of the Uruguay Round', 25 *Journal of World Trade* (1994), no. 5, pp. 3-16.

that of national firms if the situation of foreign firms is not comparable, as is the case in many service industries.[15] Any obligation for national treatment covering both the pre-entry phase and existing establishments, would amount to a right of establishment. This would go well beyond most bilateral and regional investment agreements, in which national treatment is only granted for existing establishments.[16]

Protection of the *transfer of funds* by foreign-owned affiliates into and out of the host economy are a key concern for developing countries in times of balance of payments crises. Intervention by central banks in pursuit of monetary and exchange rate stability or under obligations to the IMF should take precedence over this safeguard – which is in line with bilateral and regional agreements – and should be included in an MFI.

WTO provisions bind governments who are the only parties with rights of legal standing in dispute settlement proceedings. Such procedures have so far only been adopted in Chapter 11:B of NAFTA and in the European Energy Charter. Even though private rights of litigation might be desirable in extreme cases, WTO proceedings are unlikely to accommodate this. Provisions under the WTO Dispute Settlement Understanding (DSU) also appear more effective in inducing compliance with current and future investment provisions. Where a defendant party fails to comply with the recommendations of a dispute settlement panel the complainant will be authorized to withdraw a commensurate amount of concessions granted to this party.[17] This possibility of cross-retaliation – and the possibility of several aggrieved parties taking concerted action – would be a very effective discipline on non-compliant behaviour if the MFI comes under the WTO.

Foreign investment will give rise to the full set of issues of modern trade relations, which are already addressed in WTO agreements, particularly the competition implications of a liberal investment regime. The interaction between inward investment and market structure was recognized in the services negotiations of the Uruguay Round. Article VIII of the GATS stipulates that monopolies and exclusive service suppliers shall not act in a manner inconsistent with Members' obligations under the Agreement, while Article IX provides for consultations over restrictive business practices. In the WTO Telecommunications Agreement these articles were implemented when WTO Members entered into specific competition safeguards.

The objective of the negotiations would be to establish a common set of multilateral rules providing a simplified, secure and predictable framework for international investment. However, the proposed MFI is intended to be a

---

15 GATS Art. XVII:2 and 3.
16 The scope of these provisions in the MAI would have depended however on the number of exemptions which signatories lodged under Section IX Annexes A and B - which would have radically weakened obligations for non-discriminatory treatment.
17 DSU Art. 22.3 (c).

binding multilateral framework encompassing existing bilateral agreements and practices: it would thus replace existing international agreements on investment. The substantive obligations of any agreed text are thus unlikely to go beyond requiring national treatment for foreign investors and compensation for expropriated property. Moreover, the text will have to include a list of sectors generally excluded from the agreement, as well as a list of reservations exempting specified industries and regulatory arrangements from the agreement's provisions on a country-by-country basis.

In sum, the central core of all investment agreements is the principle of national treatment, which implies non-discriminatory treatment of foreign and domestic investments 'in like circumstances'. This would limit the application of the national treatment obligation to investments that are alike in legal and factual terms with respect to the characteristics of the investment, the sectors involved and the circumstances in which the investments were made.

## 3   SUSTAINABLE DEVELOPMENT AND AN MFI

### 3.1   Foreign investment planning and performance requirements

There exists a general agreement in principle that foreign direct investment is a desirable component of a sustainable development strategy – in the sense of macroeconomic stability, continued productivity growth and sustained poverty reduction – but less agreement exists on how best to organize such inflows in order to maximize the development potential. Three points are at issue:

a) the reaction of investors to regulatory risk;
b) the role of policy-based performance requirements; and
c) the impact of international labour and environmental standards.

According to the UNCTAD, on balance

> ... an MFI would improve the enabling environment for FDI, to the extent that it would contribute to greater security for investors and greater stability, predictability and transparency in investment policies and rules. This, in turn could encourage higher FDI flows and potentially some redistribution of those flows, particularly to countries whose investment climates would newly reflect the multilateral framework. How much difference an MFI would make, however, in terms of the quantity, quality and patterns of actual FDI flows is difficult to predict because as in the case of BITs, it is precisely the functions of an enabling framework to allow other determinants, and especially economic determinants, to assert their influence. Expecta-

tions about the impact of an MFI on FDI flows ... should therefore, not be exaggerated.[18]

This conclusion, nonetheless, probably underestimates the sensitivity of foreign investment to regulatory uncertainty, and thus the benefits of a multilateral agreement. However ambitious the scope of domestic policy reform, as long as policy instruments remain within the discretion of host authorities and thus the local political process, investors will regard themselves as exposed to regulatory risk – and thus invest less (or more short-term) than otherwise.[19] This factor is particularly strong in the case of small or weak low-income countries.

In view of the differences between the restrictiveness of investment laws and their administration – which are frequently liberalized *de facto* long before the law is changed – rigorous quantitative estimation of the effect of these restrictions on capital flows is problematic. When a country partially liberalizes its investment rules, there can be a large inflow – particularly if a large domestic market is available – even if the rules are still restrictive. In the long run, the equilibrium stock would be below that which would obtain if there were no such constraints. In other words, the fact that some restrictive countries (for example, China) enjoy sizeable capital inflows does not undermine the case for well-regulated liberalization, although it does suggest that an appropriate transition process must be planned.

Although the prevalence of performance requirements is not hard to document, their influence on investment decisions and on the pattern of foreign purchases and sales by an investment project is far more difficult to discern.[20] In addition, there is a high correlation between investment restrictions and incentives, so that the net effect is difficult to sort out.[21] The only recent database on investment restrictions and liberalization, is that compiled by the European Roundtable of Industrialists, covering 27 developing countries in 1987-1996 and based on surveys in 1992 and 1996.[22] When the scopes of individual restrictions are summed up across all countries in the sample, lack of intellectual property protection, and issues related to property rights (sector-specific restrictions, approval procedures, ownership rights) emerge as the most prevalent impediments to investment.[23] The ERT survey also looks at

---

18 UNCTAD, *supra* note 1, pp. 129-130.
19 In theoretical terms, uncertainty increases the option value of delaying investment even if it is expected to be profitable. A. Dixit and J. Pindyck, *Investment under Uncertainty* (1994).
20 S. Guisinger, 'Do Investment Incentives and Performance Requirements Work?', 9 *The World Economy* (1986), no. 1, p. 168.
21 There is also a 'political economy effect' insofar as those countries, which are most attractive anyway – due to market size, e.g. – are in the best position to impose restrictions.
22 European Round Table of Industrialists, *Investment in the Developing World: New Openings and Challenges for European Industry* (1997).
23 Even when corrected for income levels, export composition and trade openness.

changes over time, and indicates that the investment restrictions which have been at the forefront of liberalization efforts over the previous ten years still pose the largest impediments to foreign investors: protection of intellectual property rights, sector-specific and ownership restrictions, foreign exchange restrictions and approval practices.

A particular consequence of regulatory uncertainty with importance for sustainable development is that of the 'quality of investment' reflected on the technology transferred as part of affiliates' activities or joint ventures. For instance, a study of US, German and Japanese firms operating in sixteen developing host countries in the early 1990s shows that both the composition and extent of US direct investment is influenced, and that in many cases intellectual property protection is too weak to permit joint ventures with local partners.[24] Investment in R&D facilities is clearly much more sensitive than that in sales or distribution outlets, while some industries (such as chemicals, pharmaceuticals, machinery and electrical equipment) are more sensitive than others such as food processing or transportation equipment. It also appears that older technologies are transferred to countries with weak intellectual property protection.

Developing country governments have tended to use performance requirements as a condition for foreign investment licensing in order to attempt to shift investment towards sectors or activities that have priority - typically particular less-developed regions of the country, technological upgrading or export promotion. Such requirements are not usually applied to domestic investors, although it is far from clear why large domestic firms should be excluded – unless performance requirements are just a disguised form of protection.

While performance requirements are generally discriminatory,[25] their effect depends on market structure and the behaviour of foreign affiliates in the host country;[26] where they 'bind' in the sense that the affiliate (say) would not have exported anyway, then they logically generate losses which must be cross-subsidized from other operations, typically sales to the host market. It can be argued that MNCs will only be willing to invest under such conditions if compensating investment incentives are offered, such as local licenses for exclusive supply or host market protection.[27] Even though there is ample

---

24  E. Mansfield, 'Intellectual Property Protection, Foreign Direct Investment and Technology Transfer: Germany, Japan and the United States', in International Finance Corporation, *Discussion Paper 27* (1995).
25  They need not necessarily be so. In the highly successful Costa Rican export processing zones, e.g., *all* firms must comply with regulations on domestic content, not just foreign ones.
26  United Nations Centre on Transnational Corporations, *The Impact of Trade Related Measures on Trade and Development* (1991).
27  D. Greenaway, 'Why are we Negotiating on TRIMS?' in Greenaway et al (eds), *Global Protectionism* (1990).

evidence showing a correlation between investment restrictions and incentives, there is no evidence that the combination of the two sets of measures will be perceived as neutral. On the contrary, the conjunction of discretionary restrictions and incentives exposes an affiliate to additional regulatory risk.

Many developing countries have already embarked on the unilateral abolition of restrictions to foreign investment. Moreover, experience suggests that enlarging the technical and managerial skills of the domestic labour force is the best way to ensure technology transfer. In specific cases, developing countries may wish to maintain (through exceptions or reservations) some performance requirements on the grounds of public interest, but these should be specified in a negative list, and be made consistent with the national treatment and most-favoured-nation (i.e., non-discrimination) clauses. Nonetheless, an MFI should seek to restrict these constraints.

Discriminating against low-tech foreign investment through technology transfer or R&D requirements at the entry, establishment and/or expansion levels does not in itself attract high-tech investment. Furthermore, technology is difficult to define and even more difficult (and burdensome) to screen, especially when it comes to 'soft technologies' such as ideas, information, management and organizational skills. The OECD[28] argues that performance requirements (such as requirements to enter into joint venture with local firms, mandatory transfers of technology, compulsory licensing, mandatory divestiture after a number of years, local content requirements, obligatory training for employees and weak intellectual property rights) have a negative effect on the rate of technology transfer by MNCs.[29] The World Bank states that "more competition in host country markets increases the pressures and incentives for multinationals to transfer more and better-quality technology to affiliates".[30]

From another viewpoint, Dunning argues that the main role of the state regarding technology transfer should be the provision of basic infrastructure and facilities (such as scientific and telecommunications infrastructure, and the upgrading of labour skills).[31] He also suggests that the most cost-effective way of assimilating and disseminating imported technology is to ensure there are adequate local design engineering and organizing capabilities.

It is very difficult to establish whether performance requirements have a positive net effect on trade by increasing exports and forcing substitution

---

28  OECD, *The Role of Foreign Direct Investment in Economic Development* (1997).
29  "In Indonesia and the Philippines, for example, where foreign investors must phase down their participation in a company over time, this policy reportedly reduced investment and product- and process -technology flows, and it did little to enhance domestic capabilities" D. Conklin and D. Lecraw, 'Restrictions on ownership during 1984-94: Developments and alternative policies', 6 *Transnational Corporations* (1997), no. 1.
30  World Bank, *Private Capital Flows to Developing Countries: the Road to Financial Integration* (1997), p. 48.
31  J. Dunning, *Multinational Enterprises and the Global Economy* (1993).

of domestic inputs for imported ones. Even by the 1990s, a comprehensive survey of the theoretical and empirical literature on the relationship between trade and FDI could still conclude that performance requirement effects are difficult to separate from the effects of incentives.[32] However, Kokko and Blomström find no positive relationship between technology imports and technology transfer requirements in host countries for US direct investment abroad, and indeed suggest that technology imports of foreign affiliates tend to increase as the level of performance requirements imposed by the host government falls.[33]

## 3.2  Labour and environmental standards

In most developing countries (particularly low-income ones), domestic health, environmental and labour standards may already be low and largely unenforced. Therefore, the relevant issue from a development perspective is whether any multilateral agreement on investment should, in addition to prohibiting the lowering of existing standards, incorporate universal environmental and labour standards[34] and make them legally binding among signatories. This is not merely a matter of reiterating international commitments to which some developing countries have already committed themselves, because inclusion of these in an MFI would expose these countries to trade or other sanctions if successful cases were brought against them at the WTO.

There is of course a common interest of both developed and developing countries in environmental protection clauses to the extent that environmental destruction has highly negative external effects which spread across borders, and this justifies the compulsory adherence of countries to international environment treaties. In contrast, there is a conflict of interest over poor labour standards, which are seen by developed countries as both stimulating immigration flows and underpinning 'unfair competition' in international trade.

The simplest way to include labour and environmental safeguards in the MFI is to include them in the Preamble to the treaty. This could recognize certain international principles, rules and standards to which the Contracting Parties declare to be committed, including: environmental protection, sustainable development and international environmental law. Explicit reference could be made to the Rio Declaration on Environment and Development and Agenda 21, to core labour standards as defined by ILO agreements and

---

32  WTO, *The Relationship between Trade and Foreign Direct Investment* (1997), pp. 27-30.
33  A. Kokko and M. Blomström, 'Policies to Encourage Inflows of Technology through Foreign Multinationals', 23 *World Development* (1995), no. 3.
34  E.g., those established in the *Rio Declaration*, regarding the environment, and those set forth in ILO's *Tripartite Declaration of Principles concerning Multinational Enterprises and Social Policy*, with respect to labour standards.

possibly also to the (non-binding) OECD Guidelines for Multinational Enterprises. Although the direct legal applicability of preambular declarations is controversial, their fundamental role as primary sources of legal interpretation in case of ambiguity or inconsistency is not in dispute.

Alternatively, provisions to prevent the lowering of health, safety, environmental or labour standards by signatories in order to encourage foreign investment could be included in the MFI.[35] A contracting party incurring such a practice could be required to go through consultations with a view to eliminating such measure, persistent non-compliance becoming subject to dispute settlement challenge.

However, compliance with such higher standards would in fact mean greater changes for local firms than for MNCs if the principle of non-discrimination were to be applied in practice. In consequence, there is a danger that were strict international standards to be included in an MFI, developing country parties would be continually exposed to contentious disputes from competitors, and thus could not contemplate accession except under a general exemption from these conditions – which would be politically difficult at home and diplomatically embarrassing abroad.

This danger could be effectively overcome by imposing international labour and environment standards on all large domestic firms as well, thus avoiding discriminatory bias. The exception for small firms would in fact mirror similar exemptions in the domestic legislation of industrial countries. Finally, limits on the imposition of requirements concerning domestic content and purchase of (or preferential treatment to) local supplies should not prevent a contracting party from adopting measures necessary to protect human life or the environment. Indeed the NAFTA sets a precedent for generalizing the environmental exception to all the provisions of the agreement[36].

## 4 THE MANAGEMENT OF CAPITAL FLOWS AND AN MFI

### 4.1 Liberalizing capital flows

The theoretical case for liberalizing international capital flows is based on four principles. First, free capital movements can facilitate a more efficient allocation of savings, channelling resources to countries where they can be used most productively, and thereby increasing growth and welfare. Second, access to foreign capital markets may enable investors to achieve a higher degree of portfolio diversification, allowing them to obtain higher risk-adjusted returns.

---

35 A package of proposals for text on environment and labour to this effect was before the negotiators when the MAI talks broke down.
36 Although Art. 1114 of NAFTA also provides that no environmental measure shall be adopted as a disguised restriction for investment outflows or inflows.

Third, full convertibility for capital account transactions can complement the multilateral trading system, broadening the channels through which countries can obtain trade and investment finance. Fourth, more generally, by subjecting governments to greater market discipline and penalizing unsound monetary and fiscal policies, liberalization may improve macroeconomic performance.

Set against these benefits is the risk of sudden, possibly excessive, reversals in the availability of external finance caused by shifts in market sentiment. Enthusiasm for liberalizing capital flows has now diminished as the East Asian crisis spread to other regions and the after-shocks have been transmitted first to other emerging markets and then to the equity markets of the advanced economies.

It is now recognized that there is an increased risk that volatility within the financial system will destabilize real economic performance, measured in terms of output, employment and price stability. Industrial countries are actively pursuing the reform of the 'international financial architecture', of which the MFI would logically form a part.[37] More radically, some emerging market governments have begun to consider the reimposition of capital controls as a means of insulating their economies from the potentially destabilizing effects of short-term capital movements.

The instability of emerging markets is related to macroeconomic fault lines and inadequate institutional structures in the capital markets. Unlike the sovereign borrowing of the late 1970s and early 1980s, much of the flow to emerging markets in the 1990s represented borrowing by the private sector. In theory, this should have resulted in a closer link between borrowing and expected investment returns; the debt should also have been fully collateralized. However, the volume of lending to individual emerging markets clearly exceeded their capacity to invest the resources productively and at reasonable risk.

The excessive inflows were encouraged by apparent exchange rate guarantees and misallocated by poorly supervised domestic banking systems. Moreover, the lack of corporate and banking sector transparency made it impossible for foreign investors to assess investment risks accurately. Western policy-makers have responded by calling for the adoption of more rigorous accounting and banking standards, and greater openness about public and private sector debt levels, in order to improve the functioning of market mechanisms in allocating cross-border capital.

Even allowing for the problems of risk assessment, it is difficult to explain the rapid shift from optimism to pessimism that triggered crises in a number of countries, or the virulence of the contagion process by which a crisis in one emerging market has been transmitted to others. Much of this appears to be the result of herd behaviour among investors, and so may not be fully 'rational'. It is possible that in this sense globally integrated financial markets

---

37 FitzGerald et al., *supra*.

may be accentuating or even creating instability within the real side of the economy.

In many cases, the small and relatively illiquid financial markets of developing countries have been swamped by sudden shifts in the availability of external finance, causing exchange rate and monetary adjustments to overshoot.[38] The result of this overshooting may be the widespread failure of corporate and banking sector institutions: indiscriminate failures which destroy sound as well as unsound banks and corporations may jeopardize the institutional basis of a future economic recovery.

The possibility that markets may behave irrationally – and that monetary variables may overshoot as a result, destabilizing real economic performance – traditionally justifies government intervention in capital markets, in the form either of controls on capital flows or the provision of a lender of last resort facility. Both of these interventions necessarily have a discretionary element and require the ability to discriminate against foreign banks, which are not under the regulatory control of the domestic monetary authorities.

Nationally, central banks and other government institutions have assumed market-stabilizing responsibilities, offering to act as lender of last resort to troubled financial intermediaries in order to prevent the failure of one institution from impairing the functioning of the financial system as a whole. By analogy, as national financial systems become increasingly integrated, a case could be made for a lender of last resort in the international capital markets.[39]

However, the expansion and integration of national financial systems has not been coupled with a strengthening either of national central banks or the international financial institutions.[40] A key issue for an MFI would thus be whether, on the one hand, emergency measures to reduce volatility would be compatible with the treaty, and, on the other, whether the MFI would itself reduce the volatility of capital flows by reducing investor uncertainty.

4.2     Managing short-term capital surges

Recent financial market turmoil has prompted new interest in capital controls, because emerging markets are adopting a more sceptical attitude towards short-term external finance in the wake of the crisis in East Asia. Article VIII of the IMF's Articles of Agreement only requires States Parties to avoid imposing restrictions on current account transactions, such as those related to trade

---

38  E. FitzGerald, 'Global Capital Market Volatility and the Developing Countries: Lessons from the East Asian Crisis', 30 *IDS Bulletin* (1999), no. 1, pp. 19-32.
39  *Idem.*
40  "International cooperation between regulators and adequate disclosure of information at all levels are increasingly important to ensuring safe and efficient markets." World Bank, *supra* note 30.

in goods and services and the remittance of profits and dividends. Nonetheless, the IMF policy-making Interim Committee agreed in September 1997 that full convertibility for capital account transactions should be the ultimate objective for all Fund Members. The IMF staff was instructed to draw up an amendment to the Articles of Agreement that would make the orderly liberalization of capital account transactions one of the Fund's central purposes.

Several developed countries (including France, Spain and Italy) have in the recent past resorted to controls on the inflow or outflow of capital as a temporary expedient to stabilize domestic financial markets. Capital controls have distortionary consequences and may be used as a pretext to relax macroeconomic discipline, as well as discriminating against foreign investors in practice – although this is not necessarily so in principle, as domestic holders of overseas assets may also be constrained in their operations by such controls. Nonetheless, where domestic capital markets are imperfect and systems for financial supervision are not robust, there may be a strong case for not liberalizing capital account transactions fully until these problems have been addressed. The appropriate sequencing of capital account liberalization and measures to strengthen domestic banking systems, remains a central issue in the current discussions about international monetary reform.

Exposure to short-term capital flows in the form of interbank lending and portfolio investment is widely blamed for exacerbating the crisis, disrupting financial systems and destabilizing real economic performance. This has prompted many developing country governments to search for policy instruments to insulate their economies from the vagaries of an apparently crisis-prone international financial system. In September 1998, Malaysia became the first major emerging market to reintroduce controls on capital outflows; although these specifically stated to be temporary and excluded FDI inflows and profit repatriation.

Following the Asian crisis, policy-makers have shown increasing interest in the macroeconomic model pioneered by Chile, which couples trade openness and FDI encouragement with restrictions on short-term capital inflows. The model has five components, each of which are used by other emerging markets to some extent:

*Sterilized intervention.* The central bank has intervened in the foreign exchange market to prevent the real exchange rate from appreciating excessively, purchasing dollars in exchange for local currency to maintain the exchange rate within a reasonably broad band around a dollar-deutschmark-yen reference rate. The impact on the money supply has been sterilized by massive placements of central bank promissory notes, albeit at the cost of additional fiscal burdens and high domestic interest rates.

*Investment regulations.* Capital investment is subject to a number of laws and restrictions specifying minimum entry amounts and the time, which must elapse before capital can be repatriated. Decree Law 600 requires FDI to enter Chile through a foreign investment contract with a specified minimum duration, which varies according to the industrial sector concerned. Capital cannot be repatriated until one year after entry, although there are no restrictions on the repatriation of profits. Law 18,657 creates Foreign Capital Investment Funds. Foreign portfolio investment in public securities and equities is allowed, subject to a minimum amount of one million dollars, which must be invested within one year. Capital invested in these funds cannot be repatriated for a minimum of five years, but profit repatriation is not restricted.

*Reserve requirements.* The central bank has imposed reserve requirements on capital inflows, which attempt to discriminate between long-term capital investments and short-term 'non-productive' inflows. Short-term inflows are subject to a one-year reserve requirement of 30% at zero interest. The aim is to reduce speculative capital inflows and increase the proportion of direct investment and long-term credit in the capital account. These 'market-friendly' controls have proved highly effective in practice.

*Other mechanisms.* Chile has also used several other policy instruments to restrict the speculative inflow of capital, including minimum conditions for external bond and equity issues, and reductions in the availability and increases in the cost of swap facilities at the central bank. The authorities have also taken measures to encourage capital outflows, including the liberalization of pension fund regulations, in order to avoid excessive money supply growth.

These measures necessarily involve a degree of discrimination against foreign capital, particularly the portfolio entry regulations. Although in principle these could apply equally to asset repatriation by residents, effective discrimination against foreign nationals is held to be justified because they are believed to less 'committed' to the host economy.[41]

## 4.3 Capital flows management in an MFI

The most logical approach in the MFI would be to build upon a broad, asset-based definition of investment, which includes not only foreign direct investment as such, but also the direct or indirect ownership or control of any other asset. Coverage of portfolio investment, bank loans and all kinds of asset management by residents or nationals of Contracting Parties (even through offshore companies) would go considerably beyond most BITs.

At first sight, the inclusion of portfolio investment under the disciplines of an MFI (particularly national treatment and most-favoured-nation treatment) would seem to restrict the ability of governments to impose controls on volatile capital inflows. Contracting Parties would thus have to be allowed to adopt temporary non-conforming measures in the event that cross-border capital

---

41 This is because foreign investors are believed to have less information about any one emerging market than nationals, and are also in a better position to switch between emerging markets rapidly. They thus are more likely to leave in response to bad news.

transactions cause or threaten to cause external financial difficulties or serious difficulties for the conduct of monetary or exchange rate policies.[42] This safeguard - which in practice could be continued for many years - would be of crucial importance for developing countries faced with large exogenous capital surges.

Contract-based rights with governments may be proposed by industrial countries for inclusion in the definition of investment under the MFI.[43] This would affect concessions, authorizations and licenses in key development sectors such as natural resources and tourism. Even though this is a principle already included in most aid-funded investment projects, its exclusion from the MFI (or at least the facility for lodging of sector-specific exceptions) would be necessary to prevent undue harassment of developing country governments.

Finally, many foreign investors control their investments in developing countries through offshore holding companies, often incorporated in tax havens. In some cases, this is done for tax evasion or money laundering purposes. The inclusion and protection of indirect ownership under the MAI is, in this context, a potential problem for recipient developing countries and should be excluded from protection under the MFI.

MFI rules on privatization should be straightforward: all kinds of privatization, irrespective of their method, or rules regarding subsequent disposal of a privatized asset, must conform to the national and most-favoured-nation treatment clauses. The procedures and essential features of each prospective privatization shall be made publicly available, and in accordance with national treatment and most-favoured-nation treatment. An MFI should not impose an obligation on Contracting Parties to privatize, however. Nor should it prevent governments from retaining 'golden shares' or from regulating privatized utilities in the public interest.

MFI provisions should strike an adequate balance between the interests of foreign investors and those of developing countries. While they should rule out arbitrary discrimination against international investment, they should allow for specific (and domestically determined) privatization mechanisms that have proved positive in developing countries' experiences, such as: retention of 'golden shares' (with special veto rights) by the government, voucher schemes for members of the public or specific communities, preferential treatment to employees and/or managers of privatized entities, or allocation of shares to specific groups.

---

42 As was done in Section VI of the MAI draft. However, it was proposed that such measures should only be permitted with permission from the IMF, which does not seem to be a helpful restriction in view of the need for rapid action in balance of payments crises. Maintenance of such restrictions would depend on the prevailing rules of IMF membership (which are consistent with the Chilean controls, e.g.) in any case, and would not require additional restrictions in the MFI.

43 This was included in Section VI of the MAI draft.

An MFI should include specific provisions for the financial services sector, including: (a) an exception for the application of the MFI when any of its provisions need to be suspended in implementing prudential financial system regulation measures (and provisions on dispute settlement when such exception is invoked in a financial dispute); (b) procedures for the recognition of another contracting party's financial regulation standards; (c) transparency in authorization procedures; (d) national treatment by self-regulatory bodies (such as stock markets and associations); and (e) national treatment in the access of foreign investors to official funding and refinancing facilities, but not to lender of last resort facilities.

The inclusion of similar provisions in the MAI draft was an explicit acknowledgement of the unique nature of the financial system and the need for prudential regulation to ensure its stability – an aspect of particular importance to developing countries. Despite the fact that foreign investment in the banking sector can bring greater management expertise – especially in risk management – as well as stronger backing to provide liquidity, it is clear that for regulatory purposes most national authorities require a base of domestically owned banks with whom to work. The same provisions should also be included in an MFI.

The MFI should exclude domestic taxation measures (including direct, indirect and social security taxes) from the application of its provisions,[44] except those on expropriation and transparency, within the limits set by domestic or international commitments on tax secrecy and confidentiality. Thus, the MFI would exclude taxation from national and most-favoured-nation treatment clauses, thereby giving flexibility to States Parties to enter into bilateral and/or regional tax agreements or to enforce the existing ones. It would also enable developing country governments to adopt discriminatory tax laws and anti-evasion policies facilitated by technological developments. However, it might be necessary to provide that a taxation measure could effect expropriation for the purposes of the agreement if it exceeds the bounds of internationally recognised tax policies and practices.

Investor protection of financial assets would only refer, of course, to government expropriation of such assets and not to their market price or the effect of (say) exchange rate changes on their international value. Broad asset definition in an MFI would help in private debt workouts. Private debt failures have become common in the wake of financial liberalization, due to the excessive lending discussed above. Working out bad debts requires the disposal of counter party assets as bank asset values are written down. In the absence of clear internationally recognized property protection, this can become very difficult - especially in a crisis situation. In consequence, private debtors are reluctant to participate in international bailout operations such as those organ-

---

44 This was also the case in the MAI draft, OECD, *Multilateral Agreement on Investment: Consolidated Text* (1998).

ized by the US Treasury and the IMF in Korea, Russia and Brazil during 1997-1999.

Sovereign debt would continue to be covered by existing arrangements under public international law, and thus might require specific provision in an MFI, particularly since protection of sovereign debt held by private banks and bondholders could make workouts *more* difficult by allowing individual creditors faced by a debt moratorium or an internationally organized restructuring scheme to press for legal sanctions at the WTO. This would impede orderly debt workouts (such as the Brady Plan) and should be avoided in any future MFI.

MFI rules would thus be more conducive to private sector development than the present system of 'policy conditionality' operated by the IMF and other international financial institutions, where successive debt restructurings are used as a form of exogenous financial discipline. In contrast, accession to an MFI would signal to investors in a convincing way a permanent commitment to market disciplines and integration into the world economy. This would only be true of a multilateral agreement, as BITs evidently do not provide this kind of security.

## 5    NEGOTIATING ASYMMETRY

### 5.1    Asymmetric market access

In trade negotiations, there is a working assumption that the disadvantages to any one of two negotiating partners (one of whom can be 'the rest of the world') of granting the other access to its home markets by reducing import barriers can be balanced by the corresponding advantage of gaining market access for its exports. This may not apply within any one trading category, which is why negotiations may involve reciprocal concessions for different products. Moreover, the different size of negotiating states matters:[45] in extreme cases where the importing country is a virtual monopsonist, the power to maintain quotas – often for non-economic reasons – is considerable. Nonetheless, the principle of reciprocity is the starting point for all trade negotiations.[46]

The case of investment flows is quite different, for two reasons. First, the industrial countries are net capital exporters on a large scale, and developing

---

45  The *relative* advantage (and thus importance) to Bangladesh of gaining free access to the EU market is much greater than that for the EU of access to the Bangladesh market, e.g..

46  This is independent of the possibility that their might be net welfare gains to developing countries from *unilateral* import liberalization. These gains are clearly greater if such liberalization also implies improved access to export markets.

countries have no corresponding flow with which to negotiate.[47] Table 3 below indicates the scale of this asymmetry. Developed countries in 1997 had a roughly balanced set of claims against each other of over two trillion US dollars, more than six times the 1980 level. In addition they have net capital stock invested in developing countries of the order of one trillion US dollars, for which there is no corresponding recorded liability in the form of developing country assets.

Second, international capital flows are 'market rationed' in the sense that at equilibrium there is an excess of demand for funds over their supply. In consequence, developing countries have an almost perfectly elastic demand for funds at a given price. This is a market phenomenon and derives from the fact that investors have imperfect information about the quality of investments and incomplete control over the returns, so that they will tend to invest less than would be warranted if these intrinsic market failures did not exist. The task of market institutions in general, and an MFI in particular, is to reduce these obstacles to the extent possible.

Developing countries must thus compete between themselves for available investment. They are not in a strong position to negotiate with developed countries by demanding corresponding facilities for their own investors. If anything, the problem is the reverse - the encouragement and protection given by the financial centres of developing countries to capital flight is probably damaging to developing countries.

Table 3: Inward and outward FDI stocks (US$ billion)

|  | 1980 Inward | Outward | 1997 Inward | Outward |
|---|---|---|---|---|
| World | 480 | 525 | 3456 | 3541 |
| Developed countries | 372 | 509 | 2349 | 3192 |
| Developing countries | 108 | 15 | 1044 | 342 |
| · South-Saharan Africa | 9 | - | 40 | 15 |
| · Latin America & Caribbean | 48 | 3 | 375 | 36 |
| · South, East & South-East Asia | 32 | 11 | 528 | 279 |
| Least developed countries | 2 | - | 17 | 1 |

Source: UNCTAD, supra note 1.

---

47 Ironically, the factor flow that should reciprocate for the flow of capital from developed to developing countries in liberal political doctrine and neo-classical economic theory is that of labour! However, immigration is restricted by precisely those industrial countries most committed to the principles of free trade and free capital movements.

In recent years the picture has also begun to change because several of the industrializing countries are emerging as major net investors in their own right, in particular Taiwan and Korea. Among the net recipients, countries such as Chile, China, Malaysia and Brazil are emerging as key regional investors. In consequence, a number of industrializing countries are beginning to have a different objective interest in international investment disciplines, even though in negotiating practice they will clearly attempt to gain the greatest possible advantage in exchange for reducing their own controls over inward investment. The figures in Table 3 are only for officially registered outward stocks, of course. In addition, private investors from developing countries have built up considerable overseas portfolios unregistered with their home authorities ('capital flight').

## 5.2    Assistance and reciprocity in MFI negotiations with developing countries

From the above considerations it should be clear that developing countries – and the smaller low-income countries in particular – would require considerable assistance if they are to accede to any agreement of this type. Wide and discretionary exceptions are not the solution, because these would undermine the very rigour, which creates confidence among investors. The issue is thus one of raising domestic standards rather than lowering international requirements.

Such strengthening of domestic standards is a complex, lengthy and expensive undertaking. However, it could bring considerable benefits for foreign as well as domestic firms. In particular, it would involve an overhaul of the system of commercial law – including the courts – and a parallel rationalization of systems of public registries, accountancy systems, and government regulation. The role of aid donors could be crucial in this regard, providing not just financial support but, more importantly, technical expertise.

The provision of dispute settlement procedures between states is a standard feature of international agreements: the WTO rules, which would probably be applied to an MFI, are well established. The costs are, however, a source of concern for smaller developing countries. The costs of representation are usually very high and most low-income countries lack highly skilled litigants with expertise in international investment and arbitration procedures. This implies the risk that litigation be used as a form of harassment to other parties, or at least an incentive to negotiate 'off-tribunal'. And here, the bargaining power (as measured by the relative weight of each party's potential retaliation measures) would be on the side of the developed countries. This implies that the donor community should consider the provision of internationally funded arbitration tribunals and pools of litigation experts in this field.

In view of the inherent asymmetry in investment negotiations, it seems logical to explore what reciprocal concessions might be made to developing countries in exchange for market access by foreign investors from developed countries. The fact that adherence to an MFI without such concessions might still be in developing countries' own interest does not detract from the need for such concessions by developed countries. Nonetheless, such reciprocal action should be justified in its own terms as being conducive to development.

The first and most obvious type of reciprocity is that of exchanging some other form of market access, particularly the access of key developing country exports to highly protected industrial country markets. This is in effect the strategy adopted in the Uruguay Round by exporters of many agricultural products and processed raw materials in exchange for concessions on services trade and related investment issues. There are obvious limitations to this approach: it is not directly related to investment as such, so a general agreement is impossible to establish. A successful MFI agreement would thus depend upon the success of essentially unrelated changes.[48] Moreover, the ad hoc exchange of concessions would probably favour the interests of larger and/or middle-income developing countries as opposed to the smaller/poorer ones.

The second type of reciprocity takes as its starting point the investing firms themselves, and argues that as the main beneficiaries from investment in developing countries, they should take on some of the wider burdens of economic development. Specifically, they should bear special responsibilities that domestic firms in the host country do not, such as the costs of higher environmental or employment standards. This, in essence, appears to be the proposal of many NGOs and to some extent the UNCTAD, and reflects the laudable aim of ensuring that the citizens of developing countries (the poor in particular) gain an appropriate share of the global welfare increment generated by international investment process.

This form of reciprocity – even if it were acceptable to industrialized countries, which is highly unlikely – runs up against two major difficulties. On the one hand, the principle of all investment (and indeed trade) treaties is that of equal treatment, so that host country firms[49] would necessarily have to obey the same rules under international legislation translated into domestic law. Insofar as the MFI is an intergovernmental agreement, and in view of the absence of a supranational regulator for such firms, this would presumably require that the authorities in the home country cooperate with those of the host country to apply a uniform set of rules so that all firms assume their obligations. This might lead to transfer of ownership to offshore financial centres, in much the same way as happened with 'flags of convenience' for shipping lines.

The third type of reciprocity can be derived from the way in which firms (and asset owners in general) discharge their obligations to the wider community, and the way in which investors are induced to behave more respons-

---

48  Such as the dismantling of the EU Common Agricultural Policy.
49  Or at least those above a certain size.

ibly, in a market economy. This is through the imposition and design of corporation tax. The most logical form of reciprocity in international investment negotiations would be for industrial countries to ensure that profits taxes are levied on, and paid by international firms in such a way that the developing countries where they operate can obtain a fair share of the return on investment in the form of fiscal revenue and invest this in wider development objectives. In addition, international agreement could prevent the damaging competition between host countries on tax incentives caused by the market rationing of investment discussed above.

### 5.3 International tax cooperation

Free movement of capital and opportunities for the geographical dispersion of firms create new challenges for tax authorities. Different national taxation norms and interstices between different national tax administrations create conflicts of interests among all involved. International double taxation arising from the concurrent exercise by two or more countries of their taxation rights, is a phenomenon that is not conducive to business agreements in general and FDI in particular.[50]

Many developing countries – particularly the smaller ones – attempt to attract foreign investment through tax incentive policies in an attempt to compensate for local distortions and inefficiencies, or to simply prevent foreign investment from going to neighbouring or similar countries. However, the empirical evidence suggests that such incentives play a very limited role as determinants of foreign investment, and even where successful, involve significant fiscal costs.[51] Although the net benefit of tax incentives in attracting FDI is not clear in practice they are expected to become more significant as other investment barriers decline.[52] The role of the tax factor in determining location gives rise to wasteful tax competition for investment.[53] In consequence, both the OECD and the EU have recently adopted non-binding instruments for dealing with potentially harmful preferential tax regimes, and it is recognized that the association of non-OECD countries with these is important.[54]

---

50  See UNCTAD, *supra* note 1, pp. 74-88.
51  See UNCTAD, *Incentives and Foreign Direct Investment* (1995).
52  S. Plasschaert (ed.), *Transnational Corporations: Transfer Pricing and Taxation* (1994)
53  OECD, *Harmful Tax Competition: an Emerging Global Issue* (1998).
54  The OECD member countries plan to take punitive action against 47 tax havens that fail to cooperate with international efforts to combat tax evasion. 'Harmful jurisdictions' are defined as those that offered zero or low tax rates but lack legal or administrative transparency, which would allow other countries to investigate tax evasion by their nationals. It had been intended to announce the list of defaulting countries in October 1999 and initiate the sanctions in June 2000, but those measures have now been postponed until 2001. All

Since the tax systems of the major home countries are based on worldwide income taxation principles, their multinational companies are frequently subject to some degree of double taxation. This fact not only deters international investment, but also provides incentives for the use of tax havens to channel cross-border capital flows through the incorporation of offshore holding companies. The use of these schemes is detrimental to both the home and host country through reduced tax revenues and distorted investment inflows.

Only when a multilateral tax agreement is implemented, would the legal framework of international investment be logically complete.[55] Such an agreement would not only improve the fiscal revenue position of developing countries and reduce the attractiveness of tax incentives to foreign investors, but would also strengthen the effort to combat money laundering and financial fraud.[56]

However, the likelihood of an agreement on a comprehensive system of multilateral tax administration is low. Thus the prospect of fiscal issues being excluded from a future MFI (if only because they do not fall within the remit of the WTO) has serious consequences for developing countries because a multilateral coordination of investment incentive policies could help developing countries in terms of conserving fiscal resources and avoiding economic distortions.

The number of double taxation treaties (DTTs) has increased rapidly and there are now some 1,700 such treaties in existence.[57] DTTs were originally between developed countries, but the recent expansion, clearly following the course of the BITs, is both with and between developing countries: 34% of all DDTs are between developed and developing countries, and a further 17% between developing countries. The principle of non-discrimination (i.e., national treatment) has been intrinsic to DTTs since the nineteenth century; and was central to the 1935 draft tax convention prepared by the League of Nations. The application of DTTs in support of developing countries, possibly as a joint EU initiative, may thus be the only viable basis for investment-related tax cooperation. There are two models used, which are similar in their general provisions but have very different implications for developing countries: the OECD Draft Taxation Convention/Model Tax Conventions,[58] which is based

---

OECD Members (except Switzerland and Luxembourg) have pledged to change their laws by 2003 in order to meet the new reporting standards.
55 Possibly based on the model treaty proposed by the OECD, *Model Double Taxation Convention on Income and Capital* (1997b).
56 The failure of attempts to reduce narcotics traffic by demand reduction (i.e., education and repression within developed countries) and supply interdiction (i.e., eradication and police action in developing countries) has led to increased interest in the expropriation of traffickers' funds, and thus measures to monitor and regulate international financial transfers – previously a major constraint on national tax administration.
57 International Bureau of Fiscal Documentation, *Annual Report 1997-1998* (1998).
58 OECD, *supra* note 55.

on residence taxation, and the United Nations Model Double Taxation Convention between Developed and Developing Countries,[59] which is based on source (or 'territorial') taxation. The source principle may encourage nationals or residents to invest abroad, thus leading to capital flight,[60] but it is often adopted because tax administrators have great difficulty in finding out how much foreign income accrues to their residents. The residence principle, although based on overall capacity to pay, has proved to be of limited significance in countries whose residents do not have substantial (recorded) investments in other countries, and whose fiscal administration is not well equipped to ensure its application. Moreover, to the extent that developed countries apply both the source and residence principles to their own residents, they claw back tax from their own investors in developing countries, while by not taxing non-residents they stimulate capital flight from developing countries.

In theory, developing countries would benefit most from a multilateral tax treaty based on the source principle for two reasons. First, the gains from taxing income of foreign investors would be greater than the loss from not taxing income from their own residents' assets held abroad, because a developing country has a net external liability position. Second, the full taxation of these assets held abroad by the authorities in that country on the source principle would make capital flight much less attractive.[61]

For developing countries the issue is how to strike a balance between maximizing their share of revenues and maintaining a climate that attracts FDI. This involves agreement on the sharing of revenues between host and home countries in what is almost a 'zero sum game', which implies a net transfer between the taxpayers of home and host countries in the last instance, agreement on the methods to be adopted (including the definition of 'permanent establishment') and agreement on how to encourage FDI. By adopting a treaty, a developing country subscribes to international rules that promote stability, transparency and certainty of treatment.

These latter features, by reducing regulatory uncertainty are just as important to investing firms as the particular concessions or incentives that a treaty may contain. Tax incentives appear to be regarded by multinational firms as a 'windfall gain', and not the basis for long-term investment decisions as they may be subsequently reversed. This does not stop investors negotiating for such concessions of course, but at most they may affect location decisions within a country when other cost factors are unchanged.

The effect of tax treaties depends on the credits and exemptions included in them in order to eliminate or reduce double taxation. When countries are

---

59 *United Nations Double Taxation Convention between Developed and Developing Countries* (1980), UN publ. no. E.80.XVI.3.
60 Note that in principle this mainly relates to personal rather than corporate taxation, although the distinction is unclear in practice.
61 The other factor being regime uncertainty, which an MFI would help to reduce.

at a similar level of development (and there is roughly balanced two-way investment) the implicit redistribution is not a great problem, but for developing countries the marginal revenue is of greater value than to the home developed country. As the flow of income is generally from developing to developed countries, the tax credit method is the most attractive to developing countries.[62] From the point of view of developing country revenue authorities, DTTs are the only way to cover intra-firm transactions and thus overcome the problem of transfer pricing;[63] but they can of course be ineffective if offshore centres are used as transfer pricing points as well as for tax avoidance. In consequence, short of a comprehensive multilateral tax agreement, reconsideration of tax credits within existing DTTs would be desirable, as would the application of the US 'pass-through' principle to tax havens.[64]

The resolution of double taxation problems will also require a major effort from aid donors. Developing countries need help to strengthen their own administrative systems in order to make double taxation arrangements work. This help includes not only technical assistance and material resources to enhance their own tax administrations but also the sharing of information and above all the willingness to sign double taxation agreements with developing countries. The implication of this change in approach would be that developed countries would have to inspect the external transactions in developing countries of their residents with diligence, including the monitoring of transfer pricing and internal debt within multinational corporations. It would also imply that OECD countries would have to cease their tacit support for tax havens, whether under their own jurisdiction or used by their residents.

Finally it should not be forgotten that for developing countries capturing tax revenue on the income of their own residents who have assets overseas is a major problem too. In consequence, closer international collaboration, even within the existing DTT network, by sharing information and permitting joint actions could increase the fiscal resources available to developing countries dramatically.[65] Further benefits would stem from this, including: disincentives to capital flight; increased fiscal and macroeconomic stability; and greater resources available for poverty alleviation.

---

62 It is widely used in DTTs between the UK and LDCs.
63 OECD, *supra* note 55.
64 In the case of a firm (A) resident in the US, carrying out transactions with a firm (B) in another country via an offshore 'tax haven' company (C), the US authorities apply tax to the transaction A-B rather than A-C.
65 J. Williamson, 'A New Priority: Taxing Income from Capital', Paper presented at the Society for International Development meeting on 'A New Framework of Development Co-operation', Easton MD, June 26-28, 1998.

## 6 CONCLUSION

Foreign investment is important to all developing countries, not just the major recipients, because of their low levels of business investment. The upgrading of domestic law, institutions, and regulation required by MFI accession would have a strong positive effect on domestic and expatriate investors as well as on multinational companies. An MFI would represent a considerable advance over the existing pattern of bilateral investment treaties (BITs) both because it would create a transparent international standard understood by all investors and because it would reduce regulatory uncertainty by being difficult to withdraw from. The benefits would be gained by the smaller vulnerable economies in particular, which, unlike the larger developing economies, are not in a strong negotiating position.

Core requirements for an MFI are three: asset protection; national treatment; and dispute settlement. The principles of national treatment and dispute settlement established in existing WTO agreements seem appropriate for an MFI reflecting developing country interests. Asset protection would need to be defined precisely, and issues such as pre-establishment rights, privatization and compensation clarified. A broad asset definition should be adopted, including both fixed and financial assets.

Beyond this core, exceptions for developing countries should be the minimum consistent with development objectives. They should be based on a general approach derived from modern principles of competition and regulation applied to the situation of developing countries. The national security criterion employed by developed countries in the MAI negotiations will presumably also be invoked in future MFI discussions.

The internal decisions of firms on large investment projects in small economies can have major macroeconomic consequences through their effect on subcontracting, employment, exports and tax revenue. It would thus be desirable for broad criteria to be established for the regulation of foreign investment in strategic sectors of small countries. Exceptions to national treatment should be limited to sectors where large domestic firms are absent or specific monopoly concessions are involved, so that discretionary firm by firm negotiation is necessary. This will mainly refer to domestic utilities and natural resources.

There is also an evident need for clear exceptions to allow incentives to be extended to particular types of firms – particularly small enterprises and cooperatives – for social reasons, which could not be extended to foreign investors. Such exceptions would be best specified as general principles for all developing countries.

Given that host developing countries (particularly low-income countries) are credit-rationed in the international and domestic capital markets, liberalization of cross-border financial sector investment would be beneficial. However, the development of competent regulatory bodies (lacking in most low-income countries) should precede financial liberalization. Developing countries without adequate financial regulation infrastructure and capabilities will probably need specific exceptions and transitional arrangements regarding this sector in any MFI.

Some developing country governments and non-governmental organizations are concerned that an MFI might involve a loss of economic sovereignty, and thus prevent the pursuit of sustainable development strategies. All international treaties involve some pooling of sovereignty. The relevant issue is whether the economic gains exceed the 'option value' of the sovereignty pooled – that is, the economic value of the policies precluded by belonging to the agreement.

Developing countries will gain significantly by becoming part of a rules-based international system that will allow them not only to attract foreign investment, but also to regulate foreign firms more effectively. The essence of an MFI is the principle that attributes the same treatment to foreigners as to domestic investors, which is unobjectionable 'under like circumstances'. Where no domestic firms of equivalent size exist discrimination is justified on grounds of accepted competition requirements.

Trade protection for domestic producers is in any case constrained by existing WTO agreements arising from the Uruguay Round, so it is not available as an instrument of policy to the extent that it was in the traditional 'import substitution' model. Similarly, almost all developing countries are already engaged in privatization programmes, and probable MFI provisions on expropriation (compensation and non-discrimination) do not represent a real constraint on sovereignty.

It should still be possible for governments to impose across-the-board restrictions on investment under an MFI (such as regional location priorities), so long as they apply to both large domestic and foreign investors. This may be positive for countries where the levels of institutional development and investment climate are reasonable by international standards, although it may require considerable international support in order to reform and strengthen their domestic legislation and regulatory institutions.

Capital account liberalization is unlike trade liberalization as capital markets are inherently unstable. Developing countries' macroeconomic policy stance is increasingly determined by changes on international financial markets, which requires both phased and closely regulated liberalization, and promotion of FDI in order to stabilize capital flows. An MFI could play two key roles in this context: to provide more certainty to investors and thus their willingness to take long positions and to ease the process of debt workouts by making asset ownership more transparent in the wake of financial rescue operations.

The implementation of international standards on labour conditions and environmental protection is clearly desirable, and should be reaffirmed in an MFI. It would be desirable if the binding obligations on foreign firms were also those imposed on large domestic firms. Developing countries that have difficulties in meeting such standards in any but the long term could still be encouraged to join an MFI with appropriate transition arrangements and a commitment not to lower standards.

Those developing countries willing to commit themselves to high standards of investment protection under a future MFI would be free to adopt such standards swiftly within established WTO procedures. Annex IV to the Agreement establishing the WTO provides for such plurilateral agreements. Developing countries are free to negotiate 'special and differential treatment' in any WTO provision. Lengthy transition periods as well as special exemptions are part of the concessions made to developing countries during the Uruguay Round and have a long history in GATT.

Comprehensive multilateral investment negotiations within the WTO context will inevitably take many years, if not decades. On the one hand, there are severe disagreements between developed and developing countries on market access issues. On the other hand, there is the need to redefine access in terms of competition policy rather than national treatment. However, the pending review of the Trade Related Investment Measures (TRIMS) agreement[66] does provide an opportunity to start to strengthen international investment rules, although key issues of interest to poor countries, such as investor protection, do not yet lie within the WTO mandate.

---

66  These were due to start in January 2000, but were delayed by the failure to set a new WTO agenda at Seattle in late 1999.

| 4 | Comments on the MAI's General Principles for the Treatment of Foreign Investors and Their Investments. A Chinese Scholar's Perspective |

*Chen Huiping[*]*

1  INTRODUCTION

The OECD's Multilateral Agreement on Investment (MAI)[1] provides broad definitions of the terms 'investor' and 'investment', the purpose of which is to establish a wide scope of application of the provisions on treatment of foreign investors and their investments. The articles concerning the treatment of foreign investors and their investments constitute the core provisions of the MAI.[2] These articles set up core obligations for contracting parties under the MAI. In general, the treatment of foreign investors and their investments provided by the MAI consists of two categories: general principles of treatment and specific rules of treatment for specific matters under the guidance of general principles. The general principles of treatment refer to national treatment, most-favoured-nation (MFN) treatment and transparency. They apply to all aspects of the MAI, including investment protection and investment control. The specific rules of treatment are the treatment that contracting parties shall, according to the MAI, accord to foreign investors and their investments in such new issues as performance requirements, investment incentives, privatization, etc. in the field of investment. The standard of the two categories of treatment of foreign investors and their investments provided by the MAI is the minimum standard each contracting party shall accord. Compared with the standard provided by other investment treaties, the MAI's standard is the highest standard so far among existing multilateral frameworks for foreign investment, and represents the trend in treatment of foreign investors and their investments pursued by developed countries.

The present article focuses on the analysis of the general principles of treatment provided by the MAI. Some comments are made on their possible impact on international investment liberalization and on developing countries and China. The conclusion is that the final target of the MAI's general principles

---

[*] Chen Huiping is Lecturer in Law, Law School of Xiamen University, China.
[1] Draft text available at <www.oecd.org/daf/investment/fdi/mai/negtext.htm>.
[2] There are three draft versions of the negotiating text of the MAI that were published on the Internet. They are the version of February 1997, the version of February 1998 and the version of April 1998. In the present article, the MAI means the version of April 1998. As to the articles concerning the treatment of foreign investors and their investments, see Ch. III of the MAI.

of treatment of foreign investors and investments is to promote and realize the liberalization of foreign investment worldwide. But the realization of foreign investment will prejudice developing countries' state sovereignty and have a negative impact on their national economic development.

The structure of the present article is as follows. Section 2 analyzes the implications of the MAI's national treatment, MFN treatment and transparency clauses, and describes the exceptions and restrictions to the MAI's national treatment and MFN treatment rules. Section 3 deals with the impact of the MAI's national treatment and MFN treatment rules on international investment liberalization. It points out that the extension of national treatment will promote international investment liberalization, and that applying national treatment and MFN treatment to the admission of foreign investment is an important measure to realize international investment liberalization. Section 4 deals with the impact of national treatment and international investment liberalization on developing countries, and on China, in particular.

## 2  AN ANALYSIS OF THE MAI'S GENERAL PRINCIPLES FOR THE TREATMENT OF FOREIGN INVESTORS AND THEIR INVESTMENTS

Generally speaking, from the perspective of the legal regime of international investment, there are three standards of treatment accorded to foreign investors and their investments by investment treaties: national treatment, MFN treatment and non-discriminatory treatment. These three standards of treatment can be defined both broadly and narrowly.[3]

In its narrow definition, national treatment means that the host country shall extend to foreign investors any preferential treatment given to domestic investors. MFN treatment means that the host country shall extend to foreign investors any preferential treatment given to investors from any third country. Non-discriminatory treatment means that the host country shall not impose any special restrictions on foreign investors, which are not imposed on domestic investors, or the investors from any third country.[4] From the above definitions, it becomes clear that national treatment and MFN treatment are treatments provided from a positive perspective, while non-discriminatory

---

3  Xu Chongli, *A Study on Bilateral Investment Treaties* (1996), p. 106 (in Chinese, unpublished Ph.D. dissertation). Mr. Xu is Professor of Law and the supervisor of Ph.D. candidates in the Law School of Xiamen University, China. As to the specific analyses of national treatment, MFN treatment and non-discriminatory treatment, see UNCTAD, *National Treatment* (1999); UNCTAD, *Most-Favoured-Nation Treatment* (1999); G. Schwarzenberger, 'The Most-Favoured-Nation Standard in British State Practice', 22 *British Yearbook of International Law* (1945); M. Seyid, *The Legal Framework of World Trade* (1958).
4  Xu Chongli, *supra* note 3, p. 106.

treatment is the treatment provided from a negative perspective.[5] However, their purpose is the same, i.e., to ensure that foreign investors can enjoy in the host country equal legal treatment as domestic investors and the investors from any third country. When national treatment, MFN treatment and non-discriminatory treatment are defined in the narrow sense, they may be used jointly in the same investment treatment.[6]

In its broad definition, national treatment covers the implications of both the narrowly defined national and non-discriminatory treatments concerning domestic investors. MFN treatment broadly defined covers the implications of both MFN treatment and non-discriminatory treatment concerning investors from any third country in their narrow definitions. Similarly, non-discriminatory treatment covers the treatment in the narrow definitions provided both from a positive perspective and from a negative perspective.[7] Therefore, non-discriminatory treatment in its broad definition covers national treatment and MFN treatment in their broad definitions. It requires of the host country that it treats nationals of other countries in the same way as its nationals or nationals of a third country.[8] Where national treatment, MFN treatment and non-discriminatory treatment are defined in their broad sense, some bilateral investment treatments (BITs) clearly state that non-discriminatory treatment is national treatment and/or MFN treatment.[9] The North American Free Trade Agreement (NAFTA) regards the better treatment of national treatment and MFN treatment as non-discriminatory.[10] The treatments in their broad definitions may provide better protection to foreign investors and their investments.

In the draft version of February 1997 of the MAI, non-discriminatory treatment is listed together with national treatment and MFN treatment. Although the text does not state that non-discriminatory treatment means national treatment and MFN treatment, as is stated in the BIT between the United States and Russia, this was in effect the intention of the negotiators. In the draft version of April 1998, only national treatment and MFN treatment are stated. But when further analyzing the implications of the MAI's national treatment and MFN treatment, we still find that the MAI defines its national treatment and MFN treatment broadly. In addition, the MAI also requires transparency

---

5 J. Mo, 'Some Aspects of the Australia-China Investment Protection Treaty', *Journal of World Trade* (1991), no.1, p. 52.
6 E.g., there are articles concerning both MFN treatment and non-discriminatory treatment in the BIT between China and Australia.
7 Xu Chongli, *supra* note 3, p. 106.
8 J. Mo, *supra* note 5, p. 53.
9 E.g., in Art. 3(2) of the BIT between China and Japan in 1988, non-discriminatory means national treatment; in the APEC Non-binding Investment Principles (1994), as well as in Art. 1(1)(g) of the BIT between the United States and Russia of 1992, non-discriminatory treatment means a mixture of both national treatment and MFN treatment.
10 NAFTA, Art. 1104.

of all Contracting Parties' internal laws and policies relevant to foreign investment.

### 2.1 The implications of the MAI's national treatment, most-favoured-nation treatment and transparency clauses

The MAI's provision on national treatment reads as follows:

> Each Contracting Party shall accord to investors of another Contracting Party and to their investments, treatment no less favourable than the treatment it accords [in like circumstances] to its own investors and their investments with respect to the establishment, acquisition, expansion, operation, management, maintenance, use, enjoyment and sale or other disposition of investments.[11]

The purpose is to ensure that the standard of treatment of foreign investors and their investments is not lower than that of domestic investors and their investments.

The MAI's provision on MFN treatment reads as follows:

> Each Contracting Party shall accord to investors of another Contracting Party and to their investments, treatment no less favourable than the treatment it accords [in like circumstances] to investors of any other Contracting Party or of a non-Contracting Party, and to the investments of investors of any other Contracting Party or of a non-Contracting Party, with respect to the establishment, acquisition, expansion, operation, management, maintenance, use, enjoyment, and sale or other disposition of investments.[12]

Its purpose is to guarantee that the standard of treatment of foreign investors and their investments is not lower than that of investors and their investments from any third country.

According to the MAI, the relationship between national treatment and MFN treatment is that "each Contracting Party shall accord to investors of another Contracting Party and to their investments the better of the treatment..., which is the more favourable to those investors or investments."[13] The national treatment and MFN treatment provided by the MAI complement each other, so as to ensure that all foreign investors and their investments and domestic investors and their investments can operate and compete under the same treatment conditions.

---

11 MAI, Ch. III, National Treatment of Investors and Investments, para. 1.
12 *Idem*, para. 2.
13 *Idem*, para. 3.

In order to make sure that national treatment and MFN treatment are fully extended by all Contracting Parties, the MAI requires the transparency of their internal laws and policies. To be specific:

> Each Contracting Party shall promptly publish, or otherwise make publicly available, its laws, regulations, procedures and administrative rulings and judicial decisions of general application as well as international agreements which may affect the operation of the Agreement. Where a Contracting Party establishes policies, which are not expressed in laws or regulations or by other means listed in this paragraph but which may affect the operation of the Agreement, that Contracting Party shall promptly publish them or otherwise make them publicly available.[14]

This obligation requires the contracting host country to provide information that may be useful to foreign investors and other Contracting Parties. The purpose is to make these rules, regulations, and administrative practices clear and predictable to them.

Although the MAI adopts the same treatment terms as many other investment treaties, the following analysis will show that the MAI gives a broader and richer connotation to these terms. Compared with other international investment treaties, the standard of treatment of foreign investors and their investments provided by the MAI are of a relatively high level.

First, in international investment treaties, MFN treatment is by and large generally accepted as general treatment for foreign investors with a few specific exceptions, while national treatment is not universally accepted.[15] For example, most developed countries and some developing countries extend national treatment to foreign investors and their investments in their own domestic laws, and for this reason include a clause of national treatment in their bilateral investment treaties with other countries. But most developing countries do not stipulate national treatment; neither in their domestic laws nor in their bilateral investment treaties with other countries. Even those countries that have adopted national treatment still impose a variety of exceptions and restrictions.[16]

There are two reasons why national treatment is not universally accepted or fully extended. One is that the standard of national treatment is too high for the host countries to bear its full implications. The other is that many host countries still wish to retain the ability to favour their own domestic firms when needed with respect to the admission and establishment of investment,

---

14 MAI, Ch. III, Transparency, para. 1.
15 UNCTAD, *Trends in International Investment Agreements: An Overview* (1999), p. 61.
16 The exceptions may concern the pre-entry phase, or specific sectors, or other matters. For a general discussion, see UNCTAD, *National Treatment* (1999), pp. 43-51.

and in some cases with respect to the treatment of investments after their admission.[17]

The MAI features both national treatment and MFN treatment at the same time and regards them as non-discriminatory treatment. The treatment provided for in the MAI is compulsory for each Contracting Party. Irrespective of the fact that national treatment is not accepted as a universal principle, the MAI still imposes national treatment obligations on all Contracting Parties as 'hard law' obligations.[18] Therefore, it may be said that the general standard of treatment of foreign investors and their investments provided by the MAI is very high.

Second, according to the original intention of the OECD in drafting the MAI, the phrase 'each Contracting Party' shall include all levels of government.[19] Thus, all measures taken by either central government, federal government, provincial government or local government shall be applied to both domestic and foreign investors and their investments, in accordance with the requirements of national treatment and MFN treatment of the MAI. As a result, the obligations of Contracting Parties weigh much heavier than when 'Contracting Party' would only refer to the central or federal government.

Third, according to the intention of the negotiators, the term 'treatment' to be accorded to investors and their investments shall include all policies which have an impact on investment, i.e., economic policy, financial policy, tax policy, company law, etc. The term 'treatment' also includes the measures that will lead to *de jure* or *de facto* discrimination.[20] This means that where measures do not formally constitute discriminatory treatment of a foreign investor, but nonetheless limit the ability of such foreign investor to compete on equal terms, such measures would be incompatible with the MAI.[21] For example, if a law provides that, except for the existing investments, no new investments are allowed to flow to an economic sector such as natural resources, and the law is equally applied to both domestic investors and foreign investors, the law itself is non-discriminatory. But if domestic investors made all the existing investments, the law might still be regarded as *de facto* discriminatory to foreign investors. This would amount to a violation of the rules of national treatment according to the MAI. One more example: if a law itself does not prohibit the investments of foreign investors in a certain economic sector, but some technical rules in it in effect make it impossible for foreign investors to invest in such an economic sector while this law is in place,

---

17  UNCTAD, *supra* note 15, p. 61.
18  The term 'shall' is used in the national treatment clause in the MAI.
19  V. Charolles, 'National Treatment, Most Favoured Nation Treatment and Transparency', in OECD, *The Multilateral Agreement on Investment: State of Play as of February 1997*, p. 19.
20  *Ibidem*.
21  A. Bohmer, 'The Struggle for a Multilateral Agreement on Investment – an Assessment of the Negotiation Process in the OECD', 41 *German Yearbook of International Law* (1998), p. 282.

such a law might still be regarded as a violation of the MAI's national treatment rules. In sum, the standard of treatment of foreign investors and investments provided by the MAI is very high.

Fourth, the Energy Charter Treaty (ECT) and the bilateral investment treaties (BITs) of the United States only grant MFN treatment to the investment.[22] Some BITs accord national treatment only to investment.[23] Some investment agreements provide that the principal beneficiaries of MFN treatment and national treatment are 'investors' and 'investments'. The question of whether the beneficiaries of the standard of treatment are foreign investments only or also include foreign investors can have important practical implications.[24] In the MAI, it is clearly stated that the beneficiaries of national treatment and MFN treatment are both investors and investments. Moreover, the MAI uses broad definitions for both investors and investments,[25] making the scope of application of national treatment and MFN treatment wide and broad.

Fifth, the MAI's national treatment and MFN treatment clauses apply to all activities relevant to investments, such as the establishment, acquisition, expansion, operation, management, maintenance, use, enjoyment and sale of investments. They also apply to different phases of investments, i.e., the phase of pre-establishment of investment and the phase of post-establishment of investment. The phase of pre-establishment of investment is also called pre-establishment phase, pre-entry phase, admission phase, or market access phase, while the phase of post-establishment of investment is also known as post-establishment phase, post-entry phase, or operation phase. When negotiating the MAI, some delegations preferred separate articles on pre- and post-establishment, while the majority of delegations felt that a single text would better capture the intended coverage of the agreement.[26] So the MAI applies national treatment and MFN treatment not only to the post-establishment phase as many investment treaties do, but also to the pre-establishment phase. Generally speaking, national treatment only applies to post-establishment phase in those legal regimes which accord national treatment to foreign investors and their investments. The pre-establishment phase is left to the sovereign right of states in terms of deciding on admission of an investment.[27] The reason why national treatment does not apply to the pre-establishment phase is that the obligations that would arise therefrom are too heavy to bear for host countries.

---

22  See ECT, Art. 10(10); see also UNCTAD, *Most-Favoured-Nation Treatment* (1999), p. 6.
23  UNCTAD, *National Treatment* (1999), p. 18.
24  *Idem*, pp. 9-10.
25  As to the broad definitions of investors and investments, see MAI, Ch. II, Definitions, paras. 1 and 2.
26  Commentary to the MAI Negotiating Text, Ch. III, National Treatment and Most Favoured Nation Treatment, para. 1.
27  UNCTAD, *National Treatment* (1999), pp. 1 and 4.

The MAI's extension of national treatment from the post- to the pre-investment phase means a 'revolution' for many countries.[28]

Sixth, there are two different contexts as to the principle of national treatment. One is known as the Calvo doctrine supported by developing countries, which requires that the treatment to foreign investors be 'the same as' or 'as favourable as' that accorded to national investors. This doctrine emphasizes the equality of treatment between foreign investors and national investors and prevents the accordance of special privileges to foreign investors. The other is that 'no less favourable' treatment should be accorded to foreign investors. This means that foreign investors may receive better treatment than national investors where this is deemed appropriate.[29]

In the MAI, national treatment within the second meaning is stipulated. This means that the treatment of foreign investors and their investments can be more favourable than that of domestic investors and their investments. Therefore, this kind of national treatment is compatible with the preferential treatment accorded to foreign investors by a host country, which is more favourable than that accorded to domestic investors. As a consequence, the preferential policies adopted by many developing countries so as to attract more foreign investments would not be considered measures in violation of the MAI's national treatment clause, if these countries were to accede to the MAI. However, some delegations consider preferential treatment as positive discriminatory treatment, which will cause unlimited competition among countries for international investment funds and so distort investment flows. Therefore they proposed the use of terms such as 'same' or 'comparable' treatment rather than 'no less favourable' treatment. But most delegations considered that this would unacceptably weaken the standard of treatment from the investors' viewpoint.[30] These different viewpoints on the 'same' or 'no less favourable' treatment reflect the different contexts of national treatment, as mentioned above.

Seventh, in the MAI the articles concerning the standard of treatment include the phrase 'in like circumstances', marked by square brackets, to indicate that consensus had not yet been reached among the negotiating group on whether or not to use this phrase to limit national and MFN treatment. National treatment and MFN treatment are comparative standards of treatment: the specific content of the treatment is based on a comparison of the different circumstances of domestic investors and their investments and foreign investors and their investments. But in fact, it is in many regards impossible to compare domestic investors and their investments and foreign investors and their investments. Therefore, some delegations considered it necessary to clearly point out that foreign investors and their investments can only enjoy the same

---

28 *Idem*, p. 4.
29 *Idem*, pp. 5 and 7; UNCTAD, *Bilateral Investment Treaties in the Mid-1990s* (1998), p. 59.
30 See Commentary, *supra* note 26, para. 3.

treatment as domestic investors and their investments if they are in like circumstances. If the circumstances differ, so may the treatment. On the other hand, some delegations considered that the phrase 'in like circumstances' was open to abuse, since the host country could say that foreign investors and their investments and domestic investors and their investments are not in like circumstances, so as not to have to accord the same treatment. In addition, national treatment and MFN treatment themselves are relative treatment, so their comparative nature is obvious. Therefore, it is not necessary to expressly point this out.[31] Phrases such as 'in like circumstances', 'in like situations' or 'in similar situations' are used to limit national treatment and MFN treatment in most international investment treaties.[32]

Eighth, inside the regional economic integration organization (REIO), members usually confer privileges and benefits on one another. When these member countries sign investment agreements with other countries outside the REIO, they may have a REIO clause to exclude the accordance of these privileges to other countries, as is required under MFN treatment rules. Therefore, the REIO clause exists in many international investment agreements.[33] Similarly, during the MAI negotiating process, the European Union, which is the largest REIO in the world, tried to exclude the REIO from the scope of the MAI. The negotiators could not reach a consensus in this respect. The MAI kept silent on this issue in its articles concerning standard of treatment.

Ninth, the MAI requires each Contracting Party to accord the better and more favourable treatment arising out of national treatment and MFN treatment to foreign investors and their investments. The utilization of both the MFN and national treatment standards, whichever is more favourable, is a recent trend.[34] In the case when one Contracting Party accords more favourable treatment to a third country's investors and their investments than to domestic investors and their investments, the more favourable treatment shall also be accorded to any other foreign investors and their investments. As a result, foreign investors and their investments might be in a more favourable position than domestic investors and their investments.

Tenth, most international investment treaties do not contain any articles about transparency.[35] Some recent investment agreements such as the GATS,

---

31 V. Charolles, *supra* note 19, p. 20; W. Dymond, 'The Main Substantive Provisions of the MAI', in *Proceedings of the Special Session on the Multilateral Agreement on Investment*, held in Paris on 17 September 1997, p. 14.
32 See UNCTAD, *National Treatment* (1999), p. 33. Examples can be found in the United States BITs, NAFTA, the Canada-Chile Free Trade Agreement and the World Bank Guidelines on the Treatment of Foreign Investment.
33 For a discussion of the REIO, see UNCTAD, *Most-Favoured-Nation Treatment* (1999), pp. 20-22; Art. 3 of the Chile-Malaysia BIT, Art. 3(3) of the Model BIT of China and Art. V of the GATS are examples of the REIO clause.
34 UNCTAD, *supra* note 15, p. 61.
35 UNCTAD, *supra* note 29, p. 85.

the ECT and the APEC Non-Binding Investment Principles do carry the transparency clause,[36] but these agreements only require the Contracting Parties to disclose relevant laws, regulations, judicial decisions and measures. The transparency article in the MAI not only requires this of each Contracting Party, but also requires it to disclose discriminatory measures and all policies that have an impact on investments, including established policies.[37] Such a requirement lays a heavy burden on Contracting Parties.

Last, the obligation of all Contracting Parties to extend national treatment and MFN treatment under the MAI, are subject to strong dispute settlement mechanisms, including both state-to-state and investor-to-state dispute settlement. In contrast, almost all international investment treaties include the state-to-state dispute settlement provisions, but only some BITs, the NAFTA and the ECT provide for investor-to-state dispute settlement.[38]

To sum up, the above detailed analysis of the implications of the MAI's national treatment, MFN treatment and transparency clauses shows that the MAI adopts high standards as to the general treatment of foreign investors and their investments.

2.2  The exceptions and restrictions to the MAI's national treatment and most-favoured-nation treatment rules

Although the MAI sets high standards for the treatment of foreign investors and their investments, there are still some exceptions and restrictions to its national treatment and MFN treatment clauses, as is the case for most other international investment treaties. The two main reasons for this are that, first, national treatment and MFN treatment themselves are relative standards of treatment, and not absolute standards of treatment. Second, the MAI standards of treatment are so high that they will not be fully and completely accepted by all Contracting Parties. But compared with other international investment treaties, the MAI's exceptions are rather limited.

The followings are the main exceptions and restrictions to the MAI's national treatment and MFN treatment rules:

*General exceptions.* The text of the MAI shall be examined as a whole. On the one hand, it sets out obligations for Contracting Parties and, on the other hand, it provides for situations when Contracting Parties may deviate from those obligations. These situations are stipulated in Part VI, entitled "Exceptions

---

36  See GATS, Art. III; ECT, Art. 20, and the APEC Non-Binding Investment Principles under 'Transparency'.
37  V. Charolles, *supra* note 19, p. 19.
38  E.g., the BITs between Lithuania and the Netherlands (1994), and Australia and the Lao People's Democratic Republic (1994) include investor-to-state dispute settlement provisions. For a discussion of the dispute settlement mechanism, see UNCTAD, *supra* note 29, p. 87-104; UNCTAD, *supra* note 15, pp. 82-86.

and Safeguards". This part applies to the entire text of the MAI, thereby including the national treatment and MFN treatment provisions.

According to the MAI's general exceptions, a Contracting Party may take any action in contravention of the MAI so as to protect its essential security interests, to maintain international peace and security under the United Nations Charter, and to maintain its public order.[39] In such cases, a Contracting Party may refuse to fulfill its obligations under the MAI to accord national treatment and MFN treatment to foreign investors and their investments. However, such Contracting Party is under an obligation to notify its according actions or measures to the Parties Group of the MAI.[40] Most international investment treaties contain similar articles of general exceptions, but their scope is broader, including national health exceptions and moral exceptions.[41]

However, the MAI clearly stipulates that the above-mentioned general exceptions shall not apply to expropriation and compensation and protection from strife.[42] Therefore, a Contracting Party's obligation to accord national treatment and MFN treatment to foreign investors and their investments remains absolute in case of expropriation and compensation and protection from strife. The reason is that compensation in case of expropriation is considered central to investor protection and investors should be granted absolute guarantees.[43] This is not the case for most other international investment treaties.

*Subject-specific exceptions.* The MAI excludes taxation, prudential measures in financial services, and temporary macroeconomic safeguards from national treatment and MFN treatment commitments.

– *Taxation exceptions.* Although taxation is not an important component for international investment, the MAI does provide rules for taxation. However, it is stipulated that national treatment and MFN treatment do not apply to taxation, although the MAI's requirements for transparency do apply to taxation.[44] The reason is that taxation itself is a complicated matter; there exist many international taxation treaties, such as bilateral agreements for the avoidance of double taxation. Different countries bear different commitments under different treaties; one and the same country may even bear different commitments under different treaties. If they would be required to extend national treatment and MFN treatment under the MAI, it is certain that confusion and conflicts will arise.

– *Prudential measures in financial services exceptions.* Financial services form part of the MAI. However, the financial services sector is highly regulated for prudential reasons and therefore calls for specific treatment.[45] So when a

---

39  MAI, Ch. VI, General Exceptions, paras. 2 and 3.
40  *Idem*, para. 4.
41  Xu Chongli, *supra* note 3, p. 112; UNCTAD, *National Treatment* (1999), p. 44.
42  MAI, Ch. VI, General Exceptions, para. 1.
43  A. Bohmer, *supra* note 21, p. 284.
44  MAI, Ch. VIII, paras. 1 and 3.
45  MAI, Ch. VII, note 1.

country takes prudential measures with respect to financial services, it is allowed to suspend national treatment and MFN treatment under the MAI. Prudential measures include measures for the protection of investors, depositors, policy holders or persons to whom a fiduciary duty is owed by an enterprise providing financial services, or to ensure the integrity and stability of its financial system.[46]

– *Temporary macroeconomic safeguards exceptions.* It is clearly stated that national treatment, MFN treatment and transparency clauses do not apply to transactions carried out in pursuit of monetary or exchange rate policies by the central bank or monetary authority of a Contracting Party.[47] This provision in effect excludes such transactions from the MAI. It is also clearly stated that national treatment rules may not apply to cross-border capital transactions, if there are serious balance-of-payments and external financial difficulties or threats, or if movements of capital cause or threaten to cause serious difficulties for macroeconomic management, in particular monetary and exchange rate policies.[48]

There are more exceptions in other international investment agreements, for example, the intellectual property rights guaranteed under international intellectual property conventions (as in the United States model BIT, Article 11(2)(b)), incentives (as in NAFTA, Article 1108.7(a)), public procurement (as in NAFTA, Article 1108.7(b)), and cultural industries (as in NAFTA, Annex 2106).[49] These exceptions are not covered by the MAI.

– *Country-specific exceptions.* The OECD adopted the 'top-down' approach in drafting the MAI text to enable the adoption of high standards. However, in a supplement to the MAI, each Contracting Party is allowed to set out specific exceptions to its obligations under the MAI. There are two types of country-specific exceptions. One is that national treatment and MFN treatment do not apply to existing non-conforming measures or to amendments of non-conforming measures as set out by a Contracting Party in the Annex to the MAI.[50] The other is that national treatment and MFN treatment do not apply to measures in specific sectors, sub-sectors or activities that a Contracting Party set out in the Annex to the MAI.[51]

Country-specific exceptions were taken advantage of by many negotiating parties to exclude those sectors to which they did not want to apply national treatment. Therefore, there are many pages of exceptions raised by negotiating parties. The EU also issued several pages of proposed exceptions during the negotiations.[52] As far as the specific exceptions raised by Contracting Parties

---

46 MAI, Ch. VII, Prudential Measures, paras. 1 and 2.
47 MAI, Ch. VI, Transactions in Pursuit of Monetary and Exchange Rate Policies, para. 1.
48 MAI, Ch. VI, Temporary Safeguard, para. 1.
49 UNCTAD, *National Treatment* (1999), p. 45.
50 MAI, Ch. IX, Lodging of Country-specific Exceptions, para. A.
51 *Idem*, para. B.
52 A. Bohmer, *supra* note 21, p. 286.

during the negotiations are concerned, most exceptions focus on the application of national treatment to the admission phase in such service sectors as transportation and telecommunication.[53]

According to the domestic laws of many Contracting Parties, these service sectors are generally not open to foreign investors and their investments. Another sector, which is specifically excepted by many Contracting Parties, is the cultural industry. For many countries, the cultural industry is also excepted from the application of national treatment in their domestic laws. During the negotiations on the MAI, the cultural industry was a key issue of disagreement. Some countries suggested to treat it as an exception, others, such as France and Canada, suggested its total exclusion from the MAI.

As mentioned before, the MAI's national treatment rules apply both to the access phase and to the operation phase. This is not the case in most domestic laws and most other international investment agreements. The latter always regard the access phase as exempt from the application of national treatment.

3     THE IMPACT OF THE MAI'S NATIONAL TREATMENT AND MOST-FAVOURED-NATION TREATMENT RULES ON INTERNATIONAL INVESTMENT LIBERALIZATION

There are two main purposes for the MAI's high standards of treatment of foreign investors and their investments. One is to ensure that foreign investors and their investments are accorded equal legal treatment as domestic and third country investors and their investments. The other is to promote the realization of international investment liberalization.

3.1     The extension of national treatment will promote international investment liberalization

In international agreements, the principle of national treatment has been used in two different contexts:[54] national treatment may mean that no less favourable treatment is to be accorded to aliens and their property than is accorded to nationals and their property. In this context, preferential treatment of foreign investors is allowed. The national treatment principle in the MAI carries this meaning. National treatment may also mean that the same and equal treatment is accorded to aliens and their property as is accorded to nationals and their property. In this context, no more favourable treatment of aliens is allowed. This doctrine is known as the Calvo doctrine and is supported and applied by some developing countries. This is the main reason why some developing

---

53   W. Dymond, *supra* note 31, p. 15.
54   UNCTAD, *supra* note 29, p. 59.

countries include national treatment rules in their own investment codes. So national treatment acts like a double-edged sword. On the one hand, if the treatment of foreign investors is less favourable than that of domestic investors in a host country, it may be improved by invoking of national treatment. On the other hand, if the treatment of foreign investors is more favourable than that of domestic investors in a host country, it may also be lowered by invoking national treatment so as to prevent privileges from being enjoyed by foreign investors in the host country. Unfortunately, the first meaning and function of national treatment is underlined in modern international investment agreements.

To extend national treatment and MFN treatment is to remove discriminatory treatment; to accord foreign investors and their investments national treatment and MFN treatment is to make sure that they can enjoy equal legal treatment and the same treatment as domestic and third country investors and their investments. Through the two standards of general treatment, foreign investors and their investments obtain the opportunity of equal competition with all other investors and their investments.[55] Therefore, if bilateral investment treaties and multilateral investment treaties accord national treatment and MFN treatment at the same time, it is very probable that investors from one Contracting Party become 'world citizens' in other contracting countries.[56] Therefore, they can freely carry out their investments almost everywhere and thus international investment liberalization is realized.

However, countries do not have an obligation to accord national treatment and MFN treatment to foreign investors and their investments pursuant to customary international law.[57] What kind of treatment a foreign investor and his investment may enjoy in the host country depends completely on the domestic laws of the host country and the international treaties to which the host country has acceded. Whether to accord national treatment to foreign investors is an issue of state sovereignty entirely. Most developed countries usually accord national treatment with some exceptions to foreign investors and their investments, and some developing countries such as Egypt, the Philippines, Bulgaria and Argentina also provide for national treatment in their domestic laws and bilateral investment treaties.[58] Most developing countries strongly oppose the inclusion of national treatment in their domestic laws or bilateral investment treaties, due to the fact that their domestic economy lags behind and their national industry is not yet competitive. However, even those countries that do extend national treatment include exceptions and

---

55 United Nations Centre on Transnational Corporations, *Bilateral Investment Treaties* (1988), pp. 33-39.
56 Xu Chongli, *supra* note 3, p. 111.
57 K. Gudgeon, 'United States Bilateral Investment Treaties: Comments on the Origins, Purpose and General Treatment Standard', 4 *International Tax and Business Lawyer* (1986), p. 117.
58 A. Parra, 'The Principles Governing Foreign Investment, As Reflected in National Investment Codes,' 7 *ICSID Review – Foreign Investment Law Journal* (1992), no. 2, p. 436.

specific reservations in their domestic laws or treaties, and thus weaken the fundamental implications of national treatment. To sum up, the principle of national treatment has not yet become a generally applied principle.[59]

The United States is the strongest proponent of the application of national treatment. Due to the fact that the United States is the most developed country in the world and has the strongest national economy, there is a great amount of surplus capital in the national market seeking its way into the international market. Therefore, it is a matter of urgency for the United States to promote the realization of international investment liberalization, so that the domestic markets of other countries may be easily accessed. One of the measures to be taken to this end is the universal application of national treatment. As a first step, the United States always requires a national treatment clause to be included in all of its bilateral investment protection agreements with other countries.[60] The national treatment standard included in these agreements will, together with 'the multiplier effect' of MFN treatment, automatically apply to any other country that concludes bilateral treaties with countries who have entered into BITs with the United States. As a second step, the United States promotes the inclusion of national treatment clauses in both regional and multilateral investment agreements. In consequence, the North American Free Trade Agreement (NAFTA) and the Energy Charter Treaty (ECT) both include national treatment and MFN treatment.[61] The MAI's national treatment and MFN treatment clauses are mainly copies of the corresponding clauses in the NAFTA.[62] If the MAI had succeeded, its national treatment clause would have made it possible for all investors of all Contracting Parties to invest freely in all other contracting countries.

3.2 Applying national treatment and most-favoured-nation treatment to the admission of foreign investment is an important measure to realize international investment liberalization

Pursuant to customary international law, the host country has the right to regulate or prohibit the admission of aliens and their property into its territory.

---

59 UNCTAD, supra note 15, p. 61.
60 Art. II of the US Model Bilateral Investment Treaty of 1984 only provided that "Each Party *shall permit and treat* investment, ... on a basis no less favourable than ... of its own nationals or ... ", but Art. II of the Model of 1994 clearly provides that "... each Party *shall accord* treatment no less favorable than ... its own nationals... " (emphasis added). Thus, the obligation of according national treatment to foreign investment is greatly strengthened. The 1984 Model can be found in United Nations Center on Transnational Corporations, *supra* note 55. The 1994 Model can be found in UNCTAD, *supra* note 29.
61 NAFTA, Art. 1102; ECT, Art. 10(2)(3).
62 Compare the MAI, Ch. III, the clauses concerning national treatment and most-favoured-nation treatment, with NAFTA, Arts. 1102 and 1103.

This right derives from the principle of the territorial sovereignty of states.[63] So far, no country offers absolute and unconditional rights of entry and establishment.[64] Most countries, developing countries in particular, according to their specific situations, provide for legal control or restrictions to a differing extent to the admission of foreign investment in their domestic laws.[65] The admission of foreign investment was not an issue in BITs or other international investment agreements before the 1990s.

However, in the 1990s, the United States applies national treatment to the admission of foreign investments when it signs BITs with other countries.[66] With the impact of such bilateral treaties, many international investment treaties concluded in the 1990s include the clause of national treatment, and apply national treatment and MFN treatment to the admission of foreign investments. For example, the GATS, NAFTA, ECT and APEC's Non-Binding Investment Principles all contain such a clause.[67] But exceptions or reservations are still possible.[68] Moreover, the obligation to apply national treatment rules to the admission of foreign investments is mostly 'soft law'.[69] For example, the ECT requires that Contracting Parties "shall endeavour" to accord national treatment to foreign investors.[70] Merely because of this, the United States refused to ratify the ECT.[71] The APEC's Non-Binding Investment Principles are, as their name suggests, non-binding, so any obligation to apply national treatment and MFN treatment to the admission of foreign investment is unenforceable.

There are some reasons why the admission of foreign investment became an issue in the legal regimes of international investment in the 1990s. From the end of the Second World War to the 1970s, most newly independent developing countries cherished their hard-earned political sovereignty and economic sovereignty very much, causing them to impose restrictive control over the admission of foreign investment. In the meantime, the economic progress of the developed countries was limited too and the admission of

---

63 A. Fatouros, *Government Guarantees to Foreign Investors* (1962), pp. 40-41; UNCTAD, *supra* note 29, p. 46; UNCTAD, *supra* note 15, p. 39.
64 UNCTAD, *Admission and Establishment* (1999), pp. 1, 16 and 32.
65 For a discussion of admission, see *idem*, note 15, pp. 63-66 and note 29, pp. 46-50.
66 Art. II of the US Model Bilateral Investment Treaty of 1994 specifically states that "with respect to the *establishment*, ... each Party shall accord treatment no less favourable than..." (emphasis added).
67 GATS, Art. XVI(1); NAFTA, Arts. 1102(1) and 1103(1); ECT, Art. 10 (2) and (3); APEC's Non-binding Investment Principles under 'Non-discrimination between Source Economies' and 'National Treatment'.
68 UNCTAD, *supra* note 64, p. 32.
69 A 'soft law' obligation is unenforceable, while a 'hard law' obligation is enforceable.
70 ECT, Art. 10 (2) and (3).
71 T. Wälde, 'International Investment under the 1994 Energy Charter Treaty: Legal, Negotiating and Policy Implications for International Investors within Western and Commonwealth of Independent States/Eastern European Countries', 29 *Journal of World Trade* (1995), no. 5, p. 34; ECT, Preamble, Principle no. 6; ECT, Art. 10(4).

foreign investment to these countries was also restricted. As a consequence, the issue of admission of investment was not touched in BITs or other international investment regimes concluded during that period. Instead, the focus of those investment treaties was investment protection.[72]

In the 1980s, the power of the developing countries had been consolidated and stabilized. Great economic progress had been made. To further the progress of national economic growth, capital and advanced technology were in great demand. To this end, attracting foreign investments became an effective solution. Accordingly, these countries eventually relaxed their screening system of foreign investment, broadened the economic sectors in which foreign investment was allowed, softened the conditions for admission and even worked out some preferential policies and measures so as to absorb more foreign investments.

At the same time, developed countries had shown great economic development and their controls over the admission of foreign investment became rather loose. A large amount of surplus capital had been accumulated in these countries. The great demand for foreign investments and the relaxation of control over the admission of foreign investment by developing countries, plus the economic development of the developed countries and the surplus of capital: all these factors stimulated the rising tide of international investment liberalization in the world. In turn, international investment liberalization required all countries to further loosen their control over the admission of foreign investment and thus led to further liberalization.

In theory, there are four approaches to phrase the admission of foreign investment in international investment regimes.[73] First is 'an unconditional right to invest'. This was a purely theoretical notion that was not reflected in any existing agreement. Second is the 'right of establishment'. This is a narrower concept that referred to the setting up of enterprises or the provision of services by a natural person in another country. This concept existed only in a small number of agreements that aimed at far-reaching economic integration in a regional context. The third approach involved the application of non-discrimination standards to the pre-establishment phase. The application of the standards of national treatment and MFN treatment to the admission of investment was typically associated with a 'top-down' approach that provided for general application of non-discrimination standards, subject to country-specific exceptions. NAFTA and the MAI are examples. The fourth approach is the 'market access, bottom-up' approach. It was exemplified by the GATS, in which Member States had obligations regarding the admission of investment

---

72 UNCTAD, *World Investment Report 1996*, pp. 154-156; UNCTAD, *Existing Regional and Multilateral Investment Agreements and Their Relevance to a Possible Multilateral Framework on Investment: Issues and Questions*, Note by the UNCTAD Secretariat, TD/B/COM.2/EM.3/2, pp. 4-5.
73 WTO, *Report of the Working Group on the Relationship between Trade and Investment to the General Council* (1998), pp. 44-45.

only to the extent that a specific sector had been inscribed in their schedules of commitments, although the GATS also contained some obligations of a general nature, such as MFN. The scope of application of these various standards depended crucially on the definition of the term investment. Various types of exceptions qualified each of the above-mentioned approaches to the admission of investment.

The scope of the admission of foreign investment under the MAI is the broadest and widest. Almost all economic sectors of the host countries shall be open to other Contracting Parties. Moreover, the obligation to accord national treatment to foreign investments in the admission phase is regarded by the MAI as a 'hard law' obligation.

When foreign investors and their investments enjoy the same legal treatment as domestic investors and their investments with respect to admission of investment, the purpose of investment liberalization is realized. Of course, there are still some limits to such investment liberalization. For example, national treatment does not apply to those sectors listed in the country-specific exceptions. However, if one of the sectors listed in the country-specific exceptions is open to other countries through BITs or other investment treaties, this sector should be open to all other Contracting Parties, as a result of the fact that MFN treatment also applies to the admission of foreign investments.

## 4 THE IMPACTS OF NATIONAL TREATMENT AND INTERNATIONAL INVESTMENT LIBERALIZATION ON DEVELOPING COUNTRIES

The MAI was to be open for accession by all countries, especially developing countries. During the MAI negotiations, some developing countries such as China, Brazil and Chile were invited to participate as observers. Therefore, it is necessary to analyze the impact on developing countries if national treatment is extended and international investment liberalization is realized.

In general, the standards for the treatment of foreign investors and their investments set by the MAI are too high and unacceptable to developing countries at the present stage. As mentioned before, most developing countries have not included national treatment in either their domestic laws or international investment treaties, let alone that they apply national treatment to the admission of foreign investment. In those circumstances, if they accede to the MAI, they will need to change their entire current domestic legal regimes on foreign investment. This is no different from requesting them to reach the sky in a single bound. There is a famous saying that 'Rome was not built in a day'. When developed countries were in their development stage, they did not extend national treatment either, and also made many reservations with respect to the admission of foreign investment.

In order to accomplish their national development targets, most developing countries take measures to select and guide foreign investment to those areas that are in the greatest need. In order to protect their national economy and national investors, especially these countries' 'infant industries' and national industries, they prohibit foreign investments in some industries and sectors, which are left for domestic investors. According to the MAI, all such measures are prohibited. If these countries accede to the MAI, they have to eliminate all measures inconsistent with the MAI and open up almost all industries to foreign investors.

When developing countries open their doors to foreign investors, foreign investments from developed countries may flow straight in without any conditions. The domestic capital in developing countries is thin on the ground and weak; the national industries lag behind those of the developed countries. The developing countries' national investors are not able to compete with foreign investors. The possible result is that national industries and 'infant industries' such as the financial sector, service sector and public utility sector of the host developing countries would be ferociously attacked or monopolized by foreign investors. It is politically dangerous if foreign investors control a country's domestic economy.

Moreover, the MAI's national treatment not only accords to foreign investors and their investments the same treatment as it does to domestic investors and their investments, but also enables foreign investors and their investments to enjoy more favourable treatment than domestic investors and their investments. At the same time, the MAI's investment dispute settlement bestows on foreign investors the right to sue the host government in an international arbitration tribunal, which is not a possibility for domestic investors. As a result, foreign investors in effect could enjoy so-called 'supranational treatment' in a host contracting country.

As far as natural persons are concerned, immigration laws all over the world never guarantee foreign natural persons the right of completely free entry into their countries. This 'discriminatory' practice is not condemned by international society, but regarded as an established principle. In contrast, the MAI requires Contracting Parties to allow free access of foreign investments through the application of national treatment rules.

On the other hand, the requirements of the MAI constitute a restriction on the state sovereignty of developing countries.[74] The MAI prohibits host Contracting Parties to adopt special laws or policies on foreign investment in order to accomplish the national economic growth target. Although a state's existing non-conforming policies or measures on foreign investment can be retained as country-specific exceptions, according to the MAI, they shall be eliminated eventually in accordance with the MAI requirements of 'standstill' and 'roll-

---

74 A. Bohmer, *supra* note 21, pp. 273-274; C. Baumgartner, 'The Demise of the Multilateral Agreement on Investment', *Colorado Journal of International Environmental Law & Policy Yearbook* (1998), p. 46.

back'.[75] Moreover, they are no longer allowed to adopt such policies or measures after accession. All this constitutes a serious restriction to and an infringement of the national right to adopt economic laws and policies.

As far as China is concerned, it does not in its domestic legislation accord national treatment to foreign investors and their investments in the phase of operation. The Chinese government is only prepared to "gradually extend national treatment to foreign-invested enterprises in China", according to one of its official reports.[76] Most BITs concluded between China and other countries do not mention national treatment. But in the BIT between China and the United Kingdom, the Chinese government agreed to "do whatever possible" to extend national treatment.[77]

There are two main reasons for China's refusal to extend national treatment at present and in the near future. One is that the reform from a planned economy system to a market economy system is still in progress. In a planned economy system, state-owned enterprises are under more obligations and contribute more to the government and therefore enjoy more favourable treatment from the government. For instance, the government will guarantee the supply of raw materials or the sale of products, and they can invest in almost all economic areas. Privately owned enterprises account for only a small portion of the national economy. The government imposes more restrictions with regard to the areas where they can invest. They do not enjoy the same treatment as the state-owned enterprises. So discriminatory treatment exists even among Chinese enterprises themselves. The other reason is that the technology and management of domestic enterprises still lag behind the international level and so domestic enterprises are less competitive than foreign enterprises. Therefore, it is necessary to provide special treatment for the protection of domestic enterprises. Given these circumstances, it is not possible for China to extend national treatment to foreign enterprises.

In China, national treatment does not apply to the phase of operation, let alone to the phase of admission. According to China's Model Bilateral Investment Treaty, the admission of foreign investment should take place in accordance with China's laws and regulations.[78] The Chinese government draws

---

75 'Standstill' is to lock those existing non-conforming measures and prohibit the formulation of new or more restrictive measures in violation of the MAI's obligations. 'Rollback' is the liberalization process by which the reduction and eventual elimination of non-conforming measures to the MAI would take place. 'Standstill' provides the starting point for 'rollback'. See Commentary to the MAI Negotiating Text, Ch. IX, Rollback.
76 Li Peng (former Prime Minister of China), *A Report on 'the Ninth Five Plan' of National Economy and Social Development and the Compendium of Expecting Targets by 2010* (1995) (in Chinese).
77 The BIT between China and the United Kingdom, Art. 3(3).
78 Art. 2 of China's Model BIT stipulates that "each Contracting Party shall ... and admit such investment in accordance with its laws and regulations". This Model can be found in, UNCTAD, *supra* note 29, pp. 247-252.

up a Catalogue for the Guidance of Foreign Investment Industries.[79] In this Catalogue, four categories of industries open to foreign investment are listed. Each category is made up of a long, detailed list of industries. The four categories are as follows:

a) encouraged foreign investment industries (high-tech industry is an example);
b) restricted foreign investment industries (domestic commerce and foreign trade are examples);
c) prohibited foreign investment industries (agriculture and forestry are examples); and
d) permitted foreign investment industries (all those industries not covered by the above categories).

This Catalogue only applies to foreign investment in China. So national treatment does not apply to the phase of admission of foreign investors and their investments. The purpose of the Chinese government in drawing up such a Catalogue is to direct foreign investment to those areas where China is in great need of them, so as to achieve the social development target and protect national industry. If China accedes to the MAI, according to national treatment rules, China would have to abolish its Catalogue. Then foreign investment would be allowed into all areas of industry, except for those listed in the country-specific exceptions.

China is so large a country that the economic development of different districts is uneven and unbalanced. This makes it necessary to carry out different economic policies to stimulate even and balanced development. The Chinese government carries out such different economic policies and grants investment incentives with respect to foreign investment in different administrative districts. This is also not allowed under the MAI's national treatment rules.

The Chinese industries of financial services, telecommunication, transportation, automobiles manufacture, etc., are less competitive in the international market. If foreign investments are allowed into such areas without any conditions, these national industries will soon be entirely occupied by foreign investment.

In all of the above circumstances, the ability of the Chinese government to formulate foreign policies would be greatly limited. Therefore, the economic sovereignty of China would be seriously infringed.

---

79 This Catalogue was jointly published by the State Plan Committee, the State Economy and Trade Committee and the Ministry of Foreign Trade and Economic Cooperation in 1995, and was revised in 1997.

5   CONCLUSION

The MAI's general treatment principles for foreign investors and their investments are national treatment, MFN treatment and transparency. From the implications of these treatment rules and in comparison to other, similar treatment rules in other investment regimes, we may conclude that the MAI's minimum standard of treatment is the highest. The main characteristic of the MAI's standard of treatment is the adoption of national treatment and its application to the admission of foreign investment with the purpose of promoting and realizing international investment liberalization. However, this will greatly damage developing countries' national economic growth and their state sovereignty over the economy, if they accede to the MAI.

Imposing high standards of treatment on developing countries by developed countries in a single investment treaty will inevitably give rise to disputes over international investment regimes between the two worlds, and therefore result in difficulty in concluding an effective multilateral legal investment agreement. To avoid and resolve such disputes, and to conclude a worldwide legal investment agreement, the developed countries need to fully take into account and respect the right to their own administration of developing countries in the field of foreign investment and to balance the interest of the two worlds, while at the same time promoting and pursuing international investment liberalization.

# 5 | A Liberal Multilateral Investment System, Transnational Enterprises, Home and Host Countries. Some Observations

## E.C. Nieuwenhuys[*]

### 1  INTRODUCTION

Transnational enterprises may be regarded as 'merely a form or agent of FDI'.[1] They invest internationally in countries spread across a wide area.[2] The MAI, which has been the subject of negotiations within the OECD since 1995, relates to the conditions under which such investment may take place.[3] In April 1998 the negotiations in relation to the MAI within the OECD ceased because the OECD countries could not agree on a number of issues.[4] Nevertheless there is still considerable agreement in principle on the MAI between the 29 wealthy industrialized Member States of the OECD. If the negotiations on a multilateral investment treaty are continued in a different international forum, it may be assumed that the OECD countries will take most of the principles set out in the MAI as the starting point for negotiations.[5] For this reason, any consideration given to a possible future multilateral investment system may take these principles as its point of reference. As was clear during the WTO summit in Seattle in November 1999 and during the World Economic Forum in Davos in January 2000, these principles are cause for some controversy. A number of developing countries and a number of non-governmental organizations wish

---

[*] Eva Nieuwenhuys is Lecturer, Faculty of Law, Department Metajuridica of Leiden University.
[1] D. Fieldhouse, 'The Multinational: A Critique of a Concept', in A. Teichova, M. Leboyer and H. Nussbaum (eds.), *Multinational Enterprises in Historical Perspective* (1989), p. 11.
[2] In this article the term transnational enterprise is used and not the also current term multinational enterprise. These enterprises, which own or control production or service facilities in one or more countries outside the home country, can be of uni-national origin or of multi-national origin, such as the Anglo-Dutch enterprise Shell. See about the problems of definition of the term transnational or multinational enterprise P. Muchlinski, *Multinational Enterprises and the Law* (1995), pp. 12-15.
[3] The text about the MAI in this article is based on the MAI negotiating text of April 24, 1998. Draft text available at <www.oecd.org/daf/investment/fdi/mai/negtext.htm>.
[4] In France, e.g., there was a lot of opposition against the liberalization of the cultural sector and also in the United States there was insufficient political support.
[5] In the Uruguay Round, which was closed in 1994, agreements on international investments were already reached. Since the establishment of the WTO in 1995 these agreements have applied in the WTO. They are the General Agreement on Trade in Services and the new agreements on Trade Related Investment Measures and Trade Related Intellectual Property Rights.

*E.C. Nieuwenhuys and M.M.T.A. Brus (eds.), Multilateral Regulation of Investment, 89-99.*
© 2001 *E.M. Meijers Institute and Kluwer Law International. Printed in the Netherlands.*

to see international capital flows organized differently to the way proposed in the MAI.

According to the Preamble of the MAI – among others – international cooperation with regard to international investments must be improved. To contribute to the efficient utilization of economic resources, the creation of employment opportunities and the improvement of living standards, and to promote sustainable economic growth, a broad multilateral framework for international investment with high standards for the liberalization of investment regimes and investment protection and with effective dispute settlement procedures must be established on the basis of open, standardized markets. National obstacles to transnational enterprises must be removed. The conditions, which may apply to investments by transnational enterprises, must be harmonized and must comply with a number of principles on the basis of which transnational enterprises may be entitled to fair, equal, transparent, and predictable treatment.[6]

This article will address the question of whether a liberal worldwide investment system, as envisaged by the MAI, is indeed the most appropriate means to promote worldwide economic welfare. A liberal, worldwide investment system applies to the investments of transnational enterprises at home and in host countries. For this reason, attention will first be given to the question of whether a worldwide investment system will enable transnational enterprises to adopt an efficient business strategy. Following this, attention will be given to the question of whether a liberal worldwide investment policy enables home countries and host countries to adopt an investment policy aimed at increasing living standards and promoting sustainable economic growth. Firstly, however, an indication will be given of what fair, equal, transparent and predictable treatment means.

## 2  Principles for Treatment of Transnational Enterprises

According to the MAI, transnational enterprises must be treated in accordance with the principle of promoting and protecting their rights, of freedom of admission and freedom of establishment, of equitable and non-discriminatory treatment, of freedom from performance requirements and in accordance with the standstill principle.

On the basis of the principle of promoting and protecting the rights of transnational enterprises, transnational enterprises are entitled to carry out financial transactions – in the form of the repatriation of profits, dividends, royalties and other payments relating to investments – and to protection of their assets. The investments of transnational enterprises are protected against nationalization and expropriation and against measures that amount to ex-

---

6   See the Preamble to the MAI negotiating text, *supra* note 3.

propriation. The concept of investment is broadly defined and includes portfolio investments and direct investments in the form of foreign capital or in the form of tangible assets such as money and machinery and intangible assets such as trademarks, patents, technological know-how, reputation and the like, which are used to carry on a business in the host country or to participate on a contractual or any other basis in commercial activities.

The principle of free admission and free establishment gives transnational enterprises the right to be admitted to countries without prior approval by a public body authorized to grant such approval and gives transnational enterprises the right to invest in all sectors of the economy, whether or not in the form of a legal person established in accordance with the law of the host country.[7]

According to the principle of equitable and non-discriminatory treatment, transnational enterprises are entitled to be treated the same as national enterprises and to be treated the same as enterprises from the most favoured nations. Furthermore, in terms of the principle of non-discrimination and of freedom from performance requirements, the entry of a transnational enterprise may not be made dependent on meeting special requirements.

Finally, the standstill principle aims to provide transnational enterprises with legal security. On the basis of this principle, after joining MAI, existing non-conforming measures are locked and the adoption of new or more restrictive measures in violation of MAI's obligations is prohibited.

## 3 A LIBERAL MULTILATERAL INVESTMENT SYSTEM AND THE BUSINESS STRATEGIES OF TRANSNATIONAL ENTERPRISES

An investment system – as envisaged by the MAI – which would be applicable worldwide and would grant transnational enterprises entry to as many sectors as possible in as many countries as possible, subject to the least possible number of conditions, would be in the interests of transnational enterprises. After all, a system such as this offers the central management of companies the possibility of following a business strategy that enables these transnational enterprises to make optimal use of their comparative advantages. Transnational enterprises wish to ensure that the type and quantity of capital and labour at their disposal can be valued as far as possible in monetary terms. A broad definition of the concept of an investment, which includes both money and goods, and services and knowledge, enables them to do so. In addition, transnational enterprises wish to be able to use their goods, services and knowledge, valued in monetary terms, to develop as many activities as possible that meet their policy objectives. Furthermore, they wish to organize these activities on

---

[7] Although foreign investments in the army or in the police system can be forbidden for the sake of public order and safety.

the basis of an efficient internal organizational structure. They wish to be able to choose the type of organization that enables them to manage, coordinate, integrate and match their dispersed investments of different kinds across national borders in accordance with the interests of the transnational enterprise as an economic entity.[8] The principle of free admission and freedom of establishment and the principle of freedom from performance requirements enable transnational enterprises to opt for a form of organization which enables them to make optimal use of their comparative advantages. Depending on the type and quantity of capital and labour that the transnational enterprise has at its disposal, the management at the corporate level may opt for a strategy with regard to the type and quantity of commercial activities that the transnational enterprise develops, the type and quantity of the products that it produces and the way in which it produces these, the type and number of locations in which it develops activities, the type and number of markets on which it focuses and the way in which it obtains a share of these markets.[9] The managements of companies may themselves decide where, in what and in what form they wish to invest the capital and/or technological knowledge of the transnational enterprise and where they wish to locate their financial management, control and research and development facilities. This freedom in relation to corporate strategy offers the managements of transnational enterprises the opportunity to derive as much advantage as possible from developing activities at various locations.

Some enterprises have considerable capital at their disposal but do not have technological knowledge or knowledge of advanced management techniques. These enterprises may use the capital at their disposal for investments in manufacturing activities outside of their home countries without developing manufacturing activities in their home countries themselves and without being involved in the management and the organization of the activities abroad. They can concentrate on extracting raw materials outside of their home countries in support of industrial enterprises within the home country or in other countries. For this purpose, they may establish a parent company in the home country, which finances the economic activities of freestanding companies outside the home country, which are managed independently by Western or

---

8   A lot of explanations have been given for the international production activities of transnational enterprises. Based on these explanations Dunning formulated the eclectic paradigm, which explains the nature and content of cross-border production activities from firm or ownership-specific-, location-specific- and internalization factors. If the transnational enterprise possesses ownership advantages and it has an organizational structure that allows it to control investments in foreign enterprises then it can consider the use of the ownership advantages in foreign locations in its interest. See on the eclectic paradigm J. Dunning, *Multinational Enterprises and the Global Economy* (1993), pp. 76-87.
9   See about the business strategies of transnational enterprises *idem*, pp. 54-66, 66-96 and 185-210 and K. Ohmae, *Triad, de opkomst van mondiale concurrentie* (1985).

local managers and focus on the production of raw materials by exploiting natural resources, forests and plantations.[10]

There are also companies that have considerable capital at their disposal as well as advanced large-scale manufacturing technologies for the production of certain goods or services. These enterprises produce goods such as telecommunications equipment, steel, machinery, chemical, electronic, pharmaceutical, textile and food products, or certain services, such as transport or distribution, or finance and insurance for the domestic market. If the domestic market becomes saturated or profits decline, such companies seek to increase their market share. They can do so by expanding their industrial activities in their home countries and by producing for the export market. If they incur higher transport costs for this export, however, or if they have to pay higher import duties, it may be more advantageous to these enterprises to replicate the same activities that they have developed in their home countries in neighbouring countries or globally.[11] These enterprises can increases the size of their markets by investing their capital and extending their large-scale production methods horizontally within the region or through a global network of manufacturing enterprises that produce and sell the same products locally as the enterprises in the home country.[12] To protect their strong competitive position and their technological knowledge, however, such enterprises wish to have the freedom to decide for themselves on their method of financing, the organization and the coordination of the international production process.[13]

This is possible on the basis of the principle of free admission and freedom of establishment. This principle enables the parent company to not only finance the regional or global network of production companies, but also to set up, equip and manage such companies. Since no conditions apply to the form that foreign investment should take in terms of this principle, the company can opt to invest in the form of wholly foreign-owned subsidiaries. Since the control of these subsidiaries is tied to the ownership of shares, the parent

---

10  For more information about the activities of freestanding companies see M. Wilkins and H.G. Schröler (eds.), *The free-standing company in the world economy 1830-1966* (1998).
11  Chandler traces the rise of large, multi-unit industrial enterprises in "the 1880s and the 1890s in western Europe and the United States, and a little later in Japan because Japan industrialised later", see A. Chandler Jr, 'Technological and Organizational Underpinnings of Modern Industrial Multinational Enterprise: The Dynamics of Competitive Advantage' in A. Teichova et al. (eds.), *supra* note 1, p. 31.
12  See about this method Ohmae, *supra* note 9, p. 37.
13  This explanation for the international production activities of transnational enterprises is based on the theory of monopolistic competition, to which S. Hymer gave the initial impetus in 1960 and which was worked out further by C. Kindleberger and others. See about the theory of monopolostic competition Muchlinski, *supra* note 2, pp. 33-34. In addition to the theory of monopolistic competition R. Vernon developed the product cycle theory, which explains the foreign production activities of transnational enterprises from the advantages these enterprises try to get from their possession of specific products and production methods. See about the product cycle theory of R. Vernon, Dunning *supra* note 8, pp. 70-71.

company, as the sole shareholder, has full control of the subsidiaries. The subsidiaries are subject to decision-making at the centre, at the highest level of management, which, if necessary, may link decision-making power to certain specialized functions, such as finance, marketing, personnel policy and the like.[14]

In the case of enterprises that have exclusive access to considerable capital, production techniques and management techniques, a liberal worldwide investment system offers even more advantages than access to raw materials and markets. On the basis of the principle of free admission and freedom of establishment, such enterprises participate in the economies of as many countries as possible, in every sector of these economies and in any form they wish. In addition, on the basis of the principle of freedom from performance requirements, these enterprises are exempt from obligations such as the obligation to purchase their raw materials and semi-manufactures from local suppliers, or the obligation to make use of local distributors, or the obligation to transfer technology and educate and train local personnel. Since they carry out various activities in various locations and in various forms, these enterprises are also able to reduce their transaction costs, to improve the marketing and distribution of their end products, to produce as efficiently as possible, to spread any risk of a fall in demand, to strengthen their market position, to combine knowledge of production technology and to spread the cost of research and development.[15]

Through vertical investment and by including the production of various goods and services in their value chains, these enterprises are able to reduce the cost and disadvantages associated with cooperating with external suppliers of raw materials and external distributors and to circumvent certain measures taken by the government with regard to imports and exports.[16] These companies can reduce their production costs by producing parts of a particular end product at locations in the world where it is cheapest to do so and by taking advantage of favourable government policies in the area of taxation, wages, social security legislation and environmental policy.[17] By producing various products with the same or similar raw materials and production techniques, production can be increased, as can demand. Entering into strategic

---

14  See Chandler Jr, *supra* note 11, pp. 30-54.
15  See Dunning, *supra* note 8, pp. 59-61.
16  In addition to the product cycle theory (see *supra* note 13), which explains international production from factors concerning the enterprise specifically and from factors concerning the location, the internalization theory was developed. The internalization theory explains international production from factors that concern the transaction costs and from factors that concern the protection of industrial property rights. The initial impetus to the development of the internalization theory in 1930 came from R. Coase and later on several economists developed this theory further. See Muchlinski, *supra* note 2, p. 36. See about the further development of the internalization theory Dunning, *supra* note 8, pp. 75-76.
17  These sorts of vertically integrated investments can be explained with the industrial organization theory of vertical integration, which is developed by P. Krugman.

alliances in the form of takeovers or mergers with similar partners from the same or related industries can strengthen the global competitive position of these enterprises and weaken the position of competitors.

To decide how their international activities, which have increased in number and size, should be aligned and to coordinate and integrate these activities, these companies wish to determine their own organizational structures. They wish to ensure that decision-making can occur at various locations and at various levels so that the heterogeneity of markets and cooperation within non-institutionalised relationships can be taken into account.[18] For this reason, they wish to be able to spread and delegate decision-making authority to the various specialized divisional head offices. This is possible in a liberal worldwide investment system in which no conditions apply to the form that investments must take. Enterprises can organize themselves into functional divisions, geographical divisions or product divisions, spread decision-making authority and focus this on special tasks that can be linked to functions, activities, regions and products. The national managements of the dispersed specialized enterprises can be placed under the authority of these higher management bodies.

4    A LIBERAL MULTILATERAL INVESTMENT SYSTEM AND HOME AND HOST COUNTRIES

Countries participate in the international economic system through trade flows, financial transactions and capital flows in ways that are economically interdependent, although the extent to which these countries are integrated into the world economy differs considerably.[19] Nevertheless, all these countries wish to increase employment, improve living standards and promote economic growth. To realize this socio-economic policy all countries prefer to attract capital intensive investment in the form of corporate entities that exercise financial control over transnational enterprises and entities that concentrate on research into and the development and production of new products and production technologies. Through this type of investment countries benefit most from the money, goods, technological knowledge, power and employment that transnational enterprises have at their disposal. A liberal worldwide investment system, however, is a more suitable means of attracting capital-intensive investments for rich countries than for countries with middle or low incomes.

---

18  See on the changes of administrative organization of transnational enterprises, Muchlinski, *supra* note 2, pp. 55-61.
19  See about the relationship between transnational enterprises and home and host countries, R. Gilpin, *The Political Economy of International Relations* (1987), pp. 231-263.

In a liberal worldwide investment system the opportunities for investment for transnational enterprises must be increased and extended. To make the most efficient use of economic resources, the managements of transnational enterprises must be able to decide what should be produced and where, and how this should be done. Decisions with regard to the worldwide allocation of capital and labour must therefore be left to the managements of transnational enterprises so that they can utilize the capital and labour at their disposal as efficiently as possible without having to take social matters into consideration. Their decisions will be based on the comparative advantages offered by countries. Since wealthy countries have comparatively more advantages than countries with middle or low incomes, they will benefit most from a liberal worldwide investment system.[20]

The wealthy countries, or the OECD countries, have at their disposal advanced technology, a good infrastructure, highly skilled labour and, in some cases, even a large domestic market and/or natural resources. For this reason, these countries already have a favourable investment climate for transnational enterprises that are dependent on demand based on considerable purchasing power, national and regional markets, infrastructure, highly skilled labour and advanced production, and distribution networks. The majority of parent companies of the world's largest transnational enterprises and most of their subsidiaries, joint ventures, contractual partners or branches are therefore based in OECD countries. Most of the investment in the production of high-tech capital-intensive capital goods and the production of luxury consumer articles takes place in these countries. As a result, these countries have experienced

---

20  This is not only obvious from the MAI negotiations within the OECD. Already in 1961 the OECD counties accepted two codes of conduct for the promotion of the freedom of capital movements and financial transactions within the OECD countries. Besides, OECD countries have always laboured in other international organizations such as the UN, the WTO, the IMF and the World Bank for liberalization of capital transactions even outside the OECD countries. Thus, in September 1992, the Development Committee of the IMF and the World Bank approved a Report, realized by a French initiative, with Guidelines for the proper treatment of foreign direct investments of transnational enterprises by host countries. Also within the WTO agreements initiated by the OECD countries relating to the liberalization of capital transactions have applied since 1995. See *supra* note 5. From the beginning of the fifties, however, the developing countries have pleaded in the UN, an international organization in which they have the majority, for the international recognition of the sovereign rights of states in settling the movement of capital and money and goods within their territories. Note Resolution 1803 (XVII) of 1962 relating to the permanent sovereignty over natural resources, Resolution 3201 (S-VI) of 1974 relating to the foundation of a New International Economic Order and the foundation in 1975 of a Committee and a Centre of Transnational Enterprises which task it was to create a Code of Conduct for Transnational Enterprises. See about this E. Nieuwenhuys, 'Het Multilaterale Akkoord inzake Investeringen', 52 *Internationale Spectator* (1998), no. 10, pp. 509-516. Note moreover the UN Human Development Report of 1999, which pleads for an adjustment of the market on social grounds and among others, for the realization of a Code of Conduct for Transnational Enterprises.

considerable economic growth. In a liberal worldwide investment system these countries may attract new investment by utilizing their economic growth to improve their infrastructure, to strengthen their knowledge infrastructure and to create a tax regime favourable to enterprises.

The developing countries of Africa, Asia and Latin America, and the Eastern European countries that belong to the group of middle-income countries have cheap labour, a large domestic market and/or natural resources. These countries are attractive to transnational enterprises that depend on medium and low-skilled labour, markets and the availability of raw materials. For this reason, these countries mainly attract investment in the production of labour-intensive consumer goods based largely on raw materials and investment in the production of bulk products for mass consumption. In a liberal worldwide investment system the effect of this type of investment on employment, the improvement of living standards and on sustainable industrial development may prove to be small. After all, under such a system middle income countries may not make the admission and investment of a transnational enterprise subject to certain conditions and prior approval by a special government body set up for this purpose. Since transnational enterprises are also entitled to national treatment under such a system, domestic markets, companies or traditional sectors cannot be protected against competition from the investments of powerful transnational enterprises. In addition, investments cannot be used to bring about redistribution and a more balanced spread of money, goods, knowledge, power and employment. In the middle-income countries, the production of consumer goods or even of high-tech products for the world market can take place with the aid of standardized, automated production processes protected by patents, which can be serviced and maintained with low labour costs.[21]

Those developing countries and Eastern European countries belonging to the group of low-income countries, in most cases only have cheap labour. They are only attractive to transnational enterprises in search of an export base for less advanced products that have to be produced at the lowest possible cost. These countries attract least investment and therefore few legal entities of transnational enterprises are located in their territories. In a liberal worldwide investment system these countries will not be able to improve living standards and increase economic growth. If international investment increases, if they are to strengthen their competitive position relative to other low-wage countries, these countries will have to offer transnational enterprises ever larger

---

21 An example of this is Japanese production in the ASEAN countries. Stam has pointed out that the effect of Japanese direct investments on the industrial development of the ASEAN countries is small. See J. Stam, 'Eenzijdige relatie tussen Japan en Asean', 51 *Internationale Spectator* (1997), no. 5, pp. 279-285.

tax advantages, increasingly low wages and more favourable conditions in the area of social security entitlements and the environment.[22]

## 5 CONCLUSION

For transnational enterprises a worldwide investment system in which they can locate freely in as many countries as possible and in as many sectors as possible, subject to as few conditions as possible is a suitable means of promoting efficient use of their economic resources. It has been shown that a system such as this allows transnational enterprises to utilize the capital and labour at their disposal to develop international activities in such a way that they obtain as much benefit as possible from these. In the case of OECD countries, which are the home countries of transnational enterprises, a liberal worldwide investment system is a suitable means of realizing their investment policy and promoting economic growth. A system such as this enables these countries to place ownership and control of the worldwide production of transnational enterprises in the hands of enterprises that fall within their jurisdiction. The vast majority of parent companies of the world's largest transnational enterprises are located in these countries. They can use the economic growth that results from this to improve their knowledge structure and their infrastructure and can consequently attract even more capital-intensive investment in the form of parent companies. In a liberal worldwide investment system, the investment opportunities of these parent companies are also increased, while the control of the host countries of these investments is reduced. Since this system limits the supremacy of national law, host countries can no longer ensure that the rights of ownership and the control of transnational enterprises are distributed amongst foreign parent companies and their local subsidiaries. In the case of middle income countries and low-income countries, which are the host countries of transnational enterprises, a liberal worldwide investment system is therefore not a suitable means of improving living standards and promoting sustainable economic growth. A system such as this deprives these countries of the possibility of protecting their emerging economies from the adverse effects of too rapid an entry into the international market. Such systems also deprive them of the opportunity of utilizing the investments of transnational enterprises to increase their production capacity and their access to the global market. To protect the socio-economically weaker countries an

---

22  From the UN Human Development Report of 1999 it appears that countries such as Madagascar, Niger, the Russian Federation, Tajikistan and Venezuela hardly benefit from their integration into the world economy because they have insufficient access to markets and technology. By the whims of the world market and the fluctuating prices of resources these countries have even been more marginalized by their integration. See the Human Development Report, *supra* note 20, p. 2.

investment system must be created that not only focuses on economic growth, but also on a just distribution of wealth. Such a system should take into account the interests of all interested parties and the material inequality of countries, and should contain instruments aimed at reducing this inequality.

The emphasis on a just distribution of wealth and sustainable economic development may be given practical form through a system in which social considerations are included in decision-making in relation to the worldwide allocation of capital and labour. Since countries are not equal from a socio-economic perspective, an investment system must be more flexible and differentiated.[23] It must enable economically weaker countries, where necessary, to protect their domestic markets, companies or traditional sectors by temporarily closing certain sectors to investments by transnational companies or by preventing transnational enterprises from undertaking certain activities. It should also be made possible for the socio-economically weaker countries to benefit economically as far as possible from a transnational enterprise as a whole by imposing performance requirements on subsidiaries, joint ventures or contractual partners, which fall under their jurisdiction. To meet these requirements, these legal entities will have to turn for assistance to their parent companies or sister companies outside of the jurisdiction of the host country.[24]

Finally, the middle and low-income countries should be able to require the investment projects of transnational enterprises to contribute to their socio-economic development, for instance by creating a certain number of jobs, by training and educating local staff, through the transfer of technology, through an increase in exports, through the local procurement of raw materials or semi-manufactures, or through the sharing of ownership and control. A system such as this would enable transnational enterprises to do business in an ethically responsible way and to ensure that in making profits they do not do so at the expense of people, countries or the environment.

---

23 For more information about the ways and means by which investment agreements can provide for flexibility for the purpose of promoting growth and development see the work carried out by UNCTAD in the framework of its programme on a possible multilateral framework on investment as mentioned by the Trade and Development Board, Commission on Investment, Technology and Related Financial Issues, *Report of the Expert Meeting on International Investment Agreements*, 6 May 1999, TD/B/COM. 2/17, TD/B/COM.2/EM 5/3 and the Report submitted by the UNCTAD Secretariat: *International Investment Agreements: Concepts allowing for a certain Flexibility in the Interest of Promoting Growth and Development*, 5 February 1999, TD/B/COM.2/EM.5/2.
24 See R. Vernon, 'Codes on Transnationals: Ingredients for an Effective International Regime', in A. Fatouros (ed.), *Transnational Corporations: the International Legal Framework* (1994), p. 71.

# 6 | Protection Without Protectionism. Linking a Multilateral Investment Treaty and Human Rights

## S. Zia-Zarifi*

> God did not bestow all products upon all parts of the earth, but distributed His gifts over different regions, to the end that men might cultivate a social relationship because one would have need of the help of another. And so He called Commerce into being, that all men might be able to have common enjoyment of the fruits of the earth, no matter where produced.[1]

## 1  INTRODUCTION

The connection between international commerce and social transactions was obvious to Grotius, the so-called father of international law. But this connection was apparently lost to his intellectual progeny, the drafters of the Multilateral Agreement on Investment (MAI)[2] at the Organization for Economic Cooperation and Development (OECD), and their critics in the fields of international human rights, environmental law and labour law. In the debacle that was the negotiating process of the MAI, these two groups had to struggle to understand each other's positions. As a result of this struggle, however, it is now once again clear that international trade and international human rights can and must coexist. To examine this contention, this article will focus on the interaction between a particular aspect of international trade (namely, international investment) and human rights, and argues that these two topics should be linked. In other words, that any multilateral investment treaty (MIT) should include specific provisions on human rights. Section 2 discusses in general terms the existing but unacknowledged connection between some human rights and global economic regimes governing trade and investment. Section 3 synthesizes the arguments previously used for linkages of different issues with

---

* Saman Zia-Zarifi is Associate Counsel and Director, Program on Academic Freedom, at Human Rights Watch; at the time he wrote this contribution he was Senior Research Fellow at Erasmus University Rotterdam, Department of Internationl Law. The title for this article was suggested by T. Friedman, 'A Manifesto for the Fast World', *The New York Times Magazine*, 28 March 1999, p. 61.

1  Grotius, *De Jure Belli Ac Pacis* (1625) [On the Law of War and Peace, F. Kelsey trans. (1925)], Book II, Ch. II, XIII, 5, cited in I. Bunn, 'Linkages Between Ethics and International Economic Law', 19 *University of Pennsylvania Journal of International Economic Law* (1998), p. 319.

2  Draft text available at <www.oecd.org/daf/investment/fdi/mai/negtext.htm>.

international trade instruments, especially environmental and labour issues, to provide a basic framework for a discussion of linkages between human rights and international investment. Section 4 builds on the previous sections to set out some concrete proposals about how human rights could and should be linked to an MIT. This is not to examine the merits or desirability of an international investment instrument. Rather, it is simply to argue that linking an MIT with human rights is important not just because it advances the promotion and protection of human rights, but also because it supports a multilateral and liberalizing economic instrument. That these two goals are compatible is a central contention of this paper.

These considerations spring from the aborted MAI negotiations at the OECD, but the present paper focuses on the MAI only as an example of how to handle (or more exactly, how not to handle) linkages between investment rules and social issues. The MAI, which was an attempt to liberalize global investment, focused attention on the large and increasing role of international investment in the global economy. Over the last decade, the transboundary flow of capital and managerial control between private firms, so called Foreign Direct Investment (FDI), has become a central component of globalization and a potentially dominant avenue of development funds and technology transfers to developing countries.[3] Foreign portfolio investments (in which, as opposed to FDI, the foreign investor does not have a large managerial role) have also risen significantly, and became the focus of much concern regarding the globalization process as a result of the economic crisis that swept several Asian and Latin American countries in 1997 and 1998. This newfound prominence for investment naturally resulted in greater scrutiny of the social impact of international investment, with the MAI as the lightning rod for the ensuing criticisms.

The MAI failed in part due to its lack of adequate labour and environmental safeguards.[4] But at least the OECD did discuss safeguards regarding some labour and environmental issues in its MAI; human rights (except those included as labour rights) did not even receive a cursory treatment, and human rights groups were absent from negotiations about the MAI. However, in the wake of the MAI's demise and talk of introducing a similar treaty in other fora, such as the WTO or the proposed Free Trade Area of the Americas, it is important to examine the linkage between an MIT and human rights.

---

3   UNCTAD, *World Investment Report 1997: Transnational Corporations, Market Structure and Competition Policy* (1997), pp. xv – xxii.
4   For a review of the MAI's negotiating history and some of the reasons for its failure, see S. Zia-Zarifi, 'The Multilateral Agreement on Investment': Special Report, 9 *Yearbook of International Environmental Law* (1999), p. 345.

## 2 INTERNATIONAL ECONOMIC TRANSACTIONS AND HUMAN RIGHTS

### 2.1 The intimate link between economics and human rights

Discussions about the role of economics in society are far beyond this paper's ambitions, so suffice it to say that the basic point of economic policy and human rights is the same: forming a better society.[5] I repeat this basic proposition because it is often ignored by those primarily responsible for drafting economic treaties – the economists and trade diplomats. The other group of scholars and actors relevant to this discussion, namely the human rights community, has long accepted economic development as an important component of its agenda, at least since the Universal Declaration of Human Rights and the two international covenants on human rights (the International Covenant on Civil and Political Rights (ICCPR) and the International Convention on Economic, Social and Cultural Rights (ICESCR)) enumerated the right to work, the right to organize labour, and the right to earn a living wage among basic human rights. These instruments, based on arguments of absolute rights and social justice, nevertheless intimately involve economic considerations, especially where the protection of particular human rights have important economic consequences.

The increasing number of statements about economic policy emanating from human rights advocacy organs and institutions is one easy marker of their growing (albeit still weak) awareness of the link between human rights and global commerce.[6] It is also clear that the general public considers economic and social issues together, as demonstrated by the intense public demonstrations surrounding recent gatherings of international economic institutions such as the World Trade Organization, the International Monetary Fund and the World Bank. These mass outpourings of resentment against globalization build on the more focused political debates surrounding the North American Free Trade Agreement, not to mention the OECD's failure in gathering public

---

5   This contention is amply supported by a quick glance at history, through Moses' defence of private property ("Thou shalt not steal"), the Confucian advocacy of a centralized market economy, Jesus' attack on the moneylenders, Islam's support of trade and banning of usury, Marx's materialistic dialectic, to the current day, and US President Bill Clinton's "It's the economy, stupid".

6   See, e.g., the recent statements in a report from the UN Sub-Commission on Prevention of Discrimination and Protection of Minorities about the responsibility of states to create a social and economic system that supports and advances basic economic, social and cultural rights, *The Realization of Economic, Social and Cultural Rights: The relationship between the enjoyment of human rights, in particular economic, social and cultural rights, and income distribution*, publ. no. E/CN.4/Sub.2/1998/8.

support for the MAI.⁷ Thus it is important to remember that both economic policy and human rights are significant to the polity, and one set of concerns does not inherently preempt the other. Indeed, it is impossible to discuss one without the other, because any argument for human rights necessarily encompasses economic activity (the cost of providing due process, the formation of trade unions, the proper training of personnel, the cost of building classrooms) and any justification for economic policy relies on promised social improvements (the generation of wealth, the increase in development, the protection of ownership rights, the decrease of unemployment).

The point of reiterating the existing and intimate connection between economic policies and human rights is to justify and encourage examination of the social impact of economic instruments and the economic impact of human rights instruments. While proponents of free trade may see the issues as one of market freedom, to human rights defenders the question is one of meeting existing and clear international standards regarding the duty of states to redress violations of human rights.⁸ In other words, there is now growing concern about the relative primacy of international economic law *vis-à-vis* international human rights. Unless these two fields are linked explicitly, crucial questions remain: Who gets to decide if a given measure of market intervention by a state is called for by international human rights obligations, or is hidden protectionism? Should human rights bodies interpret these economic principles, or should trade bodies address human rights obligations?

2.2     Human rights intersecting with international trade and investment

It is first necessary to identify what we mean by human rights and which of these rights could and should be linked to an instrument on international investment. Unfortunately, these important analytic questions have never received sufficient attention from either human rights scholars or economists. Beyond general exhortations from the human rights community that economic treaties in general should take human rights into account, or the piecemeal

---

7   J. Dunoff, "Trade and ...': Recent Developments in Trade Policy and Scholarship, and Their Surprising Political Implications', 17 *Northwestern University Journal of International Law & Business* (1997), pp. 767-768. For a more general discussion of the importance of societal values for trade instruments, see P. Nichols, 'Trade Without Values', 90 *Northwestern University Law Review* (1997), pp. 691-709.
8   The awkward interaction between the human rights and trade communities is redolent of the similar meeting between the environmental and trade communities. In the words of one environmentalist, "environmentalists came to the table not seeking leverage for their nefarious ends, but in a purely defensive posture at first. We noticed that the world trading system was beginning to interfere with our work: People who had never heard the word GATT were told, 'You can't do that because of GATT'". Remarks by D. Schorr, quoted in J. Dunoff, 'The Misguided Debate Over NGO Participation at the WTO', 1 *Journal of International Economic Law* (1998), p. 439.

references to social and human development cited in various economic instruments, there has been no comprehensive examination of the impact of economic policies, particularly trade and investment regulations, on the fulfilment of human rights obligations.[9] Nevertheless, we can make some assumptions about those areas where human rights intersect most clearly with economic policies.

### 2.2.1 Social rights

The foremost area of interaction between international human rights standards and economic policy is naturally that body of rights set out in international treaties regarding economic, social and cultural rights, such as the ICESCR, the Convention for the Elimination of All Forms of Discrimination Against Women and the Convention for the Elimination of Racial Discrimination. In general, these treaties combine a commitment to individual rights and dignity, especially of historically disadvantaged groups, with interventionist beliefs in the state's obligation to promote the progressive attainment of such rights.[10] These rights, known as social rights, range from the right to physical and mental health, to the right to education and adequate food, clothing and housing.[11] (To the extent that these rights relate to the conditions of labour, I will address them in the next subsection.)

Although these instruments as a rule do not specify the means by which State Parties must attain the enumerated social rights, they are nevertheless clear in demanding that State Parties allocate significant resources toward promoting and protecting these rights.[12] The thrust of this approach has historically been that economic development must be combined with the

---

9 An interesting new set of quantitative research on the impact of liberalized economic principles on human rights in developing countries appeared in W. Meyer, 'Human Rights and MNCs: Theory versus Quantitative Analysis', 18 *Human Rights Quarterly* (1996), p. 368, in which the author claimed that data showed a somewhat positive association between foreign investment and improving civil, political, social and economic human rights practices. Contradicting this assertion, and suggesting a slightly negative association between foreign investment and human rights, are J. Smith, M. Bolyard and A. Ippolito, 'Human Rights and the Global Economy: A Response to Meyer', 21 *Human Rights Quarterly* (1999), p. 207. A more specific focus, indicating some negative impact on workers' rights due to investment liberalization in the automotive industries of India and Mexico, appears in M. Filbri, *The Multilateral Agreement on Investments, Liberalisation of Foreign Direct Investment and Effects on Labour Standards* (1998).
10 P. Alston and G. Quinn, 'The Nature and Scope of State Parties' Obligations Under the International Covenant on Economic, Social and Cultural Rights', 9 *Human Rights Quarterly* (1987), p. 156.
11 On the state's legal obligation to provide these rights, see G. van Hoof, *The Legal Nature of Economic, Social and Cultural Rights, The Right to Food: From Soft to Hard Law* (1984), pp. 6-29.
12 P. Alston and G. Quinn, *supra* note 9, p. 159.

realization of human rights without any compromises.[13] More recently, there are signs that human rights scholars have recognized that in order to ensure states can implement the fundamental, inalienable rights set out in the international covenants, it may be necessary to engage in a more detailed, realistic examination of the economic underpinnings of these social rights.[14] At any rate, carrying out obligations of promoting and protecting social rights clearly involves important considerations of available economic strategies for states and therefore is inextricably linked with the issues surrounding an international trade or investment treaty. This conflict manifests itself most directly in the capacity of international trade and investment regimes to hinder states' efforts to promote and protect human rights in accordance with their international obligations, and it is this conflict that requires the greatest effort at reconciliation.[15]

### 2.2.2 Labour Rights

Since labour is one of the central activities of human society,[16] the conditions surrounding labour and labourers have always been a part of human rights. In the post-World War II international legal regime, labour rights appear in Article 55 of the UN Charter, in the Universal Declaration of Human Rights, and the two main covenants on human rights mentioned above. Despite the obvious intimate connection between labour and human rights, historically human rights NGOs and labour unions seem to have operated without much overlap. Nevertheless, their concerns are in fact parallel, or, more accurately, they operate in two concentric rings focused on the right of individuals to earn the means of their subsistence.[17] It is clear that labour rights are a necessary part of human rights discourse.

Labour is also a necessary part of international trade discourse; economists as early as David Ricardo considered the cost of labour as one of the factors determining comparative advantage. The impact of global liberalization and increased competition on labour and wages is a concern for both developed and developing nations. For developed countries, the fear is that jobs will

---

13 M. Craven, *The International Covenant on Economic, Social, and Cultural Rights: A Perspective on its Development* (1995), pp. 138-143.
14 R. Steiner, 'Social Rights and Economic Development: Converging Discourses?', 4 *Buffalo Human Rights Review* (1998), pp. 40-42.
15 F. Garcia, 'The Global Market and Human Rights: Trading Away the Human Rights Principle', 25 *Brooklyn Journal of International Law* (1999), pp. 73-76.
16 See, e.g., Nichols, *supra* note 7, p. 682.
17 See V. Leary, 'The Paradox of Workers' Rights as Human Rights', in L. Compa and S. Diamond (eds.), *Human Rights, Labour Rights, and International Trade* (1996), p. 22.

migrate away to the cheaper markets of the developing world;[18] for developing countries, the fear is that competition for foreign investment will drive down already low labour standards – the so-called race to the bottom.[19] The typical governmental reaction to these developments, at either end of the development scale, is implementing protectionist measures. Therefore, any liberalizing trade and investment policy must address these concerns in order to be viable.[20] In the words of the OECD: "Properly designed labour market and social policies that provide adequate income security while facilitating the redeployment of displaced workers into expanding firms and sectors produce important equity and efficiency gains".[21]

However, the exact nature and scope of the labour rights that should or could be protected and linked to international trade are still disputed.[22] In 1998 the ILO identified four core rights which, the organization stated, have become so widely accepted as to constitute a part of customary international law,[23] and the OECD, for instance, has accepted these standards as authoritative.[24] These rights are:

a) freedom of association and collective bargaining;
b) elimination of exploitative forms of child labour;
c) prohibition of forced labour and slavery; and
d) non-discrimination in employment.

This list sets out the minimum labour rights that must be observed by all states, regardless of their development or economic strategy.[25] As such the protection and promotion of these rights has a significant impact on economic policies and international trade, and of necessity should be linked to an international trade and investment treaty.

---

18 This concern was especially acute in the US and Canada during negotiations leading up to NAFTA. The most prominent advocate of this view has been Ravi Batra, who claimed that free trade led to the decline in the real wages of US labourers in the 70s and 80s. R. Batra, *The Myth of Free Trade* (1993).
19 R. Bhala, 'Clarifying the Trade-Labour Link', 37 *Columbia Journal of Transnational Law* (1998), pp. 19-20.
20 The best analyses of the link between high labour protection and high productivity comes from the OECD itself. OECD, *Trade, Employment and Labour Standards: A Study of Core Workers' Rights and International Trade* (1996).
21 OECD, *Open Markets Matter: The Benefits of Trade and Investment Liberalisation* (1998), Policy Brief no. 6, para.6, available at <www.oecd.org>.
22 Leary, *supra* note 17, p. 22.
23 ILO Declaration on Fundamental Principles and Rights at Work and Its Follow-Up (adopted 18 June 1998). For greater conceptual description of these core rights and their acceptance internationally, see Bhala, *supra* note 19, pp. 33-37.
24 OECD, *supra* note 20.
25 For a succinct discussion on these rights, see Bhala, *supra* note 19, pp. 33-39. On other labour rights broader than these rather minimal standards, see S. Cleveland, 'Book Review: Global Labour Rights and the Alien Tort Claims Act; Review of Human Rights, Labour Rights, and International Trade', 76 *Texas Law Review* (1998), p. 1533.

## 2.2.3 Internationally recognized prohibited acts

The last category of human rights implicated by investment regulation is the one farthest from typical business school curricula on investment and, at the same time, the most notorious and attention-grabbing: unjust or illicit enrichment by directly engaging in or indirectly supporting internationally prohibited acts. These acts include:

a) genocide;
b) war crimes and crimes against humanity;
c) torture;
d) extrajudicial murder;
e) systematic racial discrimination; and
f) production and sale of internationally criminalized weapons.[26]

International law has recognized the link between commerce and violations of human rights at least since the post-World War II Nuremberg trials, during which the US Military Tribunal convicted several German industrialists for their roles in financing and/or benefiting from commercial schemes, whose activities violated acceptable rules of conduct (i.e., use of slave labour, production of chemical weapons, use or misappropriation of occupied property).[27] More recently, US federal courts have entertained lawsuits against corporations financing and profiting from the activity of foreign governments involved in genocidal practices, the use of slave labour and widespread environmental degradation.[28] Most clearly, trade sanctions have been used against some MNCs allegedly cooperating with states violating international human rights standards, for instance against apartheid-era South Africa, against Saddam Hussein's Iraq, and, by the US especially, against corporations doing business with countries failing to satisfy US standards for human rights.[29] Without

---

[26] This list draws partly from Section 702 of the Restatement (Third) of the Foreign Relations Law of the United States (1986), which recognizes under customary international law the prohibition of genocide, slavery, disappearances, official torture and systematic racial discrimination.

[27] Consider, e.g., the I.G. Farben trial, 10 *Law Reports of Trials of War Criminals*, p.1. The US Military Tribunal found the directors of this company guilty in a case whose allegations involved deportation, use of slave labour, torture, killings, plunder of occupied territory, production of internationally banned chemical weapons, and conduct of illegal experiments on unwilling human subjects. A. Clapham, 'The International Criminal Court and the Question of Jurisdiction under International Criminal Law over Legal Persons Including MNCs', in M. Kamminga and S. Zia-Zarifi (eds.), *Liability of Multinational Corporations Under International Law* (2000), p. 139.

[28] S. Zia-Zarifi, 'Suing Multinationals in US Courts for Violating International Human Rights', 4 *University of California Los Angeles International Law Review* (1999), p. 81.

[29] P. Stirling, 'The Use of Trade Sanctions as an Enforcement Mechanism for Basic Human Rights: A Proposal for Addition to the World Trade Organization', 11 *American University Journal of International Law and Policy* (1996), p. 1 (discussing utility of trade sanctions as an instrument of addressing human rights abuses).

entering the debate about the efficacy or wisdom of trade measures as a tool of advancing human rights, suffice it to say that it is clear that the profit motive is generally circumscribed by international standards of behaviour against the use of forced labour, against financing of internationally recognized crimes and against involvement, whether directly or indirectly, in violations of international law. These limits on international investment and trade, whether imposed unilaterally or multilaterally, must therefore be addressed in an MIT.[30]

This broad list is not intended as a comprehensive catalogue of possible links between economic policy and human rights protection. For the most part, the list reflects linkages expressed by various institutions representing either human rights (including labour rights) or international trade. Thus, even if the inclusion or omission of particular rights may be criticized, this list does serve as a starting point for discussing the interaction between an investment treaty with human rights. These rights, and the extent of their interaction with international investment rules, will become clearer in the following discussion regarding the reasons for linking human rights with an MIT.

3    WHY LINK AN MIT AND HUMAN RIGHTS

In order to analyze the propriety of a proposed linkage between human rights and investment policies within an MIT, it is helpful to draw upon the existing analyses on linkages between social and economic issues. To do so, this paper advocates the following schematic approach, which divides the reasons for linking, or not linking, different topics within one treaty into four categories:[31]

a)  conceptual: linkage supports, or detracts from, the policy rationale behind the two topics to be linked;
b)  instrumental: linkage aids, or hurts, implementation of the two topics' objectives;
c)  political: linkage aids, or hurts, the political process necessary for successful adoption (at the international and domestic level) of the treaty including both topics; and
d)  institutional: linkage aids, or hurts, the organization responsible for implementing the treaty including both topics.

---

30  S. Charnovitz, 'Trade Measures and the Design of International Regimes', 5 *Journal of Environment & Development* (1996), p. 168.
31  This approach is adapted from a framework suggested in S. Charnovitz, 'Linking Topics in Treaties,' 19 *University of Pennsylvania Journal of International Economic Law* (1998), p. 335.

## 3.1 Conceptual reasons

An instrument should link two different topics if their inclusion supports the rationale underlying both topics; conversely, linkage should be avoided when the linkage opposes the policies underlying either topic. Given FDI's increasing importance in international transactions, it is the environment for FDI that has become the recent focus of international attention, with the arguments previously used to justify international commerce applied specifically to FDI and the benefits of liberalization. As described more fully below, these arguments all rely on the belief that increased global commerce increases global and national wealth and thus enables greater human rights protection.[32]

Economists typically justify international commerce by some version of Ricardo's theory of comparative advantages, which claims that a perfectly free system of international trade allows countries to develop their best resources, thus maximizing their (and global) wealth.[33] The frequently unarticulated assumption behind the theory of comparative advantage is that increased wealth leads to improved human existence.[34] More recent and nuanced theories, like game theory and John Ruggie's 'embedded realism' model, whereby nations engage in international trade primarily to advance their own economic policies, essentially flesh out the invisible hand approach by explaining how international commerce simultaneously aids multilateral achievement as well as domestic agendas.[35]

The same basic rationale supports investment treaties; for instance, the OECD justified its drive for investment liberalization thus:

---

[32] This justification for international trade is particularly relevant for the Western (i.e., European and American) economic powers that dominate global trade, because of the basis of liberal democratic ideology in liberal (and liberalizing) economic policies, fundamentally stated as the individual's right of decision-making in economic and social activities. F. Garcia, 'Trade and Justice: Linking the Trade Linkage Debates', 19 *University of Pennsylvania Journal of International Economic Law* (1998), pp. 411-413 and 422-424.

[33] For a succinct description of the various theories underpinning international trade, see J. Dunoff, 'Rethinking International Trade', 19 *University of Pennsylvania Journal of International Economic Law* (1998), p. 347.

[34] Nichols, *supra* note 7, pp. 661-667. Aside from the wealth-generating benefits of trade, Nichols cites the following benefits of international trade which may be extrapolated to international investment: increased international contacts fostered by transboundary trade, supporting international peace; distribution of foreign exchange to needy developing countries; the creation of jobs through foreign investment.

[35] J. Ruggie, 'Embedded Liberalism Revisited: Institutions and Progress in International Economic Relations', in E. Adler and B. Crawford (eds.), *Progress in Postwar International Relations* (1991), p. 201 (arguing that GATT has allowed States to dismantle various barriers to international trade for a variety of internal agendas). See further J. Jackson, 'World Trade Rules and Environmental Policies: Congruence or Conflict?', 49 *Washington & Lee Law Review* (1992), p. 1231.

> Trade and foreign direct investment are major engines of growth in developed and developing countries alike. ... [W]hen individuals and companies engage in specialisation and exchange, a country will exploit its comparative advantage. It will devote its natural, human, industrial and financial resources to the highest and best uses.[36]

In more concrete terms, the OECD argued that:

> liberalisation can benefit developed and developing countries alike. As is the case for OECD countries, foreign investment brings higher wages, and is a major source of technology transfer and managerial skills in host developing countries. This contributes to rising prosperity in the developing countries concerned, as well as enhancing demand for higher value-added exports from OECD economies.[37]

International institutions whose focus is international trade and investment have begun to accept that their missions are intertwined with social considerations, even if they do cast these rights not as fundamental rights, but rather as the by-products or the distant justifications for international commerce. Most international economic institutions have recently begun to define their work more explicitly in these terms, as seen in the growing attention to sustainable development and good governance by various Bretton Woods institutions and other multilateral development banks,[38] and the World Trade Organization, which allows trade-restrictive measures relating to the protection of human health and natural resources.[39] Even bilateral trade treaties state their purpose in terms of improving economic growth and social development.[40] Other international institutions dealing with economic issues have gone farther in assessing economic performance in terms of its ability to improve a society. At the vanguard of this development has been the UN Development Programme, which has created a fuller and more nuanced view of economic development, encompassing not just factors such as national wealth and production, but also health, education and real individual income.[41] Similarly, the much-maligned UN Conference on Trade and Development (UNCTAD) has done much recently in its annual reports on international trade and investment to track not simply the volume of international commerce, but also the distribution of that trade and its real impact on the trading countries.

---

36  OECD, *supra* note 21, p. 1.
37  *Idem*, p. 3.
38  G. Handl, 'The Legal Mandate of Multilateral Development Banks as Agents for Change Toward Sustainable Development', 92 AJIL (1998), p. 642.
39  GATT, Art. XX(b), e.g., allows Members of the WTO to take trade restrictive measures when "necessary to protect human ,animal or plant life or health"; Art. XX(e) similarly allows trade restrictive measures designed to combat the use of prison labour.
40  K. Vandevelde, 'The Political Economy of a Bilateral Investment Treaty', 92 AJIL (1998), p. 621.
41  See, e.g., UNDP, *Human Development Report 1999: Globalization With a Human Face* (1999).

In terms of social rights and labour rights, then, the argument for international investment liberalization is that increased social wealth may lead to improved human rights standards.[42] There is some quantitative correlation between increasing domestic wealth and improving human rights, for instance, which indicates that nations that provide better protection for human rights are generally those countries better at generating wealth.[43] This type of empirical analysis should not be overstated; suffice it to say that there is some economic data that supports the notion that support for human rights may facilitate economic development and trade liberalization, and vice versa. If so (and this is certainly the official line of international economic bodies), the link between international investment and human rights, especially social and labour rights, should be encouraged by any trade or investment treaty.

Furthermore, an international investment treaty should prohibit economic activity that would involve investors in acts criminalized or widely proscribed by international law. Criminal acts by their nature weaken the legal regime necessary for smooth economic transactions and investor protection. Even if profitable in the short term, there is no question that such conduct is outside the pale of acceptable economic activity. Thus there is no possible economic justification for maintaining silence on such abuses of basic human rights, and an economic treaty designed for the real world should incorporate a prohibition of violations of basic international human rights standards in order to signal its awareness of the occasional crimes perpetrated by investors and its commitment to stop such acts. That such a statement would not in any way interfere with global economic transactions should make this linkage palatable to all. Presumably, economists and trade diplomats do not support those investment and trade policies that could have deleterious social results or rely on unethical conduct. At a conceptual level, then, there seems to be no reason to avoid reiterating the value and primacy of human rights in an investment treaty; in fact, such explicit recognition would go a long way toward clarifying the exact reason why international investment is beneficial for the people of the world.

### 3.2 Instrumental reasons

While economists and human rights lawyers may agree that their ultimate goal is the creation of a better society where people lead better lives, the two groups diverge sharply over the means necessary for bringing about these improvements. The position of classic economic liberal policy, at the risk of

---

42 See *supra* note 9.
43 Nichols further notes the correlation between increased national wealth and longevity, and conversely, decreasing wealth and deterioration in public health. Nichols, *supra* note 7, p. 666.

some simplification, is that the market's invisible hand is the most effective organizer and improver of societies, and that therefore any government policies that interfere with the market's operation must be minimized or eliminated. This argument or variations upon it typically militate against linkage between human rights and economic treaties because economists view these regulations as having the same distorting effect as any other state intrusion upon the market.[44] On the other hand, the international human rights regime relies on state governments to implement and ensure labour rights, social rights, and other basic human rights. Linking human rights and investment policies would help establish the range of social policies within which the state could foster a free market conducive to international investment and trade. This linkage would serve to protect and strengthen states' ability to choose those courses of action (or inaction) that would best help them compete in the global marketplace while satisfying their obligations to uphold and improve the livelihood of their citizens.

In terms of state action, economists have long admitted that the free market as such does not exist, but is rather a construct of particular forces within society that use social resources to create and protect a particular institution wherein the state minimizes its direct involvement. To explain the political ramifications of the clash over the state's role in ordering social resources, 'public choice' theory casts state economic policy as a subset of political competition over resources between various public sectors; a competition which naturally favours the rich and mighty.[45] That is, in the context of liberalizing international investment it is not enough for states simply to deregulate the investment environment. States must also protect investors, foreign or otherwise, for instance by assigning resources to judicial enforcement of foreign patents in the case of investors in intellectual property. States must actively create the necessary legal and physical infrastructure to support foreign investors. Even more active is the role of states when they attract FDI through incentives and tax breaks.

Government inaction has now also been recognized as having non-neutral effects. There is the phenomenon of social dumping, for instance, whereby lax labour standards constitute, in practice, a subsidy of particular businesses, which seriously skews the market.[46] Furthermore, any single country that tried to enforce higher labour standards would risk losing out to less scrupulous competitors. This race to the bottom continues to push states (especially developing states) to weaken their protection of human rights in order to

---

44 See P. Stephan, 'Barbarians Inside the Gate: Public Choice Theory and International Economic Law', 10 *American University Journal of International Law & Policy* (1995), p. 745.
45 See *idem*; J. Bhagwati, *Political Economy and International Economics* (1991).
46 D. Ehrenberg, 'The Labor Link: Applying the International Trading System to Enforce Violations of Forced and Child Labor', 20 *Yale Journal of International Law* (1995), p. 379.

maintain or increase their competitive advantage.[47] It is presumably the same profit motive that drives some investors to partake of ventures that directly or indirectly rely on benefiting from internationally prohibited acts, such as the use of slave or forced labour, forced resettlement of populations, or the threat or application of force. Since no single actor is willing to assume the cost of stopping this downward spiral, it is necessary to use collective action, enforced by a multilateral regime, to address this type of market distortion. Thus, any MIT must include devices that prohibit market distortions caused by (unethical) social policies of its Member States; precisely the role performed in this context by a linkage to international human rights standards.

The OECD's Guidelines for Multinational Enterprises, considered the organization's primary instrument regarding its social responsibility, put it this way:

> The common aim of the Member countries is to encourage the positive contributions which multinational enterprises can make to economic and social progress and to minimize and resolve the difficulties to which their various operations may give rise.[48]

This statement also encapsulates the other instrumental reason supporting linkage of human rights to an investment liberalization treaty: such linkage in fact aids the implementation of liberal policies by decreasing potential negative social responses to liberalization. For instance, the OECD has long recognized that liberalization can lead to social instability, which provokes protectionist measures from national governments. To avoid this protectionist urge, the OECD has advocated maintaining important social values, such as education, job training, taxation, social security nets, job provision, and health protection.[49] "In sum", the OECD argued, "a balanced mix of policies is needed to reinforce adaptive capacity in the face of all structural changes, including those stemming from trade and investment liberalisation".[50] Clearly, many, if not most, of the 'mix of policies' identified by the OECD as necessary for the smooth liberalization of a national economy implicate human rights such as the right to education, social security, health, and labour protection.[51] The OECD's conclusions should not be viewed as anecdotal, but rather as a distilla-

---

47 While this reasoning may seem commonsensical, it is not at all certain what impact regulatory measures have on comparative advantage. On the link between comparative labour standards and trade competitiveness, see Bhala, *supra* note 19, pp. 17-28. On the impact of environmental regulations on competitiveness, see R. Stewart, 'Environmental Regulation and International Competitiveness', 102 *Yale Law Journal* (1993), p. 2039.
48 OECD, *Guidelines for Multinational Enterprises* (1991), Introduction, para. 2.
49 OECD, *supra* note 21.
50 *Ibidem*.
51 E.g., the UNDP's Human Development reports measure development not just in terms of national wealth, but using a composite index in three fundamental categories: life expectancy (health), educational attainment and income. See also Steiner, *supra* note 14, pp. 35-40.

tion of the approach of the dominant international liberal economic paradigm to issues inherent in liberalization.[52]

Aside from these utilitarian arguments in favour of linkage, it is important here to point out another natural type of linkage between an MIT and human rights. This type of issue refers to what may be called 'stealth linkages', or problems of omission in a treaty where some economic principle directly interacts with human rights principles but is left unaddressed. A prime example would be a liberalizing prohibition of regulations aimed at redressing historically discriminatory employment practices, such as affirmative action measures. For instance, the OECD MAI prohibited employment requirements and performance requirements that impinged upon investors' right to hire as they pleased.[53] Such a rule would of course have a tremendous impact on existing affirmative action efforts pursuant to international obligations.[54] Similarly, investment provisions that limit the state's ability to craft domestic measures for providing social human rights, the protection and promotion of the lots of minorities, women and children, would be threatened by stealth linkages. Reconciling the state's responsibility to meet its international human rights obligations with the state's desire to attract and maintain FDI is thus a key function of the process of linking an MIT with human rights.

### 3.3 Political Reasons

The issues categorized as conceptual or instrumental find their voice through different social and governmental groups reflecting political forces, and treaty linkages are frequently necessary to build political coalitions in order to make liberalization treaties acceptable to various domestic or international constituencies. On the other hand, linkages sometimes damage a treaty by including topics unacceptable to various important constituencies. In the context of an MIT, for instance, it is likely (as was the case with the OECD MAI) that governments in newly developed countries, such as Mexico, South Korea and Brazil, would view human rights regulations, especially those regarding labour relations, as inimical to their economic development plans, which typically

---

52 For a more general discussion of the non-trade social values inextricably linked to discussions of liberalization, see J. Jackson, *World Trade Trading System: Law and Policy of International Economic Relations* (1989), pp. 16-18 (discussing market inefficiencies caused by social problems such as poor education, poor distribution of wealth, and other social problems).
53 OECD, draft MAI, Ch.III, Employment Requirements, p. 17 and Performance Requirements, p. 21.
54 Y. Klerk, 'Working Paper on Article 2(2) and Article 3 of the International Covenant on Economic, Social and Cultural Rights', 9 *Human Rights Quarterly* (1987), p. 265.

involve the attraction of massive private FDI.[55] On the other hand, in the Western democracies, where the free trade coalition is fairly narrow, an MIT would have to rely on support from important groups pushing specific aspects of the human rights agenda, i.e., labour rights, non-discrimination, environmental and health protection, and sustainable development. The balance ultimately struck between these opposing tendencies will establish the existence and strength of any linkages between human rights and an MIT. On the whole, however, given the other reasons favouring linkages, the existing legal obligations of states in terms of human rights protection, and the empirical evidence connecting better human rights protection and economic development, it is likelier than not that human rights, to some degree, will be linked to any investment treaty with a large membership.

Treaties are signed by states, and, as Professor Nichols has pointed out on the domestic front, "to the extent national governments are in some measure democratic, their abilities to support an international trade regime depend on marshalling popular support".[56] Especially in the major Western trading countries (which are all liberal democracies), human rights in general, and particular subtopics such as labour rights and women's rights, have strong political constituencies that could block a liberalizing trade treaty unless their concerns are met.[57] We have already discussed in terms of instrumental reasons the value of linkages in minimizing social disruption caused by liberalization, and thus increasing the acceptability of an MIT. An example of a successful linkage in an international economic instrument propelled by domestic political concerns comes from the negotiating history of the GATT, which specifically allowed trade barriers in some instances where domestic policies were designed to minimize job loss due to international competition.[58] The linkage between international economic obligations and domestic politics was even clearer during the debate surrounding NAFTA, which addressed concerns about its impact on labour and environmental regulation in order to mollify domestic political concerns.[59] The necessity of drafting an MIT with

---

55 These countries opposed the inclusion of binding labour standards in the MAI. At the first Ministerial Conference of the WTO discussions regarding a social clause, proposed by the US and some other developed countries, were blocked by a number of developing countries. See Bhala, *supra* note 19, p. 31. Proposals for including core labour rights in the WTO system, e.g., have met with resistance from East Asian economies who claim that such moves constitute hidden protectionism. See Ehrenberg, *supra* note 46, p. 403. See, e.g., M. Richardson, 'A Warning on Trade Talks: Discord Threatens Seattle Meeting, Asians Say', *International Herald Tribune*, 23 October, 1999, p. 13.
56 Nichols, *supra* note 7, p. 702 (footnotes omitted).
57 On the role of NGOs in molding international economic policy as regarding environmental matters, see H. French, 'The Role of Non-State Actors', in J. Werksman (ed.), *Greening International Institutions* (1996), p. 251.
58 Dunoff, *supra* note 33, p. 372.
59 On the role of NGOs, especially environmental NGOs, in first opposing and then tacitly supporting NAFTA, see D. Esty, *Greening the GATT: Trade, Environment and the Future* (1994).

sufficient linkages to satisfy domestic constituencies was most apparent in the OECD's failed MAI, where one factor for the treaty's demise was the OECD's inability to attract the support of labour and environmental groups.[60] As international economic institutions become better known as important international players, it is certain that they will also become more vulnerable to political pressures emanating from within their Member States, and any future MIT must include linkages that respond to these pressures.

While linking human rights to an investment treaty may increase the treaty's domestic and international chances of acceptance, linkages can also have the opposite effect in some instances. Politicizing economic treaties by linkages with social issues may lead to economically sub-optimal results.[61] Politically, also, linkages can cause problems by seeming to provide a pretext for increased governmental interference.[62] The OECD MAI lost support from the business lobby in part because of the possibility that the document might include some labour and environmental obligations.[63] In a similar vein, the business community, and the main home states of this community, had previously demonstrated their ability to thwart an international economic instrument during negotiations in the 1970s and 1980s over the drafting of a UN Code of Conduct for Transnational Enterprises attempting to combine a regime of investor protection along with guidelines on investor obligations.[64] The UN's effort was a victim of the last gasps of the Cold War ideological struggle and the effort to initiate a New International Economic Order, but the evidence suggests that the different constituencies involved in the draft Code actually agreed on many substantial points, including the application of some obligations to the business community.[65] While the business lobby is likely to continue to resist a strong human rights linkage, the experience of the UN Code also demonstrates that in the face of significant political pressure, or in the pursuit of significant gains such as strong investor protection, business interests will agree to some linkages. The UN's experience in this ultimate attempt at linkage may once again prove useful if an MIT is negotiated in the context of the WTO or a UN body. It is a measure of the political maturity of the business community to see whether it will use the nearly universal acceptance of free market principles as an occasion to accept greater responsibility, or rather simply as a position of power from which to dictate one-sided demands.

---

60 J. Huner, 'The Multilateral Agreement on Investment and the Review of the OECD Guidelines for Multinational Enteprises', in Kamminga et al. (eds.), *supra* note 26, p. 197.
61 F. Roessler, 'Domestic Policy Objectives and the Multilateral Trade Order', in A. Krueger (ed.), *The WTO as an International Organization* (1998), p. 226.
62 For greater development of this theme see Dunoff, *supra* note 7.
63 Huner, *supra* note 60.
64 P. Muchlinski, 'Attempts to Extend the Accountability of Transnational Corporations: The Role of UNCTAD', in Kamminga et al. (eds.), *supra* note 27, p. 97.
65 *Ibidem*.

## 3.4 Institutional reasons

Linking different topics in one treaty, aside from theoretical and political issues, affects the institutional framework of that treaty. Treaty secretariats, like all bureaucratic organizations, typically share a broad institutional ideological framework. The success or failure of a linkage within a treaty depends on whether a given treaty secretariat can, and will, benefit or suffer from the linkage. It is clear that linking human rights and investment issues in the context of an MIT will impact institutional resource allocation. But these problems are not intractable and are outweighed by the benefits of some degree of linkage. Furthermore, the overwhelming success of the liberal trade model and the elevation of economic science as determinants of international relations demand that economic treaties and their secretariats address a diverse array of non-economic problems in lieu of any alternative fora for addressing these problems.

Economists, as well as social activists like environmental and labour NGOs, seem to agree that economic institutions are not the best places to address social issues. Social activists have criticized the inability or disinclination of economic bodies like the WTO, the World Bank, and the IMF to address social issues. In partial agreement, the WTO secretariat has frankly admitted its inability to review and monitor social issues.[66] Traditional liberal economists defend the sanctity of trade organizations on the grounds of an institutional version of comparative advantage, arguing that trade bodies do not have the expertise or resources to tackle a variety of environmental, labour and human rights concerns, and that there are already international organizations dedicated to addressing these social concerns.[67] In short, to borrow a phrase from one international trade lawyer, overreaching through linkages between human rights and investment issues might turn an MIT into an economic Kellogg-Briand pact, and the MIT's secretariat into an economic League of Nations.[68]

These arguments, while important to consider, only go so far. First, arguments for the institutional sanctity of economic organizations beg the question of where to raise issues common to both the trade and the human rights discussion. The reason that trade bodies have increasingly faced pressure for linkages to social issues is that there are no other viable alternatives.[69] Witness, for instance, the UN's ECOSOC, which has no tangible influence on the

---

66 Dunoff, *supra* note 7, p. 759.
67 See, e.g., the statement by a group of economists in 1997 in favour of focusing trade liberalization organizations on trade issues and addressing human rights in other international bodies. Charnovitz, *supra* note 30, p. 341, 342 and note 48.
68 D. Palmeter, 'International Trade Law in the Twenty-First Century', 18 *Fordham International Law Journal* (1995), p. 1657.
69 Charnovitz, *supra* note 30, p. 342.

conduct of international or domestic economic policy.[70] Even the ILO lacks any input on international trade policy.[71] Second, an alternative forum for analyzing the intersection of economic and human rights policies would immediately face problems of competing jurisdiction with economic bodies. For example, it is unclear what international body would rule on the validity of new affirmative action policies aimed at increasing women's participation in the workforce, if such policies seemed to contravene economic liberalization mandated by an MIT. Third, and perhaps most simply, the problems of institutional expertise and the complexity of linked issues apply equally strongly to any human rights body. Issues involving both human rights and investment policies must be addressed somewhere, and the current predominance of economic bodies marks them as the natural fora for addressing these problems. There has already been a large amount of work performed on linkages between trade treaties and social issues, and it makes imminent sense to discuss these issues when all the economists are gathered already, instead of breaking up such discussions artificially. If this is an inconvenience for economic bodies and economists, it is the price of their own success in setting much of the current international agenda.

Linkage of social and economic issues not only makes sense from a political point of view, but also addresses some of the public choice criticisms directed at typically opaque and undemocratic international economic institutions.[72] All international bodies rely to some extent on outside groups for important expertise and information support. For instance, the WTO dispute resolution body receives information from business lobbies as well as NGOs.[73] Business interests influence the WTO not just directly, but also through their home states, as most clearly demonstrated in the *Reformulated Gasoline* dispute between the US and Venezuela, which actually was a dispute between the American Citgo company versus the Venezuelan national petroleum company.[74] Linking human rights with an MIT would require similar involvement by NGOs involved in the monitoring of human rights that could enhance an MIT secretariat's resources by providing information and analysis. It is true, as many opponents of linkage argue, that many human rights NGOs are in practice hostile to economic liberalization efforts and would use their well-organized interest

---

70 ECOSOC's Sub-Committee on the Promotion and Protection of Human Rights, e.g., has in the past few years issued a number of strongly worded statements on the negative impact of globalization on human rights issue, all to no apparent attention, much less avail. See, e.g., *supra* note 6.
71 The WTO mandate includes provisions for consultation with the ILO, though to date no such consultation has taken place. GATT (1994) Art. V.
72 D. Esty, 'Linkages and Governance: NGOs at the World Trade Organization', 19 *University of Pennsylvania Journal of International Econonomic Law* (1998), p. 719.
73 The WTO has accepted submissions from NGOs in its dispute settlement mechanism, most prominently in the Shrimp-Turtle Case, *Appellate Body Report* (1998), paras. 99-110.
74 *United States – Standards for Reformulated and Conventional Gasoline*, WT/DS2/9 (1996).

groups to exert a disproportionately protectionist impact on economic organizations.[75] However, this influence would be more than counterbalanced by the influence of the business community, and, at any rate, this kind of interest group lobbying is an acceptable and necessary part of the operating procedure of any large organization with multiple constituencies.

Institutional constraints are among the reasons most often trotted out by opponents of linkages between trade and social policies, for instance by the OECD during the MAI debate, and in rejecting calls for including detailed human rights considerations in the OECD Guidelines. While some of the arguments against linkages represent genuine considerations of bureaucratic scale and institutional resources, and thus should be carefully heeded by all proponents of linkages, other arguments, such as those claiming some kind of mission sanctity for liberalizing institutions, merely reflect the siege mentality of economists circling their wagons against a host of real and imagined antiliberal forces. But having won the battle for the hearts and souls of the world's governments convincingly, economists should now open up the circle and adopt a more inclusive attitude. They have created strong, viable institutions uniquely positioned to address some of the most important problems facing the globe. Sharing these institutions is not a sign of weakness, but rather of strength.

## 4  How to link an MIT and human rights

At this point, having exhorted the MIT's drafters to reach new heights of complexity in their efforts, it is only fair to attempt here to make some preliminary suggestions about the form of a future MIT that would create a viable global investment treaty while observing international human rights standards and obligations. To achieve these results, the MIT should follow a multilayered approach drawn from the recent work of UNCTAD on international investment treaties.[76]

The MIT should contain provisions that state the treaty's objective, within the context of an international commitment to development and growth, toward achieving better human rights. The most effective means of doing so is to allow host states sufficient flexibility to follow their human rights development strategy. To provide this flexibility, an MIT's overall structure must take into account the actual asymmetry between the State Parties so that their respective rights and obligations reflect the differences between states at

---

75  This argument, applied specifically to the WTO, appears in P. Nichols, 'Extension of Standing in World Trade Organization Disputes to Non-Government Parties', 17 *University of Pennsylvania Journal of International Economic Law* (1996), p. 295.

76  UNCTAD, *International Investment Agreements: Concepts Allowing for a Certain Flexibility in the Interest of Promoting Growth and Development* (1999).

different stages of economic development. Furthermore, the MIT's substantive provisions, and the prescribed methods for their implementation, should include, or at least not prohibit, certain minimum standards of behaviour regarding relevant human rights in order to prevent host states from engaging in a race to the bottom or otherwise using an MIT to justify deviation from human rights norms. Specifically:

a) it must clarify and express its conceptual commitment to protect and promote existing international human rights obligations;
b) it must ensure that implementing its requirements does not impinge on the protection of human rights;
c) it must expand its political constituency to include human rights advocates in an effective coalition; and
d) it must adapt its institutional resources to respond to human rights concerns.

Before addressing these recommendations, it may be necessary to acknowledge the inevitable howl of protest from the proponents of trade liberalization regimes (and the already beleaguered lawyers and economists who must make those regimes work). If they view these suggestions as another unwelcome instance of 'trade and ...' issues, they only have their own success to blame. The dominance of the free market system after the Cold War's end and the remarkable success of various international trade regimes in creating viable, vibrant multilateral frameworks naturally attracted the attention of international lawyers of all persuasions. This shift is, in fact, a tribute to the success of the liberalization regime, in that debates in fields as diverse as labour, environmental and human rights law are now cast in terms of their interaction with trade law. The free traders won the war and conquered the planet – now they must demonstrate that they can rule it wisely. [77]

4.1   Clarifying the MIT's motives

Linking investment and human rights within a single international instrument is a matter of stating the sometimes unstated premise that the point of international commerce (and its subset, investment) is the improvement of human welfare. That this is, or should be, the goal of all government actions should never be lost to us. Therefore the MIT should be clear about its commitment to this goal and, more important, about how it contributes to achieving this goal. Legislation typically addresses such basic rationales in its preamble.[78]

---

77   As Dunoff suggests, the present argument itself indicates the victory of traditional trade partisans in setting the intellectual agenda, *supra* note 6, p. 768. However, the aim here is not to defend or celebrate this victory, but rather to show that even the traditionalist approach to global commerce must heed international human rights obligations.
78   1969 Vienna Convention on the Law of Treaties, Art. 31(2), 1155 UNTS, p. 331.

The MIT should state its policy objectives and rationales clearly in its preamble. These objectives, based on respect for the human rights mentioned above, should be:

a) explicit recognition of the interaction between foreign investment and human rights, stressing the primacy of the latter and an explicit commitment to curbing the negative impact of foreign investment on human rights; and

b) explicit recognition of the differing needs of states at differing stages of economic activity for investments and investment measures.

The first objective is already part of the rhetoric of nearly all international economic regimes. In the case of an investment regime, an MIT should include among its objectives explicit recognition of the contribution, which foreign investors can make to economic and social progress in areas such as technology transfer, employment, education and labour rights. The draft MAI, for instance, explained FDI's role in improving human welfare via the following language in its Preamble:

> [A]greement upon the treatment to be accorded to investors and their investments will contribute to the efficient utilisation of economic resources, the creation of employment opportunities and the improvement of living standards ....[79]

Furthermore, among the proposals considered for the OECD MAI's Preamble was one expressing the OECD's

> commitment to the Copenhagen Declaration of the World Summit on Social Development and to observance of internationally recognized core labour standards, i.e., freedom of association, the right to organize and bargain collectively, prohibition of forced labour, the elimination of exploitative forms of child labour, and non-discrimination in employment.[80]

The basic human rights discussed above in this article, which rely on already existing international law, have even stronger normative legitimacy than the somewhat hortatory Copenhagen Declaration. But at the very least, these statements show a growing responsiveness to sentiments consistently expressed by the architects and leaders of globalization and its supporting structures.[81]

The second objective, which is aimed at creating a more realistic and nuanced view of the global economic playing field, is more easily found in existing economic instruments. UNCTAD has collated some of the better samples from the myriad international treaties that realistically address the asymmetry

---

79  OECD, draft MAI (1998), Preamble, para. 3.
80  *Idem*, para. 9.
81  For a survey of the recent shift toward accepting social obligations for commercial interests and entities, see C. Avery, *Business and Human Rights in a Time of Change* (1999).

that exists between various parties to a multilateral economic treaty and the impact of this asymmetry on their ability to meet their obligations to their people and their international partners.[82] For instance, witness the Preamble to the Agreement on Trade Related Investment Measures (TRIMS), which states its objective as:

> Desiring to promote the expansion and progressive liberalization of world trade and to facilitate investment across international frontiers so as to increase the economic growth of all trading partners, particularly those developing-country Members, while ensuring free competition ....[83]

Numerous other examples articulate the intention of multilateral economic treaties to increase global liberalization in order to assist developing countries. Any MIT should at least include a similar clear explanation of its objective in improving global well-being.

### 4.2 Improving the MIT's implementation

As discussed in the context of conceptual reasons for such linkage, the MIT must explicitly state its goal of improving human welfare by protecting and promoting human rights. Preambular statements alone, however, are insufficient because they are hortatory and unenforceable. The two basic instrumental reasons in support of linking international investment and human rights within the same treaty, namely, avoiding the negative effects of investment regulation and strengthening the positive effects, must be viably implemented in a future MIT, not just because they support international human rights obligations but also because they create the social stability necessary for economic development. Thus the MIT's substantive provisions must reflect the goals stated in the Preamble, basically by locking in existing international obligations against downward pressure from investment liberalization measures, and maintaining flexibility for states to improve their human rights protection within the liberalized investment regime.

In its work on international investment agreements, UNCTAD has identified issues that typically comprise the substance of investment regimes and some of the methods used to implement them.[84] The first issue is the correct range of the MIT, i.e., its breadth in covering what constitutes investment, how extensive the protection of investment should be, and what acts impinge on this protection. The second issue is the substantive heart of any MIT, namely

---

82  UNCTAD, *supra* note 76, pp. 7-10.
83  Agreement on Trade Related Investment Measures, Preamble, para. 2; the special requirements of developing countries are reiterated in Art. 4.
84  UNCTAD, *supra* note 76, pp. 10-20.

the notion of non-discrimination as embodied in the doctrines of national treatment and most-favoured-nation treatment. The third and final issue is the implementation mechanism used to enforce the agreed upon substance of the treaty, typically through a dispute settlement mechanism.

### 4.2.1 The MIT's range - definitions of investment and expropriation

If development in general and the advancement of human rights in particular are to be considered goals of an MIT, then the MIT should define what exactly it means by investment. The argument that the MIT benefits countries is that increased FDI, especially to developing countries, helps their development and increases wealth generally. As discussed above, there is some empirical evidence for this (although that too is disputed, as I have indicated), and at any rate this argument is the only one advanced by economists in order to justify including developing countries in an MIT. But there is no evidence that non-FDI type investments are also beneficial, or at least benign, for developing countries. Portfolio investments, for instance, are subjects of immense controversy for their value in fostering financial development, as demonstrated in the financial crisis that swept through Asia and Latin America. The particular problem associated with portfolio investments is that, unlike in the case of FDI, the foreign investor has no lasting stake in the welfare of the host state and therefore is more likely to focus on short-term gains instead of the long-term or even medium-term gains that proponents of trade liberalization ascribe to foreign investment. The IMF for instance focuses on this difference by defining FDI as

> international investment that reflects the objective of a resident entity in one economy obtaining a lasting interest in an enterprise resident in another economy .... The lasting interest implies the existence of a long-term relationship between the direct investor and the enterprise and a significant degree of influence by the investor on the management of the enterprise.[85]

The lower degree of involvement by the foreign portfolio investor lends itself more easily to investment in or profiteering from violations of international human rights standards, essentially negating the rationale for liberalizing this type of international investment.[86] Similar considerations apply to calls for liberalization (and extension of protection to) exploratory or speculative investments, otherwise known as pre-investment protection. While FDI investors with established stakes in a community may be regulated by market intangibles

---

85 IMF, *Balance of Payments Manual* (1993), 5th edn., quoted in UNCTAD, *supra* note 76, p. 11.
86 Many bilateral investment treaties between developed and underdeveloped countries define investment broadly to include direct and indirect investment by foreigners, as well as intellectual property rights. See K. Vandevelde, *United States Investment Treaties, Policy and Practice* (1992).

(i.e., consumer loyalty, reputation, management stability), these mechanisms would hardly apply to prospective investors, who could contest government action with very little concretely at stake for the investor.[87] Any MIT must define its range of protected investments narrowly to protect host states from the negative impact of shortsighted or avaricious foreign investors.

The definition of expropriation is a key concept for any MIT, since it will establish the range of actions from which the MIT seeks to protect foreign investors. In the current global political climate, expropriations are not the proclamations of revolutionary independence, as witnessed after the revolutions in Cuba and Iran, for instance, but rather matters of regulations and creeping expropriation. A definition that does not take into account national goals competing with trade liberalization will tend to generate legal conflicts, whether in developed or developing countries. In the extreme, any national human rights effort that would direct private capital into particular areas could be considered by private investors as a taking, since their interests would be infringed upon. Unfortunately, this extreme vision seems borne out at least in part by experience from NAFTA, whose broad anti-expropriation language has given rise to a number of lawsuits of dubious provenance (and certain controversy) in which investors successfully challenged government regulations intended to protect human health and the environment.[88] Without getting into the merit of these particular cases, it is important to note that the NAFTA jurisprudence indicates at least potential problems, especially in poor countries where MNCs with extensive resources could seriously challenge weak governments. To address this problem, any MIT must include a careful definition of expropriation, to distinguish it from legitimate (i.e., non-protectionist) government regulation. Another crucial mechanism for ensuring that foreign investors do not use an MIT as a sword against legitimate human rights policies (instead of a shield against purely expropriatory acts) is to allow regulations for the public purpose so as to allow sufficient flexibility to governments meeting their human rights obligations.[89]

A less direct method of preserving state flexibility in meeting human rights obligations is to carve out these state actions from the purview of the MIT either through treaty exceptions or state derogations. For instance, recognizing the

---

87 Avery suggests that these intangible forces are in fact quite powerful in directing investors toward better human rights protection, *supra* note 81.
88 E.g., a Canadian corporation filed a dispute against Mexico when the Mexican government refused to license the company's takeover of a waste disposal plant on the basis of an environmental impact assessment. Metalclad Corporation v. United Mexican States, Case ARB(AF)/97/1 (ICSID 1999); the US company Ethyl Corporation forced the Canadian government to a $13 million settlement after challenging Canada's restriction of a possibly toxic gasoline additive; and the Canadian company Methanex is challenging California's ban on another gasoline additive in a dispute requesting $970 million in damages (see <www.Methanex.com>).
89 On the public purpose element of state discretion, see P. Muchlinski, *Multinational Enterprises and the Law* (1995), p. 504.

potential clash between liberalization demands and legitimate affirmative action schemes, the OECD MAI considered limited exceptions (only) for anti-discrimination provisions.[90] Other exceptions were included in Annex B to the MAI, which was not incorporated into the final draft version of the MAI.[91] In order to maintain flexibility, the MIT must include such derogations as maintenance of public order, observance of human rights obligations, and prohibition of human rights violations. One method of providing for investor protection and transparency would be to use the standstill and rollback method already familiar to economic treaties. That is, governments would identify a number of human rights policies that would be locked into place as exceptions to the MIT's expropriation protection. Governments would also identify a number of human rights policies that would require alteration over time, and could be invoked to block particular economic activity only following due process of law (i.e., all the basic rules governing the legality of government takings).[92]

### 4.2.2 Non-discrimination

The core of any MIT is formed by the concepts of national treatment and most-favoured-nation treatment (MFN), whereby host states commit themselves to provide a level playing field for foreign and national investors. Unfortunately, these concepts do not take into account differences in power among the players on this level playing field; powerful foreign investors can thus benefit at the expense of weaker native competitors. When these weaker economic actors are comprised by or operated in areas populated by those whose protection and promotion is obligatory under human rights law, the doctrine of non-discrimination becomes problematic. The MIT must be clear that it does not impinge on legitimate affirmative action programmes, for instance as seen above in the OECD MAI. An alternative would be to include a built-in reservation in an MIT for development goals pursuant to international human rights

---

90 OECD, draft MAI, Ch. III, note 14: "It is understood that this Article [Employment Requirements] would not interfere with domestic anti-discrimination and labour laws"; note 24: "Nothing in this paragraph [prohibiting performance requirements demanding hiring of a given level of nationals] shall be construed as interfering with programmes targeted at disadvantaged regions/persons or other equally legitimate employment policy programmes".
91 OECD, draft MAI, Section IX, note 11: "It was agreed to withhold the drafting of the introduction of 'Annex B' until the Negotiating Group had taken a political decision on the status and coverage of Part B of the Article. Moreover, a number of delegations felt that the wording of such an introduction might need to be drafted in a limited way (i.e., to cover only cases of privatization or demonopolization".
92 See generally O. Schachter, 'Compensation for Expropriation', 78 AJIL (1984), p.121.

obligations, thereby ensuring a level playing field by adopting universally applicable standards.[93]

Performance requirements are the primary national tools for promoting contribution, and prohibiting damage, by FDI. The MIT should explicitly allow certain performance requirements designed to allow countries, especially developing countries, to develop their national economies, as long as the rules were applied equally following the principle of non-discrimination. The OECD MAI had gone some ways in this direction, pointing out in Paragraph 4 of Section III that "Parties could take measures necessary to protect human, animal or plant life or health or measures necessary for the conservation of living or non-living exhaustible natural resources". The GATT Agreement on Subsidies and Countervailing Measures, for instance, allows subsidies for research, but more significantly, for promoting development in "disadvantaged regions" and for one-time adaptation of existing facilities to meet new environmental requirements.[94] In this sense, the MIT should not go beyond the range of limits on performance requirements established by TRIMS, which, for instance, allows requirements for the employment of a given level of nationals, for establishment of joint ventures with nationals, and for a minimum level of local equity participation.[95] A similar approach, more explicitly tied into existing human rights standards, is necessary for an MIT.[96]

Furthermore, to counteract the potential negative effects of non-discrimination standards, the MIT should adopt an 'in like circumstances' standard that provides the context for comparing different competitors in different fields. Problems arise for instance when a powerful MNC is compared with a struggling local enterprise and treated the same way, thus not creating a level playing field but instead enforcing existing inequalities. The central point again is that the national treatment rule must not be applied against legitimate human rights goals. For instance, subsidies or investment incentives are a major tool by which governments can reallocate resources to correct the market's failure when its prices and profitability do not accurately reflect social benefits.[97] Governments typically use subsidies to encourage particular market sectors, or industries, or geographic regions. Such policies may run afoul of a proposed MIT by favouring local investment over FDI, thus violating the national treat-

---

93 This type of harmonization by reliance on existing international standards is explicitly pursued by the WTO, most prominently in its agreement on Sanitary and Phytosanitary Measures and its agreement on Technical Barriers to Trade.
94 GATT ASCM, Art. 8.2(b) (1994).
95 A. Ganesan, 'Development Friendliness Criteria for a Multilateral Investment Agreement', 6 *Transnational Corporations* (1997), p. 139.
96 The MAI's final draft did not include a final decision on this issue, instead opting to postpone the issue to further 'MAI disciplines' regarding positive discrimination. MAI, Ch. III, Investment Incentives, para. 3, p. 48.
97 M. Daly, 'Investment Incentives and the Multilateral Agreement on Incentives', 32 *Journal of World Trade* (1996), p. 5.

ment clause. Any MIT with international aspirations must include some method of distinguishing between admissible subsidies that pursue legitimate national development goals and impermissible protectionist measures.

On the flip side, many governments, especially in the developing world, actually favour FDI over local investment by subsidizing, directly or through tax benefits, foreign MNCs. Another issue associated with investment incentives is preferential treatment for foreigners in order to attract FDI, for instance by lowering applicable social and labour standards – the race to the bottom. Again, an MIT must prohibit such measures, using a 'not lowering measures' clause perhaps similar to NAFTA Article 1114(2), which states:

> Parties recognize that it is inappropriate to encourage investment by relaxing domestic health, safety or environmental measures. Accordingly, a Party should not waive or otherwise derogate from, or offer to waive or otherwise derogate from, such measures as an encouragement for the establishment, acquisition, expansion, or retention in its territory of an investment or an investor.

This clause merely suggests that the race to the bottom is 'inappropriate'. Similar, but stronger, language, designed to protect human rights from competitive forces, is necessary for an MIT.

### 4.2.3 Implementation mechanisms – conflict of obligations and dispute settlement

Obviously the impact of an investment liberalization regime on human rights obligations will depend much on how the liberalization schemes of an MIT are implemented. At the treaty level, the MIT must create at least a mechanism for resolving disputes between economic provisions and existing human rights obligations. Technically, following Article 30 of the Vienna Convention on the Law of Treaties, a new MIT could prevail over any conflicting, more general older human rights treaty obligations, thus requiring some sort of conflict resolution mechanism that would protect human rights obligations from unexpected or unintended (not to mention expected and intended) intrusion by an MIT.[98] A useful example of a beginning point is NAFTA's side agreement on the environment, which is designed to raise environmental standards and to create a dispute settlement mechanism to address failures to enforce environmental laws.[99] NAFTA clarifies that certain multilateral environmental agree-

---

98  J. Schultz, 'Environmental Reform of the GATT/WTO International Trading System', 18 World Competition (1994) p. 104, cited in T. Schoenbaum, 'International Trade and Protection of the Environment: The Continuing Search for Reconciliation', 91 *AJIL* (1997), p. 283.
99  S. Miller, 'NAFTA: A Model for Reconciling the Conflict Between Free Trade and International Environmental Protection', 56 *University of Pittsburgh Law Review* (1994), p. 483.

ments take precedence over NAFTA;[100] the same approach should be used for human rights obligations under an MIT.

The next issues who gets to resolve conflicts between investment liberalization measures and human rights obligations. The OECD MAI's dispute settlement mechanism was a lightning rod for criticism because its unprecedented wide reach exacerbated the treaty's perceived shortcomings.

Presumably, any MIT that allowed trade measures taken pursuant to human rights obligations as exceptions to its liberalization rules would use language similar to GATT Article XX(b), and apply the same kind of test for establishing the necessity of measures that could restrict trade.[101] The Article XX(b) exception for the protection of human, animal or plant life and health generally uses a three step analysis:

a) is the substance of the measure the protection of health?;
b) is the measure necessary to protect health?; and
d) does the measure avoid arbitrary discrimination?[102]

The trouble with this approach has been that in practice, the trade lawyers applying this test have interpreted necessary as 'least trade restrictive', perhaps reflecting their priorities and their understanding of the regulatory framework for environmental protection. If so, any future MIT's dispute settlement mechanism would be wise to move away from the WTO's unduly restrictive interpretation[103] and instead adopt a more lenient approach, utilizing the views of human rights experts who can point out that 'necessary' should be read as 'reasonably necessary'. A useful example of a trade agreement that seeks to balance trade against the absolute necessity of preserving human health comes from a side agreement to the GATT, the Agreement on the Application of Sanitary and Phytosanitary Measures. This agreement, for instance, allows trade restrictive measures designed to protect human health from diseases borne by foodstuffs unless a complainant can show that a better alternative exists.[104] Such a formulation of a dispute settlement mechanism's purview

---

100 J. Smith, 'NAFTA and Human Rights: A Necessary Linkage', 27 *University of California at Davis Law Review* (1994), p. 793.
101 E.g., the MAI offered a possible protective paragraph to its Performance Requirements section following GATT. This provisional para. 4 read: "Provided that such measures are not applied in an arbitrary or unjustifiable manner, or do not constitute a disguised restriction on investment, nothing in paragraphs 1(b) and 1(c) shall be construed to prevent any Contracting Party from adopting or maintaining measures, including environmental measures:
(a) necessary to secure compliance with laws and regulations that are not inconsistent with the provisions of this Agreement;
(b) necessary to protect human, animal or plant health;
(c) necessary for the conservation of living or non-living exhaustible natural resources."
OECD, draft MAI, Ch. III, Performance Requirements, p. 23.
102 Schoenbaum, *supra* note 98, p. 276, citing Tuna/Dolphin III.
103 For summary of protests following from this interpretation, see generally, Garcia, *supra* note 15, pp. 83-85.
104 GATT, SPS, Art.5.6, note 3 (1994).

would clarify that investment protection rules would be implemented without impinging on a state's obligation to improve the welfare of its citizens.[105]

Furthermore, in order to provide states with the flexibility necessary to balance internal human rights obligations with international liberalization schemes, an MIT should exempt certain provisions from review by the dispute settlement mechanism based on their human rights content.[106] Under this approach, an MIT would specify certain criteria to establish safe havens for existing and developing human rights treaties. A useful model would be something similar to Article XX(h) of the GATT that creates an exception for trade measures imposed pursuant to international commodity agreements either automatically, if they conform to enumerated criteria or on an ad hoc basis, if agreed to by GATT Members.[107] A similar system for human rights obligations is easy to envision in an MIT.

### 4.3 Expanding the MIT's political support

There is no question about the general lack of communication, not to say mistrust and antipathy, between the international investment community and advocates of human rights. Nevertheless, in the wake of the MAI fiasco, and the vehement demonstrations against the activity of the World Bank and the WTO, it seems certain that a compromise between the two groups is necessary for the expansion of the rule of international law, both in the economic field and as regarding human rights. It would be possible to create such a compromise through both substantive and procedural methods. The substantive suggestions above regarding the form and content of an MIT would aid in creating such a consensus. But it is also necessary to create proper, transparent procedures that would accommodate the needs and demands of different political constituencies. As said, politics is the art of the possible, and currently it would be impossible to push for an international trade regime, especially one on investment rules, without creating a coalition between trade economists and advocates of human rights.

Naturally, the forum chosen for negotiating an MIT will leave a strong imprint on the process and on the product itself, and thus choosing the proper venue is itself an important first political gesture. For instance, the choice of the OECD as the forum for the MAI reflected the pressure brought to bear by the United States, which believed that negotiating such a treaty between the

---

105 Garcia develops this theme in the context of proposed amendments to the GATT regime, *supra* note 15, pp. 93-95.
106 Nichols, *supra* note 7, pp. 660-661.
107 R. Hudec, 'GATT Legal Restraints on the Use of Trade Measures Against Foreign Environmental Practices', 2 *Fair Trade and Harmonization* (1996), p. 95, cited in Schoenbaum *supra* note 98, pp. 283-284.

like-minded trading countries of the OECD would be easier and would present the developing countries with a *fait accompli*.[108] Other major trading powers, such as the European countries and Canada, had instead favoured the WTO, which is generally accepted by the OECD countries but has broader membership that would have involved the developing countries in the negotiations and thus secured their eventual consent.[109] This reasoning still seems valid, as the WTO presents the only viable forum available for such discussions currently (on the other hand, as pointed out in the next paragraph, the OECD is actually better at communicating with non-trade groups such as NGOs).[110] UNCTAD also presents a strong framework for such a discussion, especially given its comfort with multidisciplinary approaches regarding trade. Unfortunately, UNCTAD is still suffering from a poor reputation in the major trading capitals of the world, and at any rate lacks the commercial expertise and acceptance of the WTO. An MIT advanced in another, less transparent forum, will also likely excite general suspicion and create political problems. Unfortunately, at the moment it seems as if investment issues will be pursued through the opaque network of bilateral investment treaties and the liberalizing demands of the IMF on debtor countries. Such underhanded approaches, while tempting as paths of least resistance for trade lawyers and diplomats, should be avoided due to the adverse political repercussions they will engender.

This is not to voice vague entreaties regarding better communication and dialogue between the trade and human rights camp. It is apparent that at least part of the international trade community has learned this lesson, as demonstrated by the recent reiteration of the UN bodies' interest in eradicating poverty and the role of business in improving human society and through programmes such as the Global Compact advocated by UN Secretary General Kofi Annan,[111] and ever increasing pronouncements by the heads of the World Bank and the WTO regarding the positive social impact of these institutions.[112] Translating these noble statements into deeds would clearly go a long way

---

108 See Zia-Zarifi, *supra* note 4.
109 A. Bohmer, 'The Struggle for a Multilateral Agreement on Investment – An Assessment of the Negotiation Process in the OECD', 41 *German Yearbook of International Law* (1998), p. 275.
110 M. Shahin, 'Multilateral Investment and Competition Rules in the World Trade Organization: An Assessment', 6 *Transnational Corporations* (1997), p. 171.
111 See <www.uncglobalcompact.org>.
112 See, e.g., how James Wolfensohn, President of the World Bank, recently reiterated that "the Bank is now working and trying to deal with the questions of poverty and trying to deal with the questions of equity because that's our job". J. Wolfensohn, *Challenges Facing the Bank in the 21st Century*, Remarks before the (US) National Press Club, 14 March 2000, available at <www.worldbank.org>; similar comments come from the WTO's Director-General, Michael Moore: "Although the WTO is not a development organization, it does a lot to alleviate poverty. After all, free trade is not an end in itself. It helps to raise living standards, which lifts people out of poverty". M. Moore, *Trade, Poverty and the Human Face of Globalization*, remarks at the London School of Economics, 16 June 2000, available at <www.wto.org>.

toward winning a broader political constituency for the international trade agenda. But the commitment of international economic bodies to such a course of action remains uncertain. The WTO, for example, declared its commitment to labour standards as long as the ILO takes the lead on this issue,[113] but has yet to create a meaningful procedure for including the ILO's concerns in its activities. On the positive side of the ledger, the OECD has been active in reaching out to environmental groups outside traditional trade and investment law. But even here, the OECD oddly excluded human rights groups in its discussions surrounding the revision of the OECD Guidelines on Multinational Enterprises during the first stages of the process; wisely, the OECD revisited its policy, likely seeking the approbation of groups such as Amnesty International and Human Rights Watch for its product. That these groups have generally responded openly to these overtures is a hopeful sign that broader coalitions can be patched together.

Political gestures aside, more prosaic procedural safeguards are necessary to help any MIT win the necessary support. The drafters of any future MIT would have to avoid the mistake made by their colleagues at the OECD, namely, to hide their product in the hope that human rights advocates would simply not see it and criticize it. The OECD's current practice of making drafts of important documents available for comment on the Internet is one easy and inexpensive policy to emulate. Similarly, regular meetings with human rights NGOs and academics would go a long way toward improving the acceptability (not to mention the quality) of any international investment treaty.

## 4.4 Strengthening the MIT's institutions

Creating the necessary framework for cooperation between the disparate groups advocating international investment rules and human rights, respectively, naturally requires institutional resources. The identity of those who interpret and implement any set of rules of course plays a great role in the impact of those rules. Whether an MIT operates under the aegis of an existing international institution or develops its own bureaucratic body, it will naturally be colonized by the constituency it generally serves, namely, the community of international investors, traders and diplomats. But it is possible to moderate the extent of this colonization. The inclusion of the suggestions presented above would foster greater understanding and acceptance of human rights with the MIT institutional structure simply by virtue of familiarizing the investment community with human rights concepts. But a few concrete institutional steps would assure that human rights issues receive adequate attention even in an international economic institution.

---

113 WTO, *Singapore Ministerial Declaration*, WT/MIN(96)/DEC W (1996).

Creating a special office or role to oversee the conformity of investment regulations with international human rights principles is crucial. Such an office could take the form of an ombudsman or, even more ambitiously, a venue at which complaints about the impact of particular investment regulations on human rights could be aired and examined. Such a panel could follow the lead of the World Bank's Inspection Panel, which has had some success in focusing the World Bank's attention on its own fealty to its mission.[114] What is important about this Panel is not just that it allows private citizens to hold the World Bank accountable for its performance (although that is of course a major step forward in increasing the transparency and accountability of international institutions). Rather, the importance of an internal watchdog mechanism is that it breathes life into the language advocating social development and welfare and assures that these promises are not forgotten.

Another necessary measure would be to increase the expertise of any MIT's secretariat, especially at the level of implementation and dispute settlement, to enable it to examine human rights issues. One step in the right direction could be to draw upon the expertise of human rights international bodies (such as ECOSOC, the UN Subcommission, the ILO, and UNCTAD) in cases of possible conflict between investment and human rights regulations.[115] A somewhat similar approach appears in the GATT's agreements on the Application of Sanitary and Phytosanitary Measures and on Technical Barriers to Trade, both of which rely on international bodies as sources for standards and expert advice.[116] Additionally, as pointed out above, an MIT dispute settlement mechanism could rely on human rights NGOs to provide relevant information and analysis in cases of conflict between investment protection and human rights. Several commentators have pointed out that such a system may face opposition from both the trade community, which would resent the intrusion of human rights values into their system, and the human rights community, which would fear the loss of control over their hard-won protection to those with different priorities.[117] But given the growing relationship between international investment and social welfare, the conceptual, instrumental and political will may now exist to create such institutional linkages.

---

114 I. Shihata, *The World Bank Inspection Panel* (1994).
115 Ehrenberg, *supra* note 46, p. 367.
116 The SPS Agreement refers to the Codex Alimentarius Commission, the World Organization for Animal Health, and the Secretariat of the International Plant Protection Convention. GATT SPS, Annex A, para. 3. The TBT Agreement refers to the International Organization for Standardization. GATT TBT, Annex 3, para. F.
117 Ehrenberg, *supra* note 46, p. 403.

## 5     Conclusion

The different types of reasons cited above for linking human rights and international investment rules demonstrate that the rules of international investment have a direct impact on the protection and promotion of human rights. Nor is there any doubt that an instrument on international investment cannot and should not be a general human rights instrument. Therefore it is necessary to define how much and how exactly an MIT should be linked to human rights in order to satisfy our central objective of maximizing the contributions of international investment while minimizing the problems. To summarize the arguments above: a number of reasons show that human rights should be linked to a multilateral investment treaty, but that the linkages must be limited and specific to those fields where human rights and investment requirements intersect, namely, social rights, which require financial support for their realization, labour rights that delineate the relative positions of workers and investors, and those core human rights, whose abuse, even by non-state entities such as private investors, constitute a violation of international law.

From a conceptual point of view, any international economic treaty is simply another attempt to improve the lives of the citizens of the States Party to that treaty, and as such is totally within the context of the existing international regime of defining and protecting human rights. However, where the means advocated for achieving this economic improvement could clash with guidelines on the protection of human rights, economic treaties have tended to support solely the economic requirements. But it is clear that a more sophisticated understanding of economics and the social requirements of supporting particular economic systems, especially the free market liberal model, indicates that social considerations for human rights cannot be ignored or even relegated to a very low priority. These instrumental debates increasingly show that strong social and labour rights support economic liberalization.

Additionally, in those infrequent instances when private investors are directly or indirectly engaged in egregious violations of human rights, there is no question that investment rules must serve to stop these transgressions on economic, political, legal and ethical grounds. Although the exact impact of international economic regimes on human rights has yet to be investigated, what is indubitable is that any current international economic treaty must take into account its impact on human rights obligations. Naturally, the exact scope of this analysis excites political passions, and the difficult task facing any drafter of an MIT is to create a text acceptable to a sufficiently large constituency so as to assure the text's passage and entry into force as a treaty. The increasingly political tone surrounding international economic bodies such as the WTO, the World Bank, the OECD and NAFTA indicates that economists can no longer expect to speak only to other economists, but rather must expand their vocabulary and their interests to include other segments of society. In other words, an investment treaty catering solely to business interests is no longer tenable, and any future MIT must assume that it will lose some support from some investors in exchange for support from groups which view the MIT as protecting their interests – groups concerned about the protection and propagation of human rights, for instance.

Finally, the demand for increasing sophistication on the part of those negotiating an MIT inevitably pressures the institutional and bureaucratic organizations linked with such a treaty to assume a more complicated view of the world, one in which economic interests are important but by no means paramount. Balancing (much less satisfying) all these demands in the context of one treaty is certainly a difficult task. But the alternative to success is more failures like the MAI.

# 7 | State-to-State and Investor-to-State Dispute Settlement in the OECD Draft Multilateral Investment Agreement

## P. Malanczuk[*]

### 1  INTRODUCTION

The negotiations within the framework of the OECD on a multilateral agreement on investment (MAI)[1] were unsuccessfully terminated on 3 December 1998, after four years of preparatory work and three years of negotiations.[2] However, the MAI was only one of a number of more recent initiatives in the 1990s to negotiate international principles and rules governing foreign investment at the bilateral, regional, and interregional levels, reflecting the importance of foreign direct investment in the globalizing world economy. The failure of the MAI may be attributed to a variety of combined political and other factors.[3] First, there was strong opposition from NGOs and other sectors of 'civil society' to the objectives of the draft agreement, some of its substantive provisions, and the non-transparent process of negotiations. Second, the business com-

---

* Peter Malanczuk is Professor of International Law, Law Faculty, Erasmus University Rotterdam; Director of the GLODIS-Institute of Globalization, International Economic Law and Dispute Settlement; Honorary Guest–Professor of Peking University; Chairman of the International Law Association (ILA) Study Group on State Responsibility; Arbitrator, China International Economic and Trade Arbitration Commission (CIETAC); Counsel, Lalive & Partners, Geneva. This article has appeared in 3 *Journal of International Economic Law* (2000), pp. 417-439; it is reproduced with the permission of Oxford University Press.
1  Draft text available at <www.oecd.org/daf/cmis/mai/negtext.htm>.
2  See, e.g., M. Geist, 'Toward a General Agreement on the Regulation of Foreign Direct Investment', 26 *Law and Policy in International Business* (1995), p. 673; W. Witherell, 'The OECD Multilateral Agreement on Investment', 4 *Transnational Corporations* (1995), pp. 1-14; T. Brewer and S. Young, 'The Multilateral Agenda for Foreign Direct Investment, Problems, Principles and Priorities for Negotiations at the OECD and WTO', 18 *World Competition* (1995), pp. 67-83; F. Engering, 'The Multilateral Investment Agreement', 5 *Transnational Corporations* (1996), p. 147; B. Ramaiah, 'Towards a Multilateral Framework on Investment?', 6 *Transnational Corporations* (1997), pp. 117-121; J. Messing, 'Towards a Multilateral Agreement on Investment', 5 *Transnational Corporations* (1996), pp. 123-135; B. Dhar and S. Chaturvedi, 'Multilateral Agreement on Investment – An Analysis', 33 *Economic and Political Weekly* (1998), pp. 837-849; W. Crane, 'Corporations Swallowing Nations: The OECD and the Multilateral Agreement on Investment', 9 *Colorado Journal of International Law and Policy* (1998), pp. 424-261; S. Canner, 'The MAI', 31 *Cornell International Law Journal* (1998), pp. 657-681; S. Kobrin, 'The MAI and the Clash of Globalizations', 112 *Foreign Policy* (1998), pp. 107-109; W. Dymond, 'The MAI: A Sad and Melancholy Tale', in F. Hampson, M. Hart, and M. Rudner (eds), *Canada Among Nations* (1999), pp. 52-54.
3  See UNCTAD, *Lessons from the MAI* (1999), Series on Issues in International Investment Agreements, UNCTAD/ITE/IIT/MISC.22.

munity lost interest in the MAI once it became clear that the degree of liberalization would not be significant and taxation would be excluded from the scope of the rules. Third, changes in government in a number of OECD countries resulted in a reconsideration of political priorities, with investment protection low on the list, at least in the area of the OECD. In the end, the announcement by France (concerned about cultural exception clauses) that it would no longer take part in the negotiations on the MAI, terminated the project.[4] France cited as its reason that the MAI would place private interests above state sovereignty and because fresh negotiations in a different forum (including the developing countries) were required.

Although proposals have been made that the issue should be taken up again in the wider forum of the World Trade Organization (WTO),[5] considering the resistance of developing countries, it is a widely held view that the MAI is dead, at least in its current draft form.[6] Be that as it may, certain useful lessons may still be drawn from the draft MAI, especially with regard to the dispute settlement provisions, as they seem to reflect modern trends in national investment codes and international investment instruments. It is upon this issue that this article concentrates.

It should be noted that the draft MAI was built upon the model of the growing network of bilateral investment treaties (BITs). Conclusions began in the 1960s and became more numerous in the 1990s, reaching a total of more than 1,500 at the beginning of 1997.[7] In addition, there are now a number of multilateral instruments that address investment issues. These include (as binding treaties): the 1981 Investment Agreement of the Organization of the Islamic Conference,[8] the 1987 ASEAN Agreement for the Promotion and Protection of Investments,[9] the investment provisions in Chapter 11 of the NAFTA Agree-

---

[4] Prime Minister of France, 'Réponse à une question d'actualité à l'Assemblée nationale sur l'Accord multilatéral sur l'investissement (AMI), Discours et interventions', 14 October 1998, <www.premier-ministre.gouc.fr/PM/D141098.htm>. For an explanation of the French position see B. Stern, 'Comments – International Economic Relations and the MAI Dispute Settlement System, The 7th Geneva Global Arbitration Forum', 16 *Journal of International Arbitration* (1999), pp 118-128.

[5] See French Government, *Rapport sur l'Accord multilatéral sur l'investissement (AMI), Rapport Intérimaire* (1998); European Commission, *Discussion Paper: Trade and Investment* (1998), Note for the attention of the 113 Committee, European Commission DG-I, M.D.642/98, 15 December 1998. For a good overview on the state of affairs of the discussion in the WTO, see *Report of the Working Group on the Relationship Between Trade and Investment to the General Council*, 8 December 1998, WT/WGI/2.

[6] See, e.g., S. Picciotto, *Lessons of the MAI: Towards a New Regulatory Framework for International Investment*, Commentary, <http://elj.warwick.ac.uk/global/issue/19991/lessonsmai>; S. Picciotto and R. Mayne, *Regulating International Business. Beyond Liberalization* (1999).

[7] See UNCTAD, *Bilateral Investment Treaties in the Mid-1990s* (1998); R. Dolzer and M. Stevens, *Bilateral Investment Treaties* (1995).

[8] Text in 'ICSID Review', 1 *Foreign Investment Law Journal* (1986), p. 407.

[9] 27 *ILM* (1988), p. 612.

ment,[10] the Colonia and Buenos Aires Investment Protocols of MERCOSUR,[11] the Cartagena Free Trade Agreement,[12] the 1994 Energy Charter Treaty,[13] and the WTO Agreements on Trade Related Investment Measures (TRIMS), the General Agreement on Trade in Services (GATS) and the Agreement on Trade Related Aspects of Intellectual Property Rights (TRIPS).[14] Furthermore, there are two non-binding multilateral instruments: the World Bank Guidelines on the Treatment of Foreign Investment[15] and the 1994 APEC Non-Binding Investment Principles.[16] Moreover, on the national level, since the mid-1980s some 65 states (mostly developing and formerly socialist countries) have adopted investment legislation to promote and protect foreign investment.[17]

This legal development reflects the increasing importance attached to private foreign investment for economic progress in the host countries.[18] Generally speaking, it has provided for stronger protective standards in the treatment of foreign investment, with a rather broad scope covering a variety of forms of investment and types of investors. Guarantees offered to foreign investors typically include areas such as: admission or entry, general standards of treatment, the transfer of currency, expropriation, and the settlement of disputes with the host state. Most BITs and multilateral instruments grant admitted investments national treatment, as well as most-favoured-nation (MFN) treatment,[19] provide for broad guarantees of fair and equitable treatment and

---

10  32 *ILM* (1993), p. 289. See D Price, 'An Overview of the NAFTA Investment Chapter: Substantive Rules and Investor–State Dispute Settlement', 27 *The International Lawyer* (1993), p. 727.
11  The text of the MERCOSUR Treaty is given in 30 *ILM* (1991), p. 1041. The Colonia Protocol was concluded on 17 January 1994, MERCOSUR/CMC/Doc No 11/93, the Buenos Aires Protocol on 5 August 1994, reprinted in *Sao Paolo Gazeta Mercantil*. While the first Protocol deals with investments made by nationals of the MERCOSUR Parties, the second one covers investments made by nationals of non-Member States.
12  Concluded on 13 June 1994 among Colombia, Mexico, and Venezuela.
13  Text in 'ICSID Review', 10 *Foreign Investment Law Journal* (1995), p. 258. See T. Wälde (ed), *The Energy Charter Treaty: An East–West Gateway for Investment and Trade* (1996). On dispute settlement under this treaty see T. Wälde, 'Investment Arbitration Under the Energy Charter Treaty – From Dispute Settlement to Treaty Implementation', 12 *Arbitration International* (1996), pp. 429-466; A. Tucker, 'The Energy Charter Treaty and "Compulsory" International State/Investor Arbitration', 11 *Leiden Journal of International Law* (1998), pp. 513-526.
14  Annexes 1A, 1B, and 1C to the Agreement Establishing the World Trade Organization, 15 April 1994.
15  Text in 'ICSID Review', 7 *Foreign Investment Law Journal* (1992), p. 295. See I. Shihata, *Legal Treatment of Foreign Investment: The World Bank Guidelines* (1993).
16  Text in C. Green and T. Brewer (eds), *Investment Issues in Asia and the Pacific Rim* (1995). See also M. Sornarajah, 'Protection of Foreign Investment in the Asia-Pacific Economic Cooperation Region', 29 *Journal of World Trade* (1995), pp. 123-128.
17  See ICSID, *Investment Laws of the World* (looseleaf 1973–).
18  For a good analysis of the development see G. Sacerdoti, 'Bilateral Treaties and Multilateral Instruments on Investment Protection', 269 *Recueil de Cours* (1997), pp. 251-460.
19  MFN treatment means treatment at least as favourable granted by the host state to investments from any third state.

full protection and security for investments, ensure the freedom to transfer abroad capital, profits, and other funds related to investment, and prohibit the expropriation of investment, unless it is in the public interest and met with prompt, adequate, and effective compensation. With regard to dispute settlement, the general trend is that, among the various methods available (ranging from direct negotiations between the parties, recourse to local courts and tribunals, to conciliation and arbitration with the assistance of third parties), binding international arbitration has become the preferred practice in international investment.[20] This is also the most important method in other fields of international dispute resolution,[21] including so-called development agreements,[22] or international commercial disputes. The experience of the Iran-United States Claims Tribunal should be particularly mentioned in this respect.[23]

The following analysis is limited to the type of remedies and the procedural aspects of dispute settlement envisaged under the draft MAI. It will not deal with the other main topics that remained at the end of the MAI negotiations,[24] such as the definition of investment, exceptions to national and most-favoured-nation treatment, intellectual property rights,[25] cultural exceptions, performance requirements, labour and environmental issues, and regulatory takings.[26] According to the latest version of the Commentary to the draft MAI, in the view of a number of delegations, further work was needed on the dispute settlement part of the MAI.[27] Different options concerning the area of multilateral consultations and the scope of dispute settlement are specifically mentioned. The draft text makes a basic distinction between state-to-state procedures and investor-to-state procedures. It is upon these two basic types of

---

20 See A. Parra, 'Provisions on the Settlement of Investment Disputes in Modern Investment Laws, Bilateral Investment Treaties and Multilateral Instruments on Investment', 12 *Foreign Investment Law Journal* (1997), pp. 287-364; T. Brewer, 'International Investment Dispute Settlement Procedures: The Evolving Regime for Foreign Direct Investment', 26 *Law and Policy in International Business* (1995), pp. 633-669.
21 See P. Malanczuk, *Akehurst's Modern Introduction to International Law* (1997), 7th edn., pp. 273 et seq., with references; P. Malanczuk, 'Streitbeilegung, einvernehmliche', in I. Seidl-Hohenveldern (ed), *Lexikon des Rechts – Völkerrecht* (1998) 4/1040, 1–5.
22 See, e.g., P. Bernardini, 'The Renegotiation of the Investment Contract', 13 *Foreign Investment Journal* (1998), pp. 411-425.
23 See P. Malanczuk, 'The Iran–United States Claims Tribunal in The Hague – Some Reflections on a Unique Institution of International Dispute Settlement Moving towards the End of Its Work' in V. Götz, P. Selmer, and R. Wolfrum (eds), *Liber amicorum Günther Jaenicke – Zum 85. Geburtstag* (1998), pp. 221–38.
24 For a discussion see UNCTAD, *supra* note 3, pp. 11 et seq.
25 See D. Gervais and V. Nicholas-Gervais, 'Intellectual Property in the MAI: Lessons to be Learned', 2 *The Journal of World Intellectual Property* (1999), pp. 257-274.
26 See E. Graham, 'Regulatory Takings, Supernational Treatment and the Multilateral Agreement on Investment: Issues Raised by Nongovernmental Organizations', 31 *Cornell International Law Journal* (1998), pp. 599-614.
27 Commentary to the MAI Negotiating Text (as of 24 April 1998) ('MAI Commentary'), p. 36.

procedures that the present analysis concentrates. Because of space limitations, the MAI dispute settlement considerations in special areas, such as intellectual property rights,[28] temporary safeguard measures and the relationship to the IMF,[29] the controversial issues of including financial services[30] and labour and environment standards,[31] or a proposal for a legal advisory body of the MAI Parties Group on the interpretation and application of the agreement,[32] are not discussed.

## 2   STATE-TO-STATE PROCEDURES

### 2.1   General provisions

The draft MAI sets out some General Provisions on the rules and procedures applying to the avoidance of conflicts and the resolution of disputes between Parties concerning the interpretation or application of the Agreement.[33] However, disputing parties may also agree to apply other rules or procedures. Certain obligations regarding notification of the Parties Group and the right of Parties to present views remain mandatory.[34] Any confidential or proprietary information revealed in the course of proceedings is protected, as long as the Party providing the information designates it as such.[35] Another provision mentions that text was being developed for the possible inclusion of the EC or regional economic international organizations as Contracting Parties.[36]

The MAI methods of dispute settlement include the usual non-binding methods, such as consultation, conciliation, and mediation, and legally binding arbitration.

### 2.2   Consultation, conciliation, and mediation

One or more Contracting Parties may request that any other Party enter into consultations regarding any dispute between them about the interpretation

---

28  See MAI Negotiating Text as of 24 April 1998 ('MAI Text'), p. 50. See for TRIPS dispute settlement, M. Geuze and H. Wager, 'WTO Dispute Settlement Practice Relating to the TRIPS', 2 *Journal of International Economic Law* (1999), pp. 347-384.
29  MAI Text, p. 80.
30  See MAI Text, Ch. VII, pp. 81 et seq. and p. 84, note 6.
31  MAI Commentary, pp. 25 et seq.
32  MAI Text, Annex 1: Country-specific Proposals for Draft Texts, p. 137.
33  Art. A.1
34  Reference is made to Art. B, paras 1.a and 4.c, and Art. C, paras 1a, 4, and 6e.
35  Art. A.2.
36  Art. A.3.

or application of the agreement.³⁷ The requested Party has 30 days to enter into consultations. Consultation is a mandatory phase before any arbitration proceedings can be initiated. Arbitration can only start if consultation has been requested and a period of 60 days has elapsed thereafter.³⁸

Provision is further made for multilateral consultations involving the Parties Group.³⁹ If the bilateral consultations fail to resolve the matter within 60 days, the disputing parties may agree to ask the Parties Group to consider the case. The Parties Group can then make recommendations. It has to conclude its deliberations within 60 days after the receipt of the request.⁴⁰

If consultations fail, the Parties may then have recourse to good offices, mediation, or conciliation under such rules and procedures as they may agree.⁴¹ All proceedings involving consultations, mediation, or conciliation are confidential.⁴² Moreover, no party may, in any binding legal proceeding, invoke or rely upon any statement made, or position taken, by another party in the aforementioned proceedings, except for factual representations.⁴³ Finally, there is an obligation to notify the Parties Group of any mutually agreed upon solution reached in consultations, mediation, or conciliation proceedings.⁴⁴

The next step in dispute settlement proceedings is legally binding arbitration.

## 2.3 Arbitration

A dispute about whether a party has violated the agreement may be submitted to an arbitral tribunal for decision, provided the consultation requirements mentioned above have been complied with.⁴⁵ It is clear that this provision not only covers positive acts, but also the failure to act, if the Agreement so requires.⁴⁶ In principle, legislative acts of a party may also be challenged in arbitration proceedings. It is left to the tribunal to decide, however, under which conditions a dispute over a legislative act is ripe for arbitration, if its provisions considered to be in breach of the MAI have not yet been applied to a concrete case.⁴⁷

---

37  Art. B.1.a.
38  Art. B.1.b.
39  Art. B.2.
40  Art. B.2.c.
41  Art. B.3.
42  Art. B.4.a.
43  Art. B.4.b.
44  Art. B.4.c.
45  Art. C.1.a.
46  MAI Commentary, p. 36.
47  Ibidem.

Another question that the delegations addressed concerns the 'local remedies rule'. Under the customary law of diplomatic protection, a state can only bring an international claim against another state for the injury of its nation if the nation has exhausted the local remedies in the courts and tribunals of the defendant state.[48] In the ELSI Case,[49] an expropriation case between the United States and Italy, the International Court of Justice clarified that this rule requires only the exhaustion of 'all reasonable' local remedies.[50] There was full agreement that the exhaustion of local remedies should not be required before MAI dispute settlement could be invoked.[51] The reason why this was not clarified in the draft MAI and left to the Commentary is that the Parties wanted to avoid doubts that could be placed on the dispute settlement provisions of other investment agreements having the same intent and being silent on the matter.

Parties may also be in dispute over whether one of them has violated a substantially similar obligation under the MAI and another agreement to which both are Parties. Under the draft MAI, the complaining party has the right to choose under which agreement it wishes to proceed. In that case, however – at least in terms of the MAI – it is deemed to have waived its right to submit the matter for decision under the agreement not chosen.[52]

With regard to the formation of the tribunal, it should be first noted that the parties have to maintain a roster of highly qualified individuals for serving on arbitral tribunals under the MAI.[53] Each Contracting Party can nominate up to four persons for this roster for a period of five years per term. Generally speaking, the arbitrators should be appointed from this roster, except if special expertise is required on the tribunal itself, rather than solely through expert advice in the arbitration.[54]

If a request for arbitration has been made, the parties to the dispute have 30 days time to appoint by agreement three members of the tribunal and designate one of them as Chairman.[55] The members shall be persons proposed by the Secretary General of the International Center for the Settlement of Investment Disputes (ICSID), which belongs to the World Bank Group.

If the parties do not agree on the arbitrators or the chairman within the 30-day period, following the appointing authority model of the UNCITRAL rules, the ICSID Secretary General can be called upon to make the necessary appointments, to the extent feasible, in consultations with the parties.[56]

---

48  See Malanczuk (1997), *supra* note 21, pp. 267 et seq. with references.
49  ELSI (Elettronica Sicula S.p.A.) Case (US v. Italy), *ICJ Rep* (1989), p. 15.
50  See also MAI Commentary, p. 36.
51  *Ibidem.*
52  Art. C.1.c.
53  Art. C.2.f.
54  Art. C.2.c.
55  Art. C.2.a.
56  Art. C.2.b.

Certain consultation rights are also granted to third parties.[57] Any Contracting Party, without being required to show any particular interest, may request to be granted an opportunity to present its views orally or in writing to the tribunal on legal issues in dispute. Such a Party has access to the documents of the proceedings, except for those that have been designated as confidential or proprietary information.

In the proceedings, the advice of scientific or technical experts may be required. The tribunal may appoint experts at the request of one of the parties or on its own initiative, unless the disputing parties disagree. It may ask for a written report of a scientific or technical review board, or expert, 'on any factual issue concerning environmental, health, safety, or other scientific or technical matters' raised by a disputing party, subject, however to such terms and conditions as the parties may agree.[58] The board, or expert, needs to be selected by the tribunal in consultations with the parties and the scientific or technical bodies named by them.[59] The rights of the parties are also secured in the process of the preparation of the expert report.[60]

With regard to the applicable law, the draft MAI states that the tribunal shall base its decisions on the Agreement, "interpreted and applied in accordance with the applicable rules of international law".[61] The latter is considered to be restricted to the rules of international law concerning the interpretation and application of treaties, as laid down for example in the 1969 Vienna Convention.[62] It is important to note that it does not give a tribunal the power to decide upon a dispute based on whether a party has complied with other international legal obligations.[63]

The tribunal is also expressly given the power, at the request of a party, to "recommend" provisional measures, which either party should take "to avoid serious prejudice to the other pending its final award".[64]

The award, at the request of a party, may grant different forms of relief,[65] including:

a) a declaration that an action of a party is in contravention of its obligations under the MAI;
b) a recommendation that a party bring its actions into conformity with its obligations;
c) pecuniary compensation for any loss or damage; and

---

57  Art. C.4.
58  Art. C.5.a.
59  Art. C.5.b.
60  See Art. C.5.c and d.
61  Art. C.6.a.
62  Vienna Convention on the Law of Treaties, text in 8 ILM (1969), p. 679. See Malanczuk (1997), supra note 21, pp. 130 et seq.
63  MAI Commentary, p. 36.
64  Art. C.6.b.
65  Art. C.6.c.

d) any other form of relief to which the party against whom the award is made consents, including restitution in kind.

The process of rendering the award, which has to set out the findings of law and fact with the reasons thereof,[66] also involves the parties.[67] The award has to be drafted in accordance with the requirement of confidentiality mentioned in the General Provisions and is issued in provisional form to the parties on a confidential basis. The draft MAI lays down time limits for the proceedings, stating that the award, as a general rule, must be issued within 180 days after the tribunal was formed. The parties then have the opportunity to submit written comments on the award within 30 days. The tribunal, in considering such submissions, may solicit additional written comments of the parties. The final award shall be issued within fifteen days after closure of the comment period. A copy of the award is transmitted to the Parties Group, which makes it publicly available.[68]

Apart from including provisions on the costs of proceedings,[69] the draft MAI also clarifies that awards shall be "final and binding",[70] subject, however, to possible nullification proceedings.[71] The annulment of an award can be requested by a party to the dispute on the grounds that:

a) the tribunal was not properly constituted;
b) it manifestly exceeded its powers;
c) there was corruption;
d) there has been a serious departure from a fundamental rule of procedure; or
e) the award has failed to state the reasons on which it is based.

## 2.4 Default rules

The draft agreement contains a back-up clause referring to default rules that are to apply to supplement the dispute settlement provisions.[72] These default rules are the Permanent Court of Arbitration's (PCA) 'Optional Rules for Arbitrating Disputes between Two States'.[73] In addition, the Parties Group may adopt supplemental provisions "to ensure the smooth functioning of these rules", in particular to clarify the interrelationship between these rules and the PCA Optional Rules.

---

66 Art. C.6.c.
67 Art. C.6.d.
68 Art. C.6.e.
69 See Art. C.6.g.
70 Art. C.6.f.
71 For the details of the procedure see Art. C.7.b–d.
72 Art. C.8.
73 32 ILM (1993), p. 572.

## 2.5 Non-compliance and countermeasures

The draft MAI dispute settlement provisions also address the consequences of non-compliance of a party with an award. However, the relevant text was circulated separately and contains a number of brackets, indicating the controversial issues.[74] Generally speaking, there was agreement among the Parties that there should be strong procedural safeguards for resort to countermeasures in order to prevent the problems frequently arising from unilateral action.[75] However, the role of the Parties Group in this respect was not settled.

In the case of such non-compliance by a party within a reasonable period of time, it is obliged, at the request of the succeeding party, to enter into consultations with a view toward reaching a mutually acceptable solution.[76] If after 30 days the matter is still unsettled, the precise rights of the successful party are not clear from the text. One bracketed alternative is that it may take countermeasures against the non-complying party ("take measures in response").[77] The other alternative mentions the lesser right to "suspend the application to the other Contracting Party of obligations under this agreement". At any rate, the non-complying party and the Parties Group must be notified of such intention.

Whether 'responsive measures' or 'suspension' are allowed, the principle of proportionality must be respected.[78] The language used states that the effect "must be proportionate to the effect of the other Party's non-compliance". But there is also a proposal to use language based upon the WTO agreements, such as: "The level of the suspension of benefits ... shall be equivalent to the level of the nullification or impairment of benefits, which the aggrieved Party reasonably expected to accrue to it, resulting from the non-compliance."[79]

It is clear from the Commentary that the expropriation of investments and denial of treatment in accordance with international law, presumably referring to the so-called customary international law minimum standard of the treatment of foreign nationals,[80] are not considered permissible countermeasures.[81] This reflects the general willingness in the Negotiating Group to discourage countermeasures taken against established investment through establishing some form of hierarchy of responses. There were different opinions,

---

74 Art. C.9. For a different text proposed by one delegation see MAI Text, Annex 1: Country-specific Proposals for Draft Texts, p. 136.
75 MAI Commentary, p. 37.
76 Art. C.9.a.
77 On countermeasures in general see P. Malanczuk, 'Countermeasures and Self-Defence as Circumstances Precluding Wrongfulness in the International Law Commission's Draft Articles on State Responsibility', in M. Spinedi and B. Simma (eds), *United Nations Codification of State Responsibility* (1987), pp. 197-286.
78 Art. C.9.b.
79 See note 3 to Art. C.9.
80 See Malanczuk (1997), *supra* note 21, pp. 260 et seq.
81 MAI Commentary, p. 37.

however, on the proper approach. A broad approach would generally permit any responsive measure available under customary international law, including measures in the field of trade. A narrow approach would limit the responses to the suspension of benefits under the MAI itself.

This dispute raises some questions concerning the relationship between the draft MAI, the WTO dispute settlement procedures, and the international law of state responsibility, as presently being codified by the International Law Commission.[82] The GATT, the GATS, and other WTO agreements modify the customary rules of state responsibility regarding the permissible countermeasures in case of violation of WTO obligations by a Party.

This could have led to problems in relations between MAI Parties, which at the same time belong to the (currently) 136 Members of the WTO. If, in terms of the MAI, a Party would be allowed to invoke alleged rights of retaliation under the customary law of state responsibility – the usual law of reprisals and retortion[83] – this may be considered as not being in conformity with WTO obligations in the same area. The WTO dispute settlement system, in contrast to the previous GATT mechanisms, is more judicialized, based on legally binding dispute settlement, and permits countermeasures only on the basis of authorization and under certain specified conditions in which countermeasures may be adopted.[84] A WTO panel or the Appellate Dispute Settlement Body, which is developing case law in quite a large number of disputes submitted to it since 1995, could not have relied on the classical rules of state responsibility in the same case had it been brought under the MAI, but must have limited itself to the obligations following from the WTO agreements. In that case the adoption of certain measures that are considered legal under the MAI might be assessed as illegal within the WTO framework between the same Parties.

This problem reflects the legal uncertainties that exist with regard to the right to react to the violation of one treaty by adopting measures that are not in conformity with obligations under a different and unrelated treaty.[85] One possible way of avoiding this conflict would have been to expressly authorize MAI Parties to suspend benefits under other international agreements, and to preclude the challenge of such retaliation under the WTO Dispute Settlement Understanding. The difficulty remains, however, that third parties not bound by the MAI may nevertheless be affected, or at least allege to be affected, by the countermeasure at issue and resort to WTO or other dispute settlement mechanisms. On the other hand, it must be noted that the coverage of invest-

---

82 See Malanczuk (1997), *supra* note 21, pp. 254 et seq. with references.
83 See *idem*, pp. 271 et seq.
84 See E.-U. Petersmann, 'The GATT/WTO Dispute Settlement System', 1 *Journal of International Economic Law* (1998), pp. 175-327, Special Issue on the WTO dispute settlement system (contributions by various authors); J. Jackson, 'Dispute Settlement and the WTO. Emerging Problems', 1 *Journal of International Economic Law* (1998), pp. 329-351.
85 See MAI Commentary, p. 37, referring to the view of some delegations.

ment issues by WTO rules at present is rather mixed, "with significant coverage in some services sectors, but minimal coverage in manufacturing, and no direct, explicit coverage in agriculture, textiles, or mining".[86]

After the 30-day consultation period, any party to the award may request the Parties Group to consider the matter.[87] A suggestion in brackets bars the taking of responsive measures until 20 days after the Parties Group received the request. The Parties Group has several options. First, it may make recommendations. Second, it may suspend the non-complying party's right to participate in the decisions of the Parties Group. Third, in a bracketed alternative, it may decide that some or all of the responsive measures intended to be taken by a party shall not be taken, obliging that party to comply with the decision. In the first two cases, the decisions are to be adopted by consensus, excluding the disputing parties; in the third case the vote of the party, which had intended to take responsive measures, is excluded.

A dispute on alleged failure of a party to comply with an award or on the legality of any countermeasures can be submitted again to arbitration at the request of a disputing party.[88] The case is heard by the original tribunal, which rendered the award, or if it is unavailable, by a single member or three-member tribunal appointed by the ICSID Secretary General. The procedure generally follows the rules applicable to the original proceedings. However, the tribunal is free to make modifications as it deems appropriate and the final award must be issued no later than 60 days after the date of the request. A bracketed alternative further provides that "[n]o responsive measures may be taken from the time of submission of a dispute unless authorised by the tribunal as an interim measure or found lawful".

## 3 INVESTOR-TO-STATE PROCEDURES

### 3.1 Scope and standing

The rules governing investor-to-state procedures, disputes between a private investor of a Contracting Party and another Contracting Party, are somewhat more detailed than the state-to-state dispute settlement procedures. Investor-to-state disputes refer to alleged breaches of the MAI by a Contracting Party causing "loss or damage to the investor or its investment".[89] This includes

---

86 T. Brewer and S. Young, 'Investment Issues at the WTO – The Architecture of Rules and the Settlement of Disputes', 1 *Journal of International Economic Law* (1998), p. 458.
87 Art. C.9.c.
88 Art. C.9.d.
89 Art. D.1.a.

effects on the investor and applies to all the investor's rights, including those relating to establishment.[90]

It is clear that there must be a causal link between an alleged violation of the MAI and the loss or damage. However, standing for the investor to bring a claim against the host state – as clarified in the Commentary[91] – does not require that the damage has been actually incurred; it must only be "imminent". It is also important to note that there is a consensus that an investor can bring an establishment dispute alleging that an opportunity was lost to profit from a planned investment. This means that the term 'loss' is meant to cover instances where the investment has not yet been made. This raises a number of questions concerning the proper distribution of risks that are naturally connected with any investment.[92] It is understood, however, that such standing of the investor to claim compensation for lost opportunities is without prejudice to the question of whether lost profits may actually be recoverable as damages in the proceedings on the merits of the case.[93] They may be denied as being too remote or too speculative.

In addition, investors may also submit to arbitration "any investment dispute concerning any obligation which the Contracting Party has entered into with regard to a specific investment of the investor" through two modalities. The first modality mentions an "investment authorisation granted by its competent authorities specifically to the investor or investment". The second modality refers to "a written agreement granting rights with respect to" – and now in brackets – categories of certain subject matters, which are not specified. An additional requirement for both modalities is that the investor must have relied on them "in establishing, acquiring, or significantly expanding an investment".[94] There was no consensus on the types of agreements to be covered and there was also dispute on whether reservations should be permitted.[95]

### 3.2 Methods of dispute resolution

Regarding the dispute settlement methods, the draft MAI stipulates that investor-to-state disputes, if possible, should be settled by negotiation or

---

90 MAI Commentary, p. 38.
91 *Ibidem.*
92 On the issue of whether lost profits are recoverable in the case of the expropriation of a 'going concern' see Malanczuk (1997), *supra* note 21, p. 238.
93 MAI Commentary, p. 38.
94 Art. D.1.b.
95 MAI Commentary, p. 38. It is also noted that "[p]rovided that the law specified under Article D.14.b were applicable under both options, and the respect clause were excepted from state–state dispute settlement, the full respect clause and the procedural solution would appear to be similar in their legal effect."

consultation.[96] Apart from these non-binding bilateral means, non-binding third party methods, such as mediation or conciliation, are not explicitly listed. Rather, if bilateral efforts fail, the investor is given the option to submit the dispute for resolution to any competent courts or administrative tribunals of the Contracting Party to the dispute, either under any dispute settlement procedure agreed upon prior to the dispute arising, or by arbitration under the ICSID Convention, the ICSID Additional Facility, the UNCITRAL Rules, or the ICC Rules.[97]

There are two comments to be made with respect to these choices available to the investor. First, states retain the possibility of not making the MAI directly enforceable in their national legal system.[98] This means that the recourse to 'any competent courts' of the state at issue would not be a feasible option in such cases. Second, the various options of international arbitration offered to the investor may also be limited by reservations stating that UNCITRAL and ICC proceedings may only be chosen if the ICSID and ICSID Additional Facility options are not available.

### 3.3 International arbitration

There are a number of requirements for instituting international arbitration in investor-to-state disputes under the draft MAI. In principle, by accepting the MAI, the Contracting Parties also give their unconditional consent to the submission of such a dispute to international arbitration.[99] A Contracting Party can limit its consent only to the effect that it "applies on the condition that the investor and the investment waive in writing the right to initiate any other dispute settlement procedure with respect to the same dispute and withdraw from any such progress before its conclusion".[100] Such limitation must be notified to the Depository upon deposit of the instrument of ratification or accession and it may subsequently be reduced in scope by notifying the Depository.

The ICSID Convention,[101] the ICSID Additional Facility Rules, the UNCITRAL Arbitration Rules,[102] the ICC Rules of Arbitration, and the 1958 New York Convention on the Recognition and Enforcement of Foreign Arbitral Awards[103] all require the written consent and the written agreement of the parties to the dispute to its submission for settlement for the purposes of the

---

96 Art. D.2.
97 Art. D.2.
98 MAI Commentary, p. 38.
99 Art. D.3.a.
100 Art. D.3.b.
101 Ch. II.
102 Art. 1.
103 Art. II.

instruments. The draft MAI provides that the unconditional consent of a Contracting Party to international arbitration by accepting the Agreement, together with either the written submission of the dispute to international arbitration pursuant to the Agreement, or the investor's advance written consent to such submission, fulfils the requirements of other instruments.[104]

Finally, a bracket provides for text on the possible inclusion of the EC or regional economic international organizations as Contracting Parties.[105] With regard to the EC, it is well known, from the context of the WTO also, that considerable problems arise on the international level from the mixed or unclear division of competences between the Community and the Member States.[106] The purpose of the envisaged article was to ensure that both the Community and the respective Member State would be defendant in the proceedings to cover the responsibility fully, without placing the burden upon the investor.[107] It was also considered whether to extend this to Parties that are regional economic international organizations with legal capacity and competence in matters covered by the Agreement.

The draft MAI includes provisions on the composition of the tribunal. It normally includes three arbitrators, unless the parties decide otherwise. As is usual in international practice, each party appoints one arbitrator and the chairman is appointed by agreement of the parties.[108] The draft also provides for the intervention of an appointing authority, at the request of one of the parties, if the tribunal has not been constituted within 90 days following the submission of the claim.[109] The appointing authority varies according to the type of arbitration selected. In the case of ICSID procedures or arbitration under the UNCITRAL Rules, the ICSID Secretary General is designated as the appointing authority; in case of ICC arbitration, it is the ICC International Court of Arbitration.[110]

As regards the selection of individual arbitrators,[111] the provisions largely follow the model envisaged by the Contracting Parties for state-to-state disputes, as has been described above. A problem that requires separate treatment arises from the right of parties in ICSID proceedings to appoint arbitrators of their own nationality on three member tribunals.[112] The MAI settles this issue

---

104 Art. D.5.
105 Art. D.6.
106 See, e.g., R. Frid, *The Relations Between the EC and International Organizations* (1995); M. Hilf, 'The ECJ's Opinion 1/94 on the WTO – No Surprise, but Wise?', 6 *European Journal of International Law* (1995), pp. 245-259; A. Appella, 'Constitutional Aspects of Opinion 1/94 of the ECJ Concerning the WTO Agreement', 45 *International and Comparative Law Quarterly* (1996), pp. 440-462.
107 MAI Commentary, p. 39.
108 Art. D.7.a.
109 Art. D.7.b.
110 Art. D.7.b.
111 See Art. D.7. c and d.
112 Art. 39 ICSID Convention and Art. 7 Schedule C, ICSID Additional Facility Rules.

by two provisions. First, it lays down that the disputing Contracting Party agrees to the appointment of each individual member of a tribunal established under ICSID Convention or ICSID Additional Facility proceedings. Second, it further provides that an investor may initiate or continue such proceedings only on the condition that agreement in writing is submitted to the appointment of each individual member of the tribunal.[113] These rules are without prejudice to each party's right independently to select an individual for appointment as arbitrator or to object to an arbitrator on grounds other than nationality.

Another special problem concerns the so-called 'standing of the investment'. It relates to the situation in which a company was constituted or organized under the national law of one Contracting Party, but later, from the time of the events leading to the dispute until its submission to international arbitration, became the investment of another Contracting Party. The Agreement would have resolved this problem by stipulating that, for purposes of disputes concerning that investment, it is to be considered "an investor of another Contracting Party" under the MAI and "a national of another Contracting Party" in the sense of the provisions of the ICSID Convention[114] dealing with a dispute which is not submitted by the investor owning or controlling the investment.[115] This provision reflects clauses that can be found in bilateral investment agreements.[116] States, however, are allowed to make specific reservations to this clause. They may also annex a list of countries to which it would not apply.

The draft MAI also contains detailed provisions on the consolidation of multiple proceedings, which shall not be further addressed here.[117] Such proceedings concern two or more disputes that have been submitted to arbitration that have a question of law or fact in common.

Provision is further made for preliminary objections.[118] Preliminary objections can be raised against the jurisdiction of the tribunal or to the admissibility of the application, but no later than in the statement of defence. In such cases, the tribunal may suspend the proceedings on the merits and should render its decision, after hearing the parties, within 60 days after the objection was filed.

In proceedings it may occur that a Contracting Party (a state) alleges that the investor has received indemnification or other compensation for all or part of the damages claimed, or that it will be received in accordance with an indemnity, guarantee, or insurance contract. The MAI bars a Contracting Party

---

113 Art. D.7.e.
114 Art. 25(2)(b).
115 Art. D.8.
116 MAI Commentary, p. 39.
117 Art. D.9. See also MAI Commentary, p. 39.
118 Art. D.10.

from asserting such instances as a "defence, counter-claim, right of set-off or for any other reason".[119] A note to the relevant provision, however, suggests that it does not prevent the Contracting Party from invoking the fact that it has already paid indemnification or other compensation to the subrogee or assignee of the investor's rights in the matter.[120]

In investor-to-state disputes, certain third party rights are also granted to other Contracting Parties.[121] The tribunal has to notify the Parties Group that it has been established and, consulting the disputing parties, it may grant any Contracting Party an opportunity to submit written views on the legal issues at dispute. The condition is, however, that the proceedings are thereby not unduly delayed. In this respect, the position of third Contracting Parties is clearly weaker than in the case of state-to-state disputes. The matter is different if the third Contracting Party can show that it has "a legal interest" on issues in dispute. In this case, any Contracting Party so requesting within 30 days after the notification of the formation of the tribunal "shall be given an opportunity to present its views".

The provisions on scientific and technical expertise, which the tribunal may wish to call upon in investor-to-state disputes,[122] are identical to those applicable in state-to-state proceedings.

The rules on the applicable law in investor–state disputes differentiate according to the subject matter.[123] Disputes concerning the alleged breach of an obligation of a state under the MAI causing loss or damage to the investor would have been decided in accordance with the MAI, "interpreted and applied in accordance with the applicable rules of international law". Disputes concerning the alleged violation by a state of obligations arising from an investment authorization or a written agreement granting rights with regard to certain categories of subject matter (still unspecified in the text) on which the investor has relied shall be decided in accordance with "such rules of law as may be agreed by the parties to the dispute". If there is no such agreement, the applicable law is the national law of the Contracting Party (including its rules on the conflict of laws), the law governing the authorization or agreement and "such rules of international law as may be applicable".[124]

This provision is specifically made for interim measures of relief which the tribunal may recommend "to preserve the rights of a disputing Contracting Party or to ensure that the Tribunal's jurisdiction is made fully effective".[125]

---

119 Art. D.11.
120 Note 4.
121 Art. D.12.
122 See Art. D.13.
123 Art. D.14. a. and b.
124 The MAI Commentary, at p. 39, notes "Unlike cases under Article 14 (b) in which domestic law may be applicable as law, domestic law may be considered as a relevant fact under Article 14 (a)."
125 Art. D.15.a.

Presumably, it is the last part of the sentence upon which the investor, who is not explicitly mentioned, may also rely in requesting interim measures. It may also occur that a party to an investor-to-state dispute submitted to arbitration under the MAI seeks interim relief from judicial or administrative tribunals in order to preserve its rights and interests pending resolution of the dispute. If such a request for interim relief does not involve the payment of damages, it is regarded as permissible under the MAI arbitration proceedings.[126]

The forms of relief that a final award of the tribunal may provide in investor-to-state proceedings differ to some extent from those available in state-to-state procedures. They may include:

a) a declaration that the Contracting Party has failed to comply with its obligations under the MAI;
b) pecuniary compensation, including interest from the time the loss or damage was incurred until time of payment;
c) restitution in kind in appropriate cases, provided that the Contracting Party may pay pecuniary compensation in lieu thereof where restitution is not practical; and
d) with the agreement of the parties to the dispute, any other form of relief.[127]

Moreover, it is specifically mentioned that

> [i]n appropriate cases where the loss or damage was incurred by an investment which remains a going concern, the tribunal may direct that the compensation or restitution be made to the investment.[128]

One delegation has proposed adding an interpretative note to this article explaining 'restitution in kind' to mean 'factual restoration of property and property rights'.[129] The award is final and binding among the parties[130] and to be made a publicly available document.[131] The losing party is required to carry it out without delay, "subject to its post-award rights under the arbitral systems utilised".[132]

While there are also provisions on the protection of confidential or proprietary information[133] and on fees and expenses to be paid to a member of an arbitral tribunal,[134] only two other final provisions in investor-to-state disputes should be mentioned. An important provision in practice concerns the

---

126 Art. D.15.b.
127 Art. D.16.a.
128 Art. D.16.b.
129 MAI Text, Annex 1: Country-Specific Proposals for Draft Texts, p. 135.
130 Art. D. 16.c.
131 For details see Art. D.16.d.
132 Art. D.16.c.
133 Art. D.17.
134 Art. D.19.

place of arbitration and the enforceability of awards.[135] The draft MAI makes sure that any investor-to-state arbitration must be held in a state that is Party to the 1958 New York Convention. It further clarifies that investor-to-state claims submitted to arbitration under the Agreement "shall be considered to arise out of a commercial relationship or transaction for purposes of Article 1 of that Convention". This is designed to overcome any objection as to the applicability of the New York Convention based on the argument that the nature of the award is non-commercial. Furthermore, each Contracting Party is obliged to provide for the enforcement of pecuniary obligations imposed by an award rendered pursuant to the draft MAI's investor-to-state proceedings. It should be noted that this provision does not require MAI Parties to become Parties to the New York Convention. It does require them to ensure the national enforcement of awards granting compensation under the MAI.[136] Finally, a back-up clause gives the Parties Group the power to adopt supplemental provisions "to ensure the smooth functioning of these rules, in particular to clarify the interrelationship between these rules" and the rules of the international arbitration proceedings available for investor-to-state disputes under the agreement.[137]

3.4    The relationship between state-to-state procedures and investor-to-state procedures

A special provision deals with the relationship of the right to initiate arbitration proceedings in state-to-state disputes and in investor-to-state proceedings in the same matter.[138] If an investor has submitted, or agreed to submit, to arbitration under the Agreement, a State Party may initiate arbitration proceedings only if the other party has failed to abide by and comply with the award rendered in that dispute or if those proceedings have terminated without resolution by an arbitral tribunal of the investor's claim.

This provision is based upon Article 27 of the ICSID Convention.[139] Its intention is to ensure that the commencement of any form of investor-to-state arbitration under the MAI would restrain parallel state-to-state proceedings to the same extent as the initiation of ICSID arbitration for a Party to the MAI that is also an ICSID Party. The scope of this preclusion is rather limited and concerns the right to bring the very same claim. ICSID Article 27 does not preclude a state-to-state arbitration on treaty interpretation or application

---

135 Art. D.18.
136 MAI Commentary, p. 39.
137 Art. D.20.
138 Art. C.1.b.
139 For a commentary on Art. 27 see C. Schreuer, 'Commentary on the ICSID Convention', 12 *Foreign Investment Law Journal* (1997), pp. 59 et seq.

issues, which are also part of the investor-to-state disputes, as far as this does not amount to an espousal of the claim of the investor.[140] An award in such a state-to-state procedure does not affect an award rendered in the investor-to-state proceedings.

## 4  CONCLUSION

The draft MAI has been subject to a broad variety of general criticisms as to its substance and approach.[141] The fact that, at a relatively late stage in the negotiations, pressure from public opinion also moved the investor-to-state dispute settlement provisions into the forefront of attention, however, came as a surprise. Initially, it was thought that such dispute settlement issues were not difficult to deal with because they had already been addressed in numerous international investment agreements, such as BITs, NAFTA, MERCOSUR, and the Energy Charter Treaty.[142] It is notable that NGOs, in their crusade against the MAI, found it useful to adopt the argument that foreign investors would be given special privileges, as compared to domestic investors, to challenge decisions of the host state. This point was argued only by one state delegation in the negotiations. An additional argument, following the experience with the Ethyl Case under the NAFTA,[143] was that the powers of governments to adopt legislation in the public interest would be curtailed. Other countries were not opposed to investor-to-state arbitration in principle, but were concerned about the extension of the mechanism to the pre-establishment phase.

With regard to the dispute settlement mechanisms, the draft MAI in fact reflects the development of modern BITs and multilateral investment protection instruments, especially as regards direct international arbitration of disputes between host states and foreign investors.[144] The non-applicability of the rule that local remedies of the host state must be first exhausted also conforms

---

140 As noted by the ICSID observer, see MAI Commentary, p. 36.
141 For a defence of the stalled draft MAI and a plea to move the issue to the WTO see E. Graham, 'Trade and Investment at the WTO: Just Do It!', in J. Scott (ed), *Launching New Global Trade Talks. An Action Agenda* (1998), pp. 151 et seq.
142 See UNCTAD, supra *note* 3, pp. 19 and 24.
143 Under the NAFTA investor-to-state procedures, Ethyl, an American corporation, brought a case against Canada in 1997 concerning an environmental and health regulation prohibiting the import and trade between Canadian provinces of a gasoline additive produced by Ethyl. Ethyl argued that Canada had violated its NAFTA obligations relating to expropriation and compensation, performance requirements and national treatment, and claimed damages in the amount of $250 million. In the end the parties settled the case. However, in early 1999 Canada sought to introduce interpretative changes to NAFTA in order to limit the ability of private companies to seek compensation for government regulations that affect their business.
144 Sacerdoti, supra *note* 18, p. 452.

to modern standards, as in the case of the ICSID Convention.[145] Whether such recourse of private parties to international arbitration in investment relations among industrialized OECD countries (as distinct from investment disputes with developing countries) is required and politically desirable in reality, may be a different matter, considering that only 10% of the existing BITs have been concluded among OECD countries. At any rate, the number of arbitrations actually held under dispute settlement clauses of BITs has been limited in practice and only recently was there an increase in cases brought before ICSID.[146]

In order to put the dispute settlement mechanisms in the draft MAI into a proper perspective, however, it does not suffice to merely consider the technical methods of dispute settlement. What also matters is the scope of the draft agreement to which such methods would apply. As such, this issue is beyond the limit of the present analysis. Only some brief remarks should be made in this regard. The scope of the draft MAI is much broader than the existing network of BITs in attempting to create a single multilateral regime for the acquisition of assets and all kinds of rights.[147] First, the provisions guaranteeing national treatment and MFN treatment, as well as the protection against expropriation, were to apply to a rather wide scope of 'investors'[148] and 'investments'.[149] Second, the national treatment provision was designed to grant foreign investors the unusual right of entry in an unqualified manner. Moreover, the draft MAI envisaged obligations of states regarding the transparency of relevant laws, regulations, and decisions, regarding performance requirements prohibiting export, domestic content and purchase, trade balancing and foreign exchange balancing requirements, and regarding labour and immigration laws, such as rights to temporary entry, residence, and work of investors and their employees essential to the company.

It must be admitted that there is a potential deterrent effect of an existing effective legal framework for the settlement of investment disputes. Such deterrence can work in two ways. It may protect foreign investment from unjustified measures of host states and thereby help to increase investment flows. But it also may deter host states from adopting measures in the public interest (i.e., environmental protection) out of fear of large compensation claims, especially if the scope and type of investment protected is defined in a rather broad manner, including, for example, the pre-investment phase.

---

145 See P. Peters, 'Dispute Settlement Arrangements in Investment Treaties', 22 *Netherlands Yearbook of International Law* (1991), pp. 133 et seq.
146 Sacerdoti, *supra* note 18, pp. 453-454.
147 Picciotto, *supra* note 6.
148 Including nationals and permanent residents.
149 Including all forms of contractual rights and money-claims. On the scope of and definitions in international investment agreements see UNCTAD, 2 *Series on Issues in International Investment Agreements* (1999), UNCTAD/ITE/IIT/11.

Finally, as mentioned above, the interaction of the draft MAI with other relevant international instruments[150] also raises a number of problems with regard to dispute settlement. The draft MAI addresses its relationship to other international agreements in Chapter X. The only two agreements mentioned, however, are the Articles of Agreement of the IMF and the OECD Guidelines for Multinational Enterprises. The OECD Guidelines were supposed to be annexed to the Agreement. The text clarifies that "[a]nnexation of the Guidelines shall not bear on the interpretation or application of the agreement, including for the purpose of dispute settlement; nor change their non-binding character."[151] This particular reference to the OECD Guidelines may be indicative of the dominant role in foreign investment of multinational companies,[152] considered as the driving forces of the current process of economic globalization.[153]

It may be concluded that many arguments against the MAI, at least as far as the draft dispute settlement provisions are concerned, were indeed to a large extent based on misunderstandings.[154] The real concern appears to be the impact that investor-to-state arbitration options may have on state sovereignty. One author observed that

> it is not acceptable to give a private body composed of persons specialised in international commercial arbitration, the final say on the evaluation of a State policy, with no recourse or appeal for the State and with a very efficient procedure of enforcement of the award rendered.[155]

Apart from discussing the general ambiguity of the concept of 'state sovereignty' in modern times, one could counter this argument by pointing to the possibility of selecting appropriate arbitrators in such instances and of preparing the defence more professionally.[156] State-to-state dispute procedures alone are not sufficient to protect foreign investment effectively (and thereby increase investment flows) because the investor must then rely on the discretion of the

---

150 See S. Picciotto, 'Linkages in International Investment Regulations: The Antinomies of the Draft MAI', 19 *University of Pennsylvania Journal of International Economic Law* (1998), pp. 731-768.
151 MAI Text, p. 96, Art. 1.4.
152 See T. Brewer and S. Young, *The Multilateral Investment System and Multinational Enterprises* (1998); P. Malanczuk, 'Multinational Enterprises and Treaty-Making – A Contribution to the Discussion on Non-State Actors and the "Subjects" of International Law' in V. Gowlland-Debbas (ed), *Multilateral Treaty-Making: The Current Status of Challenges to and Reforms Needed in the International Legislative Process* (2000), pp. 35-62.
153 See P. Malanczuk, 'Globalization and the Future Role of Sovereign States' in F. Weiss, P. de Waart, and E. Denters (eds), *International Economic Law with a Human Face* (1998), pp. 45-65.
154 Y. Kodama, 'Dispute Settlement under the Draft Multilateral Agreement on Investment', 16 *Journal of International Arbitration* (1999), p. 86.
155 Stern, *supra* note 4, p. 127.
156 See the comments by H. Van Houtte, 16 *Journal of International Arbitration* (1999), pp. 133-134.

home state to exercise diplomatic protection and other political considerations. This aspect would also need to be thoroughly tackled if more comprehensive rules for the protection of foreign investment were discussed within the framework of the WTO whose dispute settlement mechanism is government based and does not allow direct participation of non-state actors.

At any rate, the intricate relationship of the draft MAI to WTO agreements puts one question on the agenda of future international rule-making, not only in the field of investment. The question is how to reconcile conflicting norms of multilateral regimes in view of the proliferation of international dispute settlement mechanisms and the lack of an ultimate arbiter in the international legal system.

# 8 How to Establish a Multilateral Framework for Investment?

*M.W. Sikkel*\*

## 1 INTRODUCTION

International investment is one of the main manifestations and causes of globalization. According to the 1999 UNCTAD World Investment Report,[1] foreign direct investment climbed in 1998 for its eighth consecutive year, to a record level of $649 billion. Total assets of the 500,000 foreign affiliates of some 60,000 transnational corporations are $14.6 trillion. Their estimated sales of $11 trillion top worldwide exports ($7 trillion) and sales of foreign affiliates have grown faster than world GDP and exports of goods and services.

As in the field of trade, governments have tried to support and develop international investment by concluding treaties. In the first place there is a large network of bilateral investment treaties (BITs). Since the early 1960s these were concluded mainly between developed and developing countries, but since the 1980s increasingly also amongst developing countries. In the second place there are regional efforts, such as the OECD Codes of Liberalisation of Capital Movements and of Current Invisible Operations of 1961, the North American Free Trade Agreement (NAFTA) between Canada, Mexico and the United States and the 1994 non-binding investment principles of APEC. The Energy Charter Treaty is an example of a sectoral agreement. At the multilateral level, three of the 1994 Uruguay Round agreements (GATS, TRIMS and TRIPS) address topics directly or indirectly related to investment.[2] However, unlike in the field of trade, there is no comprehensive multilateral agreement covering investment.

This article does not discuss the (un)desirability of multilateral investment rules. It addresses the question of *how* to establish a multilateral framework for investment, if governments would want to do that. The second section examines why a recent effort at the OECD could not be concluded successfully. The third section tries to establish which lessons can be drawn from that

---

\* Marinus Sikkel is Head of the Investment Policy and International Organizations Division of the Netherlands Ministry of Economic Affairs. He was Head of the Netherlands Delegation in the MAI negotiations and chaired Drafting Group 3 of the MAI (draft text available at <www.oecd.org/daf/investment/fdi/mai/negtext.htm>. This article reflects his personal opinions. It benefited from comments received from Jan Huner, Joachim Karl and Bram van Overbeeke.

1   UNCTAD, *World Investment Report 1998: Trends and Determinants* (1999), pp. xvii-xix and 9.
2   For a detailed overview of existing investment treaties see UNCTAD, *International Investment Instruments: A Compendium* (1996).

experience and the last section explains how, based on that experience, any future effort should be undertaken.

## 2 WHY COULD THE MAI NOT BE CONCLUDED?

### 2.1 Something small and technical can turn into something big and political in a very short period of time

#### 2.1.1 Six years of technical work went unnoticed

Appreciation of investment has fluctuated importantly over time. Within the OECD the 1961 Capital Liberalisation Codes can be seen as the expression of the will of the Member States to stimulate capital flows. The Guidelines for Multinational Enterprises on the other hand, while being part of a larger package aiming at the stimulation of international investment,[3] can be seen as an answer by the OECD Member States to the growing concern about negative side effects of such flows. In the late 1980s and the early 1990s investment was widely seen as something positive and desirable. It could, *inter alia*, provide growth, employment, tax income, access to the world market and modern technology. Many countries, including developing countries that had been hesitant earlier on, were actively trying to attract investment. Most changes in investment legislation were directed at liberalization, many BITs were concluded and the Multilateral Investment Guarantee Agency was established.

In this overall climate the OECD countries tried to negotiate a binding National Treatment Instrument. This turned out to be difficult, one of the problems being that the United States felt that the scope of this instrument was too limited to attract sufficient support in the US Congress. It was therefore decided in 1991 to study the advantages and feasibility of a so-called 'wider investment instrument'. In a report to the OECD Council at the Ministerial level of June 1994 the Committee charged with the study concluded that there was a strong case for developing a new multilateral investment agreement, with legally binding obligations and enforcement procedures. The ministers endorsed "a new phase of work aimed at elaborating a multilateral investment agreement, with a report to ministers in 1995".[4] Five working groups were established to develop the framework for the MIA, as it was called at that time. The groups dealt with liberalization obligations under existing OECD instruments, liberalization obligations in new areas, investment protection, dispute

---

3 OECD, *The OECD Declaration and Decisions on International Investment and Multinational Enterprises*, OECD/GD(92)16, see also OECD website at <www.oecd.org/daf/investment/guidelines/index.htm>.
4 OECD, SG/PRESS(94)41.

settlement and the involvement of non-members and institutional matters. Their work resulted in a report to the May 1995 Ministerial Council of the OECD which stated that the time was ripe to negotiate a multilateral agreement on investment (MAI) in the OECD. The Council took note of the report and agreed to the immediate start of negotiations in the OECD aimed at concluding a MAI in 1997.

Between September 1995 and April 1997 the negotiatiors made remarkable progress. In the negotiating group, its three drafting groups and five expert groups, large 'building blocks' of the agreement were drafted. Although 'nothing was agreed until everything was agreed' it was clear that some 90% of the text was ready to be finalized. Decisions had to be taken on the outstanding issues. The main element that was still missing was the list of country-specific reservations with regard to the admission of investments. This was the main reason why the negotiating group had to ask for a one-year extension of its mandate. At that moment almost six years of technical work had passed, which had gone almost completely unnoticed by those not directly involved.

This is not to say that the negotiations were secret. In the months before the 1995 Ministerial Council, articles appeared in *The Wall Street Journal*[5] and the *Financial Times*.[6] The start of the negotiations was mentioned in the communiqué of the 1995 OECD Ministerial Council[7] and in The Netherlands by a press release of the leading Dutch press agency ANP.[8] Later articles in international and Dutch newspapers followed.[9] The Netherlands government informed its parliament in 1995,[10] 1996[11] and 1997.[12] This information provoked hardly any reaction. Most people were not interested at all; this was just another technical exercise somewhere in the international economic rule-making machinery.

---

5   D. Aaron, 'After GATT, U.S. Pushes Direct Investment', *The Wall Street Journal Europe*, 3 February 1995.
6   G. de Jonquières and D. Buchan, 'US to Seek Freer Rules on Foreign Investment, *Financial Times*, 19 May 1995.
7   OECD Press Release, 24 May 1995, SG/PRESS(95)41, p. 3.
8   ANP, 'OESO gaat afspraken maken over buitenlandse investeringen', 23 May 1995.
9   *Inter alia:* P. Lalkens, 'Investeringsverdrag volgende stap in liberalisering', *Financieel Dagblad*, 13 December 1995; J.-P. Robin, 'L'OCDE reporte de quelques mois son accord sur l'investissement', *Le Figaro*, 27 March 1997.
10  Dutch Parliamentary Papers 1995-1996, 24400 XIII, no. 21, Second Chamber.
11  Letter to Parliament by Mrs. A. van Dok-van Weele, 31 May 1996, BEB/DHZ/IINV 96031797.
12  Letter to Parliament by Mrs. A. van Dok-van Weele, 18 June 1997, BEB/DHI/IO 97037214.

## 2.1.2 Highly politicized in little over a year[13]

In early 1996 local groups in Canada and the United States, which had been active in the debate about NAFTA, began to take note of the MAI negotiations. They started to collect information and tried to get involved in the negotiations. Initially they tried to do so through their established contacts in the field of environmental policy-making. Thus, when the Environment Ministers of the OECD consulted NGOs prior to a meeting of the Environmental Policy Committee they were confronted with questions about the potential impact of the MAI on national and international environmental regulation. This eventually led to a discussion on the environment in the negotiating group in October 1996, more than a year after the negotiations had started. Meanwhile, environmental and other NGOs had been building up pressure, both in Paris at the OECD and in other capitals. In Paris, the NGOs that are consulted regularly in the framework of OECD Committees began to ask for similar consultations with the MAI negotiating group. The group decided it did not want to meet with NGOs but it did agree to an informal meeting between the bureau of the negotiating group and some selected NGOs in December 1996.

After that meeting the situation evolved quickly. Although the negotiators tried to respond to the concerns raised, *inter alia* by developing the so-called three-anchor approach,[14] the NGO-campaign against the MAI further intensified throughout 1997. Their intensive use of the Internet proved to be a very effective instrument to involve groups with other interests and in countries all over the world. The NGOs also started to receive attention from a non-specialized public. In April 1997, for example, a Canadian columnist wrote an article stating "While we've been sleeping, a group of bureaucrats from the world's richest countries ... has been meeting in airless rooms in Paris to plot the overthrow of their own democratically elected governments".[15] The fact that the original deadline of May 1997 for concluding the negotiations was not met provided the NGOs with a window of opportunity. They used it so effectively that eventually the negotiating group had to accept that a direct

---

13  For a more detailed description see J. Huner, "Environment regulation and international investment: Lessons from the MAI", speech delivered at the Conference on Trade, Investment and the Environment, October 1998, Royal Institute of International Affairs, Chatham House, London, Earthscan Publications Ltd., 2000, ISBN: 1 85383 628-1.
14  The first anchor would be the Preamble, which should reaffirm Parties' commitment to the ILO, the relevant principles of the Rio Declaration and to other relevant multilateral agreements. The second anchor would be a provision built on NAFTA Art. 1114, stating that environmental and social standards as contained in national laws and regulations should not be lowered in order to attract an investment. The main debate here has been whether or not this should be a binding provision. NAFTA Art. 1114 only says that such lowering of standards is "inappropriate". The third anchor was investor performance: this would have to be ensured by associating the existing OECD Guidelines for Multinational Enterprises.
15  S. Riley, 'Capitalist agents plot world domination', *Ottawa Citizen*, 25 April 1997.

dialogue between NGOs and the negotiators was inevitable. Thus, in little over a year the character of the negotiations had changed from technical and largely unnoticed by the outside world to highly visible and politicized.

The meeting of the negotiating group with NGOs on 27 October 1997 would prove to be a turning point. Some 50 national and international NGOs took part, representing a wide range of interests and a varied intensity of opposition to the MAI. They managed to agree on a joint position[16] and on a single moderator on their behalf. This had been requested by the negotiating group, because it seemed the only way to conduct an efficient and productive meeting.

They also succeeded in convincing many negotiating group members that a few draft provisions, particularly those on expropriation and on performance requirements, could be interpreted in unexpected ways. And, most of all, the meeting was an enormous boost to the morale and self-confidence of the NGOs as witnessed by their press release:

> Our presence today should put the OECD on notice. NGOs and citizens' groups will be scrutinising every move in the negotiation of this agreement. The MAI needs radical reform before it is acceptable... . We will be looking for meaningful responses for the proposals we present today. If not, the OECD should prepare itself for a vigorous challenge to the MAI from many quarters.[17]

### 2.1.3 The rest is history

Although everyone in the negotiating group agreed on the usefulness of the NGO hearing, this did not bring consensus on how to deal with the unresolved issues in the MAI any closer. These remaining issues were difficult ones. In his conclusion of a special high-level meeting in February 1998,[18] the chairman mentioned three areas: labour and environment, liberalization and exceptions, and extraterritoriality. Labour and environment included the issues of not lowering environmental or labour standards to attract foreign investment, the relationship between the exercise of normal regulatory powers of a government and expropriation and investors' responsibilities in this field. Under 'liberalization and exceptions' the discussion focused on the treatment of measures taken for reasons of national security, public order, regional economic integration organizations, culture, subsidies and government procurement. Extraterritoriality comprised issues arising from conflicting requirements, secondary investment boycotts and illegal expropriations. Apart from these three areas, there were also differences regarding the dispute settlement mechanism and other (relatively) less important issues.

---

16  Joint NGO statement on the MAI of 27 October 1997.
17  *Global Investment Treaty Challenged by International Coalition of NGOs*, Press Release by International NGOs, 27 October 1997.
18  OECD Press Release, SG/COM/NEWS/(98)15, 18 February 1998.

Although these issues may have constituted a small part of everything covered by the MAI, it would take strong political will to overcome the remaining difficulties. However, in early 1998 it became ever clearer that the political will to strike a deal on the outstanding issues would not be available. Because of the strong resistance against, and the weak support for the MAI, approval by the US Congress of the MAI was far from secure.

There were also signals from the French that it would be difficult for them to sell the MAI politically. In France it was not so much the environment, labour or the position of developing countries that played the key role. Here the artistic and intellectual community had discovered the MAI and branded it yet another American-inspired instrument of ultra liberalism, posing a threat to artistic and literary freedom and cultural diversity in France. This led to protests by influential politicians, thus giving the MAI opposition a much greater impact than in other countries.

The chairman of the negotiating group made a final attempt in March to bridge the gap by proposing packages of compromise texts, including provisions on labour and the environment. He did not succeed. Although there was praise all around for this credible effort, the Europeans saw too many NAFTA-inspired texts, and the Americans opposed making the not- lowering-of-standards clause binding.

At the OECD Ministerial Meeting in April the ministers decided on "a period of assessment and further consultation between the negotiating parties and with the interested parts of their societies" and that "the next meeting of the Negotiating Group will be held in October 1998."[19] On 14 October 1998 Prime Minister Jospin announced that France had decided to withdraw from the negotiations, leaving the other negotiators no other option but to end the negotiations.

2.2 The MAI was not the real problem

2.2.1 *Concerns about globalization*

The MAI was not the real problem; it was just a good focal point for concerns about globalization in general. With the strong upsurge of investment the appreciation of the phenomenon started to change again. Where most governments were still positive about investment and were actively trying to attract it, NGOs started to discuss the possible negative effects of globalization in general. A general uneasiness was emerging about a process that has many, and often important, consequences for the daily lives of many people and which, at the same time, is perceived by some as being out of control. The

---

19 OECD, *Ministerial Statement on the Multilateral Agreement on Investment (MAI)*, SG/COM/NEWS/(98)51.

market forces are seen as anonymous, calculating, not sensitive to anything but profit and shareholder interests and beyond the control of labour unions and national governments. Whereas governments are still organized on a national, or at best regional, level, business is increasingly organized on a global level and no longer linked to any country in particular. Thus fears about 'the power of the multinationals', which had no longer really been heard since the 1970s, started to reemerge.

An important element of that power is the power to (re)locate the activities of an enterprise. People working for an enterprise, any enterprise, purely national or multinational, fear that one day management will decide to close the plant they are working for and to reopen it elsewhere. This is particularly harsh when the reasons quoted for relocation are that labour is cheaper or more flexible abroad. Of course, this is not usually the reason for investment in other countries, but these things do happen and they do lead to concerns about jobs and, by extension, about globalization. The fact that the loss of jobs in one country may lead to the creation of (sometimes even more) jobs in another country may be of interest to economists, but is scant consolation for those who just lost their jobs. For labour unions this signal given off by their members is strengthened by the fear that their bargaining power will be undermined if employers use the threat of relocation in wage negotiations. Added to that is the concern that labour conditions in countries that do not respect fundamental labour rights may cause a loss of jobs in countries that do respect those rights. Whether this concern is motivated by genuine anxiety about the position of workers in other countries, by protectionist self-interest of the unions or by some mix of these motives, is irrelevant in this context. The result in either case is resistance against globalization.

A similar argument is made regarding environmental degradation. Multinational enterprises could play one government off against the other by promising to invest in the country with the lowest environmental standards or the weakest implementation of such standards. Alternatively, an enterprise might threaten to leave a country that wants to raise the level of environmental protection. Here again research[20] does not demonstrate that multinational enterprises see the level of environmental protection as a decisive element in their investment decisions. But in the eyes of some the track record of Western multinationals in developing countries, for example, in the field of mining or logging, is such that suspicion is warranted.

Environmental concerns are certainly not only related to foreign investments. Economic growth as such, independent from its source, is also seen as the cause of growing pollution. Whether tropical timber is harvested and then sold on the world market by foreign or local enterprises, does not change the objections of the defenders of tropical forests. If products are made in one country in a way considered to be environmentally unfriendly, they cannot

---

20  OECD, *Open Markets Matter: The Benefits of Trade and Investment Liberalisation* (1998), p. 71.

be stopped at the border of another country due of WTO rules. The result is once again distaste for globalization.

To end this very incomplete list of concerns about globalization, the cultural aspect should be mentioned. Many forms of globalization, not only of trade and investment, but also of travel, communication, movies, music, etc., are perceived as leading to a loss of local culture and values and to the predominance of 'Western' or 'American' culture. Needless to say, this is strongly resented by different groups in society, ranging from religious authorities to artists and from students to publishers. That this latter group may also have a commercial interest in keeping out competition, will only add to their enthusiasm in protesting against globalization.

### 2.2.1 Private versus public interest

The MAI was also a good focal point for the debate about the balance between private and public interest. This is an old debate that can perhaps best be illustrated by the case of expropriation. Many countries have laws and regulations concerning expropriation and apply them regularly. It is quite common that a local government that wants to construct a road, and cannot acquire the land necessary for such construction on a voluntary basis, resorts to expropriation. The expropriated landowner would normally have the right to go to court and start a case about the legality of the expropriation and the amount of compensation offered him. The judge(s) would have to decide whether the public interest (the construction of the road) outweighs the private interest (retaining the property) and, if that's the case, what should be the amount of compensation. Over time an important body of jurisprudence about such matters has accumulated in many countries, which would guide the judges in their decisions. Whereas all this may seem to be quite simple and straightforward, it is not. The mere fact that there are still cases concerning expropriation demonstrates that there are still differences of opinion about the conditions under which governments may take property belonging to individual persons or enterprises.

The situation is further complicated by the dynamic developments in this field. Governments see new reasons to take measures that may be conceived by those subjected to such measures as measures that are tantamount to expropriation. A recent example in the Netherlands is the action by the government to limit pig farming. The intensive pig farming methods used are increasingly becoming cause for concern. The government wants pig farmers to take responsibility for the environment, look after animal welfare and help to reduce the risk of diseases as far as possible. An important element of the pig farming policy is the Pig Production Restructuring Act [Wet Herstructurering varkens-

*houderij]* of 1 September 1998.[21] The Act aims at the reduction of the manure surplus and at the reduction of pig herd numbers. To achieve the last objective the Act introduced "pig production rights". This gives the government control over the average number of pigs that can be kept on a farm each year. The introduction of these rights serves to reduce herd numbers, which could amount to a total of 25% reduction in all. Farmers were supposed to give up those rights without compensation. The latter provision triggered strong resistance from the farmers and their organizations. They started a first judicial procedure, in which they claimed that the reduction amounts to expropriation and that compensation should therefore be paid. Although this procedure was not yet finally settled at the time of writing, the court decided in an intermediary decision that the Act is not in conformity with the European Convention on Human Rights (ECHR) and that thus compensation should be paid.[22] In a second procedure the court decided that the implementation of the part of the Act concerning the reduction of pig herds has to be suspended until compensation is paid, or until it is finally decided whether or not the Act is in conformity with the ECHR.[23]

Whatever the final result, the start of this case demonstrates that in a purely national context a legal and political battle about the balance between public and private interest can be fought. No foreign investors, no investment treaty rights, no international arbitration are involved. (And, ironically, the one treaty that is involved is a human rights treaty.) Nevertheless the issue is to a certain extent similar to that of the Ethyl Case. In this case the Canadian government had banned the import and interprovincial trade in MMT, a fuel additive, believed to present a serious health risk. The US based Ethyl Corporation, the only producer of this additive in Canada, claimed that the Canadian measure amounted to an indirect expropriation, mainly because it was impossible to continue producing MMT if it was no longer possible to sell it in other provinces. Using its rights under NAFTA, Ethyl invoked the investor-to-state dispute settlement mechanism to challenge the measures of the Canadian government and claimed a US $ 250 million compensation. A striking difference between the two cases is that nobody had any objection regarding the right of the pig farmers to bring their case to an independent (national) court, while many observers strongly objected to the right of the Ethyl Corporation to bring

---

21 Available at <www.minlnv.nl/herstructurering/>.
22 Rb. 23 December 1998, no. 98/2340.
23 Rb. 23 February 1999, no. KG 99/58. Four more decisions were rendered in this case, ending with the judgment of the Appellate Court of The Hague of 20 January 2000 (no. 99/104) in which it was found that part of the measures in question were necessary and proportionate in relation to their aim and that they did not violate the European Convention on Human Rights, but that another part of the measures was, in fact, disproportionate and did violate the Convention. All decisions in this case are available (in Dutch) at <www.minlnv.nl/herstructurering/>. See also the article by P. de Haan in *NRC Handelsblad*, 15 September 1999.

its case to (international) dispute settlement. The difference between a national and an international procedure is of course relevant. However, the objections against the Ethyl Case were often against the fact than a multinational enterprise had the right to sue a foreign government, without the consent of its own government. "Under the MAI as currently drafted, little or no public policy filter would stand between the special interests of a company that felt it had suffered loss or damage as a result of an 'alleged breach of an obligation' under the MAI."[24] There were also objections against the fact that "arbitration consists of a few trade experts",[25] again implying displeasure with a lack of political control. "[The MAI should] eliminate the investor-to-state dispute resolution mechanism and put into place democratic and transparent mechanisms".[26] These arguments seem to undervalue the importance of an independent judiciary, accessible without political interference.

### 2.2.2 Concerns placed in the MAI context

The concerns described above could easily be translated into concerns about the MAI. NGOs concerned about 'the power of the multinationals' would of course object to an agreement that would create additional rights for multinational enterprises. They would have preferred an agreement that would have created additional opportunities to regulate the behaviour of multinationals. Thus they contended that an agreement with only rights and no obligations for multinational enterprises was unacceptable. The MAI should, according to NGOs, "require multinational investors to observe binding agreements incorporating environment, labour, health, safety and human rights standards to ensure that they do not use the MAI to exploit weak regulatory regimes" and "ensure that an enforceable agreement on investor responsibilities takes precedent over any agreement on investor rights."[27]

The lack of control by governments was 'demonstrated' by referring to the Ethyl Case. Although Canada was expected to win the dispute, it eventually went for a settlement, which reportedly involved the sum of $ 13 million and a public recognition that "there is no new scientific evidence to modify the conclusions drawn by Health Canada in 1994 that MMT poses no health risk."[28] This settlement was invoked by NGOs to demonstrate the need for clarity in the MAI as to what expropriation really means. Above all, they insisted that the MAI should clearly state that the expropriation clause could

---

24 WWF, *Is the Multilateral Agreement on Investment Sustainable?* (1997), A WWF International Discussion Paper, p. 9.
25 Friends of the Earth, *License to Loot, The MAI and How to Stop It* (1998), p. 10.
26 Joint NGO statement on the MAI, *supra* note 16.
27 *Idem.*
28 Statement by the Canadian Government, 20 July 1998.

never be interpreted to prevent governments from adopting rules and regulations on environmental protection.

The fear that multinational enterprises might use their power to attain lower labour or environmental standards, or that governments might be tempted or forced not to raise their standards or not to implement existing ones was turned into the argument that the MAI would stimulate a 'race to the bottom'. The three-anchor approach described earlier was dismissed as insufficient, although the 'not-lowering-standards clause' was perhaps more far-reaching than any other international instrument available. Accordingly some NGOs recommended adopting binding requirements in the MAI that multinational corporations and governments should operate in ways that respect the ILO core labour standards.[29]

With regard to the position of developing countries there was an interesting collision of ideas. From the 'power of the multinationals' point of view, the developing countries are potential victims of multinational enterprises, which could abuse their power even more easily in those weak countries than they could in the OECD countries. Also taking into account that developing countries were not participating in the negotiations, this led to the objection that the MAI posed a serious threat to the sovereignty of developing countries. From the 'race to the bottom' point of view however, NGOs feared that the governments of some developing countries might lack the willingness and/or the ability to enact or implement sound labour or environmental legislation. This led to the conclusion that the MAI should ensure that minimum standards in these fields are respected in all countries in the world,[30] even in those countries, which are, for example, not willing to ratify the ILO conventions covering the so-called core labour standards. That this would amount to extraterritorial legislation and that this would certainly not be appreciated by developing countries, which would see this as an infringement of their sovereignty, was no problem for the NGOs.

Sensitivity about cultural domination played an important role in the negotiations, long before unrest was inspired in society about the MAI. Canada had fought long and hard over a clause in NAFTA that provides Canada with the possibility to protect its culture against the strong influence of its big neighbour. Understandably the Canadians asked for a similar cultural exception clause in the MAI. While they could count on warm support from France and some other countries, the majority of the negotiating group was opposed to a sweeping exception. The Netherlands for example, while desiring to

---

29 IRENE (International Restructuring Education Network Europe) and SOMO (Centre for Research on Multinational Corporations), *The Multilateral Agreement on Investments, Liberalisation of Foreign Direct Investment and the Effects on Labour Standards in the Automotive Industry* (1998), p. 37.
30 See Friends of the Earth, *supra* note 25, p. 33: "International investors should be required to follow the stronger of either home or host country environmental and labor standards wherever a corporation and its affiliates operate".

continue to be able to promote Dutch language filmmaking, theatrical performances and book-publishing, was of the opinion that this could be achieved through less drastic means than a general exception. This issue, just one of at least five major issues in the negotiations, turned out to be the decisive stumbling block. The assessment of the MAI by France showed that the cultural issue combined with the threat against French sovereignty, much more than labour, environment or the position of developing countries, was the insurmountable problem that forced France to withdraw from the negotiations.

To summarize the debate it can be said that when the negotiations started in the early 1990s this happened in a climate of positive appreciation of globalization, in which the consolidation and strengthening of an instrument to promote investment was deemed desirable. Probably some NGOs would not have liked such an instrument, even at that time. However, they did not know about the negotiations and did not yet have the Internet at their disposal. In the mid-1990s this climate changed dramatically. Globalization was seen by vocal groups in society as something negative, or at least as something with important negative side effects. An instrument to promote investment under these circumstances to them was a very undesirable thing. They knew about the MAI and, using the Internet, acted against it.

2.3     Why was resistance so strong?

*2.3.1   Four reasons can be mentioned here*

In the first place there was time pressure. By the time the NGO movement had gathered momentum in its battle against the MAI the original deadline of April 1997 had already expired. The OECD ministers had given their negotiators just one additional year to solve the remaining problems. This meant that when the meeting between the negotiating group and NGOs took place in October 1997 the negotiations had almost entered their final phase. It was no surprise therefore that the most urgent claim of the NGOs at that time was "to suspend the MAI negotiations and extend the 1998 deadline to allow sufficient time for meaningful public input and participation in all countries."[31] Since the NGOs, rightfully, estimated that the negotiating group, after four years of preparation and two years of negotiations, had every intention to fulfil its mandate at the time set for it by the ministers, they felt, probably correctly again, they had to pull hard on the emergency brake of this speeding train.

In the second place there was the complexity of the issue. Globalization as such is not an issue that can be easily analyzed. What are the consequences of globalization for the different parties involved? What are the consequences in the short run; what are the consequences in the long run? What would have

---

31  See joint NGO Statement, *supra* note 16, p. 3.

happened if no globalization had taken place? What is the role of investment in this process? How does it influence growth, employment, the balance of payments, the transfer of technology, labour standards and the environment? And how does an investment agreement like the MAI influence investment? What is the content of the MAI and how should its provisions be interpreted? Here the NGOs had a point. The consolidated text of the MAI[32] counted no less than 144 pages, not including the many country-specific reservations. The text contains many square brackets and footnotes. Even among negotiators a common view had not yet emerged about the correct interpretation of all the clauses. How could one expect that newcomers in this field could oversee the ins and outs of the text and its consequences for the real world? Many NGOs interpreted the text in a manner that had nothing to do with what the negotiators had in mind. Although some NGOs learned fast and produced thorough analyses of the text and its possible consequences, it should be no surprise that a complex text, with an uncertain influence on a phenomenon that in itself is complex and not fully understood, led to a strong desire for better explanations before that text would attain the status of a binding treaty.

In the third place there was the impression of secrecy. To some extent the NGOs had a point here to. The MAI negotiations, like most negotiations, were conducted behind closed doors. In any negotiation there has to be a certain level of confidentiality if one wants the negotiation to be successful. Normally negotiations are not started by putting all the cards on the table nor can they be conducted effectively by making every move public. To reach a mutually acceptable result in any negotiation, certainly in a negotiation involving 29 countries, confidential exchanges of options and possibilities are necessary instruments. Having said that, it must be added that the MAI negotiations were one of the most open of its kind. As mentioned earlier, the start of the negotiations was publicly announced. Press briefings by the chairman of the negotiating group and the secretariat of the OECD were given after every meeting of the group. Ambassadors in Paris of non-OECD countries were briefed after every meeting. So-called outreach seminars were organised in every continent to inform non-participating countries about contents and progress of the negotiations. Although all the negotiating group documents were classified 'confidential', so-called 'sanitized' versions (i.e., with country names removed) of the records of group meetings were made available and later it was also decided that 'sanitized' versions of documents might just as well be published. When the pressure from NGOs began to mount a consultation process both in Paris and in other capitals (with of course differences between the different OECD countries) was set up. Internet sites were opened, letters from the public were answered, negotiators participated in seminars and hearings organized by NGOs and, of course, parliaments were briefed and in more than one country parliaments changed their previous lack of interest into close scrutiny of the

---

32 OECD, *Multilateral Agreement on Investment, Consolidated Text*, DAFFE/MAI(98)7/REV1.

negotiations. Notwithstanding all these efforts the reproach of secrecy never disappeared.

In the last place, and probably most importantly, there was a collision of ideologies. As pointed out before, the MAI served as a focal point for concerns about globalization in general. Friends of the Earth put it as follows:

> [T]he MAI would also likely interfere with long-term efforts to reorient the world's economy in a more environmentally friendly, sustainable direction. A sustainable future will require worldwide use of natural resources to be reduced below the earth's carrying capacity and redistributed equitably to all the world's people. The MAI is dedicated to an entirely different vision of the future: the right of multinational corporations to enter all markets and bid against local people for access to resources and consumers. As the MAI gives corporate investors access to restricted economies, the supply of natural resources hooked into international markets would grow, leading to more resources being consumed rather than less, more efficiently. The MAI's open access regime would also allow rich countries to live beyond their borders, consuming more than their share of land, wood, mineral and other resources. Because breaking this cycle will require more control on international investment, not less, the MAI is hopelessly flawed from an ecological point of view.[33]

This collision is even reflected in the subtitle of the seminar at which the present paper was given: 'Free Markets or Institutional Framework?' and in the text of the invitation for that seminar where the question is asked whether the MAI should reflect the liberal values of a global free market economy and leave the investment relations between transnational corporations and political and civilian society to the free and self-regulating markets. This question is a false one in the sense that there are no real defenders of the position that there should be completely free markets. What the MAI tried to establish was more liberalization, without denying governments their sovereign right to regulate their economies in a non-discriminatory manner. Of course, to answer another question in the invitation for the seminar, markets are dependent on clear regulations and on instruments to enforce these regulations. The real point was whether additional rules on, for example, labour standards should be included in the MAI or should be agreed on in other fora, such as the ILO. Nevertheless, opponents of the MAI often depicted the MAI and its proponents as ultraliberals trying to get rid of any form of government regulation. Needless to say that in a situation with such strong ideological overtones, denying such allegations did not convince the opponents.

---

33  See Friends or the Earth, *supra* note 25, p. 15

## 2.4 Why was support so weak?

Strong resistance against a proposal does not necessarily lead to its rejection, provided there is equally strong support for it. In an open and democratic procedure a compromise can be found that would be acceptable to all involved. In the case of the MAI, politicians had an easy task. On the one hand they found a large and very diverse group of opponents of the proposal, while on the other, they faced a number of government departments with some backing from business. Not only in France but also in, for example, the United States this quickly led to the conclusion that no political efforts should be spent in an effort to save the MAI.

Why was there only limited support from business? In the first place business did not face many problems with regard to investment in the OECD area. For European investors, whose investments are predominantly made within the European Union, the EU rules provide adequate protection, market openings and dispute settlement procedures. North American investors already had the NAFTA. With regard to the treatment of established investors regarding subjects like expropriation or transfers of currency, no real problems exist. Dispute settlement may not always be quick or cheap, but in general there is a lot of trust in the instruments available at present.

There are some problems relating to market access, government procurement, aids, subsidies and other government instruments to support enterprises, which are not always available on a non-discriminatory basis for foreign investors. There are differences in the degree of openness between the OECD Member States. It would have been in the interest of enterprises if the MAI had solved those problems and differences for them. However, although the MAI did address these issues, it did not provide an immediate solution. The MAI 'only' provided a standstill (and perhaps also a rollback) mechanism, whereby a country that at present does not allow foreign investment in certain sectors, could list those sectors in its schedule of country-specific reservations. This means that, although the obligations of the MAI are applicable in principle, they are in practice not applied to that sector as long as it remains on the list of reservations. Thus, there is no immediate solution for limitation of market access. Of course, the OECD in the framework of the Codes has used the standstill and rollback mechanism very successfully. But the advantage of such a system over a longer period of time, the advantages of a rule-based system in general and of the detailed elaboration of, for example, rules on transfer, are of an almost ideological nature. Thus it was to be expected that from the outset there would be little support for the MAI from practical organizations like enterprises, that would like to see some immediate benefits from this new instrument and that there would be resistance from organizations that had a different ideology. Indeed, international business did support the MAI negotiations, but certainly not with the same enthusiasm with which NGOs attacked it.

Business' initial support only weakened when negotiations progressed and went in a direction, which was not seen as positive by enterprises. First it became clear that an almost total exception of taxation was inevitable. Then there was the debate on binding clauses regarding labour and environmental standards. Next the proposals on the annexing (and updating) of the Guidelines for Multinational Enterprises to the MAI. By then businesses, most of all in the United States, started to change their view of the MAI. It changed from something that, at least in theory and, perhaps, in the longer term, also in practice, would be of value to them into something that in the short term would be more of a liability. The resulting erosion of support for the MAI was certainly noted by politicians. This may have been as strong a reason for the demise of the MAI as the opposition from the NGOs.

## 3 LESSONS LEARNED

### 3.1 Take concerns seriously

Globalization is a phenomenon with many aspects. Its positive and negative sides evoke strong sentiments in different quarters of society. Many questions about its effects in the short and the long run have not yet been fully answered. Individual persons are sometimes strongly affected by it. Interest groups fighting for issues as different as the environment, the position of developing countries, human rights, labour standards, consumer protection, gender problems or animal rights see a link between their chosen issues and globalization. Some are opposed to globalization and growth as such; many see that globalization offers opportunities as well, provided it is adequately managed. Although different groups have different, and sometimes even conflicting, concerns, they are united in a growing uneasiness about globalization. They have demonstrated a willingness and an ability to make their views heard and politicians have shown they are sensitive to the concerns of those groups. It follows that any organization interested in globalization in general and in investment rules in particular should take these concerns very seriously if it hopes to have those rules approved by parliaments and supported by society in general.

### 3.2 An integrated approach is necessary

Since different concerns have to be addressed, expertise from different quarters has to be used. Both at the national and at the international level, experts in the field of investment and finance, development, environment, labour standards, human rights and any other field considered relevant by interested groups, should be consulted. Not only government experts but also academics and NGOs can provide valuable input. In the national administrations all interested ministries or departments should be involved in the development of national positions. At the international level, the involvement of both developing and developed countries must be ensured.

### 3.3  NGOs have become important players

NGOs were the first to voice uneasiness about globalization. In a way they overtook traditional players like political parties and organized labour as the first interlocutors of government agencies. Of course, ministers ultimately only have to answer to parliaments, but the initiative for critical questioning was on more than one occasion taken by NGOs. Although NGOs are many and diverse, they managed to reach coordinated positions and stage coordinated actions. They also used a certain 'division of labour': radical groups created a sense of urgency, the more established groups provided studies and arguments and used the openings made by groups operating on the fringe.

### 3.4 Transparency is a must

Confidentiality is important in complex international negotiations, but it should be used wisely. Secrecy, or even just the impression of secrecy, is a time bomb in today's information society. On the other hand, openness can provide important guidance for negotiators. The additional inputs from different groups in society shed more light on the priorities to be given to the subjects under negotiation and on the scope of contentious issues. Using the additional analytical capacity can lead to a better understanding of the problems in hand and to finding improved solutions. Accepting to be challenged on both principles and content of an agreement and actively participating in the ensuing debates will lead to better end results.

The Internet plays a crucial role in providing transparency. One of the reasons why the NGO campaign was so effective was their intensive use of the Internet. Exchange of information and ideas can take place on a global scale. An analysis made in Canada can lead to parliamentary questions in Australia and the answers given there may give rise to a letter campaign in European countries. Governments can benefit from this instrument by studying the information available and by posting their own views on the net as well.

## 4 HOW TO ESTABLISH A FRAMEWORK?

Like in 1991 the start could be a feasibility study. However, unlike in 1991 that study should not only address technical issues but also the politically sensitive issues, such as:
a) the relationship between investment protection and the right to regulate;
b) the relationship between investment and labour standards and protection of the environment; and
c) the position of developing countries and the balance of rights and duties of investors.

It would probably be too ambitious to try to cover all these subjects in one study. Preliminary studies would be needed, for example, regarding the relation between investment and the environment. What are the short-term and long-term impacts of different types of investments on the environment? What is the specific role of *foreign* investment in this respect? What can be done to maximize the benefits of foreign investment and to minimize its possible negative effects? What could be the role of an investment treaty and what would be the relation between such a treaty and national rules and other international treaties? It is likely that such studies will not lead to unanimous conclusions, neither on the facts nor on the desirable policies. Thus political choices will have to be made on whether to proceed and if so, how to proceed.

Political choices about sensitive issues will also have to be made, making it absolutely necessary to assure political support for the process from the outset. Parliaments will have to be informed well before the start of any negotiations and should receive regular progress reports after that. To ensure that informed policy choices can be made and to create the necessary support from society as a whole it is vital that all interested parties can actively participate in the preparatory process. Thus not only governments but also business representatives, labour unions, NGOs and academics from both developed and developing countries should be involved. This may not be all that easy to organize. In the MAI negotiations the business community was regularly consulted through the standing OECD Business and Industry Advisory Committee (BIAC). A similar committee (TUAC) was used for consulting trade unions. NGOs were invited on a self-selection basis. There were sometimes doubts as to the representativeness of the different organizations. Are BIAC's views really those of international business? The only worldwide business organization, the International Chamber of Commerce (ICC), has never been a strong supporter of the MAI. The ICC's view was that a multilateral investment agreement in an era of globalization would necessarily have to be worldwide. Thus the ICC saw the WTO as the relevant framework for such an agreement. The MAI would at best be a useful intermediate step towards a WTO agreement. There were also doubts as to whether BIAC did not actually represent only the views of a limited number of large companies in a limited number of countries. Could BIAC, or indeed the ICC, represent the views of small and medium-sized enterprises? With regard to labour, problems may arise when governments that do not recognize independent trade unions in their country would be asked to consult such unions in an international context. However, the possible problems regarding business and labour representation are to a large extent alleviated by the fact that there are well-established organizations that represent those interests in international fora.

This is not the case for 'the NGOs'. There are thousands of them, they are very different in size, they may be single-issue or interested in many issues, they may have been in existence for decades or months, they may have acquired extensive knowledge about certain subjects or be completely ignorant, they may want to take responsibility or just be interested in blocking certain developments. Notwithstanding all these differences, it turned out to be quite feasible to organize efficient meetings with NGOs, both at the national and the international level, during the MAI negotiations. Valuable input, in meetings or otherwise, might just as well come from a small, young, radical, single-issue organization as from an organization like the WWF. Thus it seems advisable to continue the pragmatic self-selection approach employed this far. Of course, when it comes to political decisions, governments and parliaments may also want to take into account the political importance they attach to the different participants in the process. In order to make participation of all interested parties possible, transparency must be ensured. Using the Internet will be an important, though in itself not sufficient, condition to achieve that.

The question of where studies, discussions and ultimately perhaps negotiations have to take place seems a bit premature to answer now. OECD, WTO, UNCTAD, World Bank, UNEP, ILO and other organizations all have a role to play. The OECD as an interdisciplinary organization is well placed to contribute to some of the issues mentioned above. The UNCTAD is very experienced with regard to the position of developing countries; the ILO is the guardian of international labour rules. Contributions from these and other organizations can all underpin the political decision to start negotiations on a framework for investment. The choice of forum for such negotiations will depend on their scope and content. There may be one comprehensive negotiation or there may be several parallel negotiations. Elements of the framework may be deemed to be ripe for negotiation in one organization, while other elements are studied further in other organizations. This is something that will have to be decided at a later stage. What is more important is that a start is made now. Globalization is here to stay, so we had better agree on how to manage it.

# 9 | Foreign Investment in the WTO

M. Koulen*

## 1 INTRODUCTION

The recent evolution of the international legal framework governing foreign investment has been marked by a proliferation of bilateral investment treaties, an increase in the number of regional and plurilateral economic arrangements that include provisions on foreign investment,[1] and a renewed interest in the creation of global rules on foreign investment.[2] These developments reflect the increasing importance of international agreements, as compared to customary international law, as sources of international law on foreign investment. In addition, while international consideration of foreign investment during the 1960s and the 1970s focused on the protection of foreign investment, a significant number of recent arrangements also provide for rules aimed at the removal of impediments to the entry of foreign investment.[3]

The last decade has also witnessed the emergence of a closer relationship between the evolving multilateral trading system, on the one hand, and international cooperation in the area of foreign investment, on the other, particularly as a result of the establishment of the World Trade Organization (WTO). The purpose of this chapter is to discuss two main dimensions of this changed relationship between the multilateral trading system and foreign investment.

---

* Mark Koulen is Counsellor in the Trade and Finance Division of the Secretariat of the World Trade Organization, Geneva. The views expressed are those of the author in his personal capacity.
1 For comparative and historical analyses of the existing international legal framework for foreign investment, see, e.g., T. Brewer and S. Young, *The Multilateral Investment System and Multinational Enterprises* (1998); D. Carreau and P. Juillard, *Droit international économique* (1998), 4th edn.; G. Sacerdoti, *Bilateral Treaties and Multilateral Instruments on Investment Protection* (1997); P. Juillard, 'L'Evolution des sources du droit des investissements', 250 *Recueil de Cours (1994)* (1997); UNCTAD, *World Investment Report 1996 – Investment, Trade and International Policy Arrangements* (1996); P. Muchlinski, *Multinational Enterprises and the Law* (1995); M. Sornarajah, *The International Law on Foreign Investment* (1994); A. Fatouros (ed.), *Transnational Corporations: The International Legal Framework* (1994).
2 See, e.g., Brewer and Young, *supra* note 1; E. Graham, *Global Corporations and National Governments* (1996); P. Sauvé and D. Schwanen, *Investment Rules for the Global Economy – Enhancing Access to Markets* (1996); D. Julius, 'International Direct investment: Strengthening the Policy Regime', in P. Kenen (ed.), *Managing the World Economy: Fifty Years after Bretton Woods* (1994), pp. 131-151.
3 See Juillard, *supra* note 1.

First, unlike its predecessor, the General Agreement on Tariffs and Trade (GATT), the WTO provides rules and a framework for further negotiations on certain aspects of foreign investment, even though the WTO Agreement does not contain a separate legal instrument specifically dedicated to foreign investment. WTO rules relevant to investment differ in scope and orientation from the rules on the entry, treatment and protection of foreign investment that can be found in bilateral and regional investment arrangements. Questions have recently arisen in various contexts regarding the implications of the interface between WTO rules and dispute settlement procedures and investment rules contained in other international agreements.

Second, while negotiations launched in May 1995 in the framework of the OECD on a Multilateral Agreement on Investment (MAI) ended unsuccessfully in December 1998,[4] the creation of a comprehensive, multilateral framework of rules on foreign investment has also been raised as a possible subject for new negotiations in the WTO. Following a period of study and exchange of views in a WTO Working Group on the Relationship between Trade and Investment, proposals to start multilateral negotiations on investment in the WTO were made by several WTO Members in connection with the third WTO Ministerial Meeting held in Seattle from 30 November to 3 December 1999. The debate in the WTO has revealed the existence of divergent views with respect to the desirability of launching negotiations on multilateral investment rules. It has also raised questions regarding the appropriate scope, architecture and content of such rules and their implications for the pursuit of domestic policy objectives of WTO Members. Disagreement whether to start negotiations on investment was one of the factors contributing to the failure of the Seattle Ministerial Meeting.

This chapter first contains a brief description of the historical evolution of the relationship between foreign investment and the multilateral trade system. This is followed by an overview of the main WTO provisions relevant to investment. The discussion then describes the controversy on whether a multilateral framework of rules on investment should be negotiated in the WTO. Finally, some concluding observations are made.

---

4   On the MAI negotiations, see, e.g., Société Francaise Pour le Droit International, *Un accord multilateral sur l'investissement: D'un forum de négociation à l'autre?* (1999), Proceedings of a symposium on the MAI reproduced in 31*Cornell International Law Journal* (1998), pp. 477-728; M. Trebilcock and R. Howse, *The Regulation of International Trade* (1999), 2nd edn., pp. 357-366; F. Engering, 'The Multilateral Investment Agreement', 5 *Transnational Corporations* (1996), no. 3, pp. 147-162; OECD, *Towards Multilateral Investment Rules* (1996); W. Witherell, 'The OECD Multilateral Agreement on Investment', 4 *Transnational Corporations* (1995), no. 2, pp. 1-14. Draft Mai text available at <www.oecd.org/daf/investment/fdi/mai/neg-text.htm>.

## 2 FOREIGN INVESTMENT IN THE ITO CHARTER AND THE GATT

The predecessor of the WTO, the GATT, was concluded in 1947 as a temporary agreement pending the entry into force of the envisaged Charter for an International Trade Organization (ITO). This proposed ITO Charter, which was adopted in March 1948 but which never came into effect, addressed a wide range of matters, including employment and economic activity, economic development and reconstruction, commercial policy, restrictive business practices and commodity agreements.[5] It contained rules on foreign investment in a Chapter on 'Economic Development and Reconstruction'.[6] These rules were among the most contentious subjects in the negotiation of the Charter as a number of developing countries opposed the traditional international property protection standards advocated by the industrialized countries.[7]

While the ITO Charter would thus have provided for a single, multilateral forum for international cooperation on trade and foreign investment, the non-entry into force of the Charter resulted in an institutional divide between the multilateral trade regime embodied in the GATT and international cooperation with respect to foreign investment. Until the launch of the Uruguay Round of Multilateral Trade Negotiations, the GATT did not constitute a significant avenue for multilateral consideration of foreign investment issues. The only action taken by the GATT Contracting Parties with respect to foreign investment was the adoption in 1955 of a Resolution on International Investment for Economic Development. This Resolution recognized that an increased flow of capital into countries in need of investment from abroad and, in particular, into developing countries, would facilitate the objectives of the General Agreement. In its operative part, the Resolution recommended that Contracting Parties enter into negotiations aimed at the conclusion of bilateral and multilateral agreements on the security of foreign investment, the avoidance of double taxation and the transfer of earnings upon foreign investment.[8] There is no record of any action taken by the GATT Contracting Parties to follow up on this Resolution.

---

5 J.-C. Graz, *Aux sources de l'OMC – La Charte de La Havane 1941-1950* (1999); R. Gardner, *Sterling-Dollar Diplomacy in Current Perspective* (1980); W. Adams Brown, *The United States and the Restoration of World Trade* (1950); C. Wilcox, *A Charter for World Trade* (1949).
6 United Nations Conference on Trade and Employment, *Final Act and Related Documents* (1948), Arts. 11 and 12.
7 See C. Lipson, *Standing Guard – Protecting Foreign Capital in the Nineteenth and Twentieth Centuries* (1985), pp. 86-87. See also Wilcox, *supra* note 5, pp. 145-146; Adams Brown, *supra* note 5, pp. 102-104 and 152-153 and G. Schwarzenberger, *Foreign Investment and International Law* (1969), p. 136.
8 GATT, *Basic Instruments and Selected Documents*, Third Supplement (1955), pp. 48-49. The Working Party which had recommended the adoption of this resolution had failed to reach agreement on a proposal by the Federal Republic of Germany to amend the GATT to introduce new provisions on freedom of establishment. *Ibidem*, p. 243.

The first significant consideration of foreign investment issues in the GATT framework since the adoption of the above-mentioned Resolution occurred in the early 1980s when the United States raised concerns regarding the use of certain investment policies as non-tariff trade barriers.[9] In March 1981, the United States proposed in the GATT Consultative Group of Eighteen that a survey be undertaken of investment performance requirements and incentives to ascertain if any of these practices violated specific GATT provisions or nullified or impaired GATT benefits.[10] However, at the GATT Ministerial Meeting held in November 1982 the GATT Contracting Parties were unable to reach agreement on the inclusion of this subject in the GATT's work programme. Subsequently, this matter became the subject of negotiations in the Uruguay Round on trade-related investment measures.

The United States also raised the issue of investment performance requirements in a GATT dispute settlement proceeding regarding the implementation by Canada of its Foreign Investment Review Act.[11] This Act provided for a mechanism for the review and approval of most proposed foreign investments in Canada to determine whether such investments were or were likely to be of significant net benefit to Canada. The implementation of this Act often involved negotiations between the Canadian authorities and foreign investors resulting in specific, written undertakings by the investors regarding a range of aspects of the performance of their Canadian subsidiaries. The United States challenged the consistency with the GATT of undertakings obliging foreign investors to purchase goods of Canadian origin or from Canadian sources, undertakings by foreign investors to manufacture goods in Canada, and undertakings by foreign investors to export specified quantities or proportions of their production. In its Report, the Panel stressed that the GATT did not prevent Canada from exercising its sovereign right to regulate foreign direct investment and that its examination was thus limited to the issue of the consistency of the undertakings with Canada's trade obligations under the GATT.[12] In respect of the purchase undertakings, the Panel determined that such undertakings were 'requirements' within the meaning of Article III:4 of the GATT[13] which were inconsistent with this provision because they provided

---

9 R. McCulloch and R. Owen, 'Linking Negotiations on Trade and Foreign Direct Investment', in C. Kindleberger and D. Audretsch (eds.), *The Multinational Corporation in The 1980s* (1983), pp. 344-358.
10 GATT, *Basic Instruments and Selected Documents*, Twenty-Eigth Supplement (1982), pp. 75-76.
11 'Canada – Administration of the Foreign Investment Review Act' (adopted on 7 February 1984), in GATT, *Basic Instruments and Selected Documents*, Thirtieth Supplement (1984), pp. 140-168 (hereinafter: FIRA Panel Report).
12 FIRA Panel Report, paras. 5.1and 5.2.
13 Art. III:4 of the GATT provides in relevant part: "The products of the territory of any Contracting Party imported into the territory of any other contracting party shall be accorded treatment no less favourable than that accorded to like products of national origin in respect of all laws, regulations and requirements affecting their internal sale, offering for sale, purchase, transportation, distribution or use."

less favourable treatment to imported products than to like domestic products.[14] In this regard, the Panel rejected an argument advanced by Canada that the word 'requirements' in GATT Article III:4 should be interpreted in light of the ITO Charter so as to exclude requirements connected with the regulation of foreign investment.[15] The Panel rejected the claim of the United States that undertakings by foreign investors to export specified quantities or proportions of their production were contrary to Article XVII of the GATT.[16] The Panel did not make findings on the undertakings to manufacture products in Canada as it considered that this issue was not within its terms of reference.

3  WTO PROVISIONS RELEVANT TO FOREIGN INVESTMENT

The WTO Agreement includes as an integral part a number of Annexes that contain Multilateral Agreements on Trade in Goods, a General Agreement on Trade in Services and an Agreement on Trade-Related Aspects of Intellectual Property Rights. Although the WTO Agreement thus does not include a separate legal instrument on foreign investment, some of the agreements annexed to the WTO Agreement pertain directly or indirectly to foreign investment.[17] In some cases such agreements provide for obligations of WTO Members with respect to the entry and treatment of foreign persons and enterprises or to the protection of certain property rights of foreign persons. Provisions contained in other agreements are relevant to foreign investment in a different, less direct manner in that they circumscribe the ability of Members to apply certain kinds of measures designed to attract investment or to influence the operations of foreign investors. The plurilateral Agreement on Government Procurement, the General Agreement on Trade in Services and the Agreement on Trade-Related Aspects of Intellectual Property Rights fall into the first category while the Agreement on Trade-Related Investment Measures and the Agreement on Subsidies and Countervailing Measures belong to the second category.

---

14  FIRA Panel Report, para. 5.4.
15  *Idem*, para. 5.12. Canada referred to the provision in Art. 12 of the ITO Charter which recognized the right of a Member of the ITO "to determine whether and to what extent and upon what terms it will allow future foreign investments, to prescribe and give effect on just terms to requirements as to the ownership of existing and future investments and to prescribe and give effect to other reasonable requirements with respect to existing and future investments." *Idem*, para. 3.9.
16  *Idem*, para. 5.18.
17  See T. Brewer and S. Young, 'Investment Issues at the WTO: The Architecture of Rules and the Settlement of Disputes', *Journal of International Economic Law* (1998), pp. 457-470; P. Sauvé, 'Qs and As on Trade, Investment and the WTO', 31 *Journal of World Trade* (1997), no. 4, pp. 55-79; WTO, *Annual Report 1996, vol. 1*, pp. 69-73; P. Sauvé, 'A First Look at Investment in the Final Act of the Uruguay Round', 28 *Journal of World Trade* (1994), no. 5, pp. 5-16.

Historically, government procurement has been the first area in which GATT rules have begun to address the treatment accorded by governments to foreign enterprises operating within their territories. The current *Agreement on Government Procurement*, which was concluded in 1994 as a plurilateral agreement and which entered into force in January 1996, is the successor to a previous agreement on government procurement, which resulted from the Tokyo Round of Multilateral Trade Negotiations and retains the basic national treatment and non-discrimination requirements contained in the previous Agreement.[18] In respect of the covered procurement operations, the Agreement requires not only that there be no discrimination against foreign products, but also no discrimination against foreign suppliers and, in particular, no discrimination against locally established suppliers on the basis of their degree of foreign affiliation or ownership. Another investment related aspect of this Agreement is the provision in Article XVI that procuring entities shall not, in the qualification and selection of suppliers, products or services, or in the evaluation of tenders and award of contracts, impose, seek or consider offsets. Offsets are defined as

> measures used to encourage local development or improve the balance-of-payments accounts by means of domestic content, licensing of technology, investment requirements, counter-trade or similar requirements.[19]

The *General Agreement on Trade in Services* (GATS)[20] is the most prominent example of the incorporation of foreign investment into the WTO. The GATS essentially treats the supply of services through foreign investment as a form of trade in services. Article I of the GATS provides that the GATS applies to all measures by Members affecting trade in services and defines trade in services as encompassing four modes of supply, including the supply "by a service supplier of one Member, through commercial presence in the territory of any other Member". The term commercial presence is defined in Article XXVIII(d) of the GATS as "any type of business or professional establishment, including through (i) the constitution, acquisition or maintenance of a juridical person, or (ii) the creation or maintenance of a branch or a representative office, within the territory of a Member for the purpose of supplying a service". Thus, the

---

18 Trebilcock and Howse, *supra* note 4, pp. 199-202; B. Hoekman and P. Mavroides (eds.), *Law and Policy in Public Purchasing: the WTO Agreement on Government Procurement* (1997).
19 This prohibition of the use of offsets is subject to an exception for measures, which may be negotiated by developing countries at the time of their accession.
20 See Trebilcock and Howse, *supra* note 4, pp. 278-291; W. Zdouc, 'WTO Dispute Settlement Practice Relating to the GATS', 2 *Journal of International Economic Law* (1999), no. 2, pp. 295-346; B. Hoekman, 'Assessing the General Agreement on Trade in Services', in W. Martin and L. Winters (eds.), *The Uruguay Round and the Developing Countries* (1996) pp. 88-124; P. Sauvé, 'Assessing the General Agreement on Trade in Services – Half-Full or Half-Empty?', 29 *Journal of World Trade* (1995), no. 4, pp. 125-146.

GATS covers forms of establishment that correspond to the notion of foreign direct investment. Another investment related mode of supply covered by Article I:2 is the supply "by a service supplier of one Member, through presence of natural persons of a Member in the territory of any other Member". This mode of supply is closely related to the commercial presence mode of supply in that it includes temporary entry of business visitors and intra-company transfers of managerial and other key personnel.

Although the GATS constitutes a multilateral framework covering foreign investment in service sectors, it differs significantly in its scope and architecture from other international agreements on foreign investment. First, the enterprise-based definition of commercial presence in the GATS is narrower than the asset-based definition of the term investment found in many international investment agreements. Second, because the focus of the GATS is on commercial presence as a modality of trade in services the GATS does not provide for the kind of rules on the treatment and protection of foreign investment typically contained in international investment agreements. For example, the GATS does not address matters such as expropriation and compensation and protection from strife. Third, the obligations of the GATS differ in respect of their general applicability. Certain obligations, such as the obligation to accord most-favoured-nation treatment, are in principle applicable to all Members and all service sectors. In contrast, obligations under the GATS relating to market access and national treatment are not general in scope. Rather, such obligations arise from specific commitments made by individual Members that are reflected in their schedules of commitments. Specific commitments regarding market access and national treatment apply only to service sectors listed in these schedules and are subject to conditions and qualifications specified therein. Thus, with respect to market access and national treatment the GATS involves a combination of a positive list approach to the identification of the specific sectors that are covered by a Member's commitments with a negative list approach to limitations on market access and national treatment in those sectors. Therefore, the inclusion in the GATS of the concept of commercial presence does not mean that the GATS provides for a generic right of establishment and national treatment for foreign investment in service sectors. In contrast, most international investment agreements that contain binding obligations regarding the admission of foreign investment do so under a negative list or top down approach whereby all sectors are presumed to be covered by a party's obligations, except those sectors that have been specifically excluded.

Detailed analyses of the specific commitments scheduled under the GATS have demonstrated that the vast majority of such commitments do not provide for the elimination of existing restrictions to trade and investment in services.[21] Article XIX of the GATS provides for successive rounds of negotiations

---

21  See, e.g., Hoekman, *supra* note 20. It should be noted that after the Uruguay Round further negotiations have taken place on financial services that resulted in improvements to the

with a view to achieving a progressively higher level of liberalization and requires that the first such round of negotiations be initiated in 2000. WTO Members started work pursuant to this mandate in February 2000.

Because the GATS covers foreign investment in services, questions concerning the interface between the GATS and other international agreements on foreign investment have arisen in various settings. In the WTO, there has been discussion of the legal implications of the most-favoured-nation requirement of the GATS for bilateral investment treaties concluded by WTO Members, particularly as regards the procedures for investor-to-state arbitration typically contained in such treaties. As a result, a number of WTO Members have taken time-limited exemptions from the most-favoured-nation obligation of the GATS in relation to bilateral investment treaties.[22] In addition, in the context of the OECD negotiations on the MAI concerns have been raised regarding the obligation arising from the GATS most-favoured-nation requirement to extend to all WTO Members the benefits of any liberalization pursuant to the MAI of restrictions to investment in services.[23]

The *Agreement on Trade Related Aspects of Intellectual Property Rights* (TRIPS Agreement)[24] requires WTO Members to accord in their territories certain standards of protection to the intellectual property of the nationals of other WTO Members. In respect of each category of intellectual property covered by the Agreement, it lays down minimum standards of substantive protection that must be available in the national law of each Member. In addition, the Agreement contains detailed provisions on the procedures and remedies that each Member must provide within its national law so that the nationals of other Members can effectively enforce their intellectual property rights. The provisions of the TRIPS Agreement on minimum standards for the protection of intellectual property, domestic enforcement procedures and international dispute settlement are directly relevant to the legal environment affecting foreign investment. In addition, the relationship between the TRIPS Agreement and foreign investment is also evident from the fact that virtually all modern investment agreements which lay down standards for the promotion and protection of foreign investment include intellectual property within the definition of investment. As a result, the question arises as to the relationship between the application to intellectual property of rules contained in inter-

---

commitments initially scheduled in that sector. Another important negotiation that was successfully concluded after the Uruguay Round concerned commitments in basic telecommunications services.

22 See Sauvé (1997), *supra* note 17, pp. 65-67 and A. Wimmer, 'The Impact of the General Agreement on Trade in Services on the OECD Multilateral Agreement on Investment', 19 *World Competition* (1996), no. 4, pp. 109-120.
23 Wimmer, *supra* note 22.
24 See Trebilcock and Howse, *supra* note 4, pp. 307-334 and C. Primo Braga, 'Trade-related Intellectual Property Issues: the Uruguay Round Agreement and its Economic Implications' in Martin and Winters, *supra* note 20, pp. 341-379.

national investment agreements, on the one hand, and rights and obligations contained in international agreements on the protection of intellectual property rights, such as the TRIPS Agreement, on the other. An example of a question that has been raised in this regard is whether the wide definition of the term expropriation in international investment agreements could be considered to prohibit certain measures that governments are explicitly permitted to take under the TRIPS Agreement, such as compulsory licensing.[25]

The *Agreement on Trade Related Investment Measures* (TRIMs Agreement) was negotiated during the Uruguay Round on the basis of a mandate that focused on the trade effects of investment measures and precluded consideration of possible disciplines on investment measures *per se*.[26] Article 2 of this Agreement requires Members not to apply any trade-related investment measure that is inconsistent with Articles III or XI of GATT 1994.[27] Thus, the TRIMs Agreement does not go beyond the rules of GATT 1994 but essentially reaffirms and clarifies the applicability to trade-related investment measures of certain obligations of GATT 1994.[28] The TRIMs Agreement applies only to trade in goods and not to trade in services. The Agreement does not offer a generic definition of the term trade-related investment measures but an Annex contains an illustrative list of TRIMs that are inconsistent with Article III:4 or Article XI:1 of GATT 1994. The measures covered by this Annex are prohibited not only

---

25 Sauvé (1997), *supra* note 17, p. 68. See also A. Hertz, 'Shaping the Trident: Intellectual Property under NAFTA, Investment Protection Agreements and at the World Trade Organization', 23 *Canada-United States Law Journal* (1997), pp. 261-325.
26 See D. Price and P. Bryan Cristy III, 'Agreement on Trade-Related Investment Measures (TRIMS): Limitations and Prospects for the Future', in T. Stewart (ed.), *The World Trade Organization – The Multilateral Framework for the 21st Century and U.S. Implementing Legislation* (1996), pp. 439-462; P. Low and A. Subramanian, 'Beyond TRIMS: A Case for Multilateral Action on Investment Rules and Competition Policy?', in Martin and Winters, *supra* note 20, pp. 380-408; P. Civello, 'The TRIMS Agreement: A Failed Attempt at Investment Liberalization', 8 *Minnesota Journal of Global Trade* (1999), no. 1, pp. 97-126.
27 The prohibition contained in Art. 2 is qualified by Arts. 3 and 4. Art. 3 provides that all exceptions under GATT 1994 shall apply, as appropriate, to the provisions of the TRIMS Agreement while Art. 4 provides that developing-country Members may deviate temporarily from the provisions of the Agreement in accordance with WTO balance-of-payments provisions. Art. 5 of the TRIMS Agreement provides for a transition procedure whereby Members, which notified existing TRIMS that were inconsistent with the TRIMS Agreement within three months after the date of entry into force of the WTO Agreement, were allowed to maintain such measures during a transition period, the length of which depends upon the level of development of the Member concerned (two years for developed-country Members, five years for developing-country Members and seven years for least developed-country Members). The TRIMS Agreement allows for the possibility of a further extension of this transition period for developing-country Members and least developed-country Members upon decision by the WTO Council for Trade in Goods. At the end of 1999, a number of developing countries submitted requests for such an extension of the transition period.
28 See the Panel Report in *European Communities – Regime for the Importation, Sale and Distribution of Bananas*, Complaint by Ecuador, WT/DS27/R/ECU, 22 May 1997, adopted 25 September 1997, para. 7.185.

if they are mandatory or enforceable under domestic law or under administrative rulings but also if they are applied as conditions that must be met by enterprises in order to obtain an advantage.

While relevant to foreign investment, the TRIMs Agreement focuses on measures that involve discriminatory treatment of products and does not govern the entry and treatment of foreign investment as such. In addition, the TRIMs Agreement is not limited to trade-related investment measures applied in connection with the regulation of foreign investment but is equally applicable where such measures are imposed on domestic enterprises.[29] The trade-oriented nature of the TRIMs Agreement also means that its obligations are narrower in reach than the provisions on performance requirements, which can be found in some existing investment agreements, such as the NAFTA and certain bilateral investment treaties. Measures such as export performance requirements and transfer of technology requirements, which are prohibited in some existing international investment agreements, are not covered by the TRIMs Agreement because such measures are not inconsistent with the provisions of the GATT 1994.

The TRIMs Agreement is also relevant to foreign investment in that it contains a mandate for future consideration of investment issues in the WTO. Article 9 provides that the Agreement shall be reviewed not later than five years after the entry into force of the WTO and that in this review consideration should be given to whether the Agreement should be complemented with provisions on competition policy and investment policy. The review was formally started in October 1999 but at the time of writing (April 2000) no substantive work had taken place in the context of this review.

The *Agreement on Subsidies and Countervailing Measures* defines the concept of subsidy and establishes disciplines on the provision of subsidies. One aspect of this Agreement that is particularly relevant to investment concerns its implications for the granting of investment incentives by governments. Financial incentives, such as the direct provision by a government of funds through grants and subsidized credits, and fiscal incentives, such as tax credits, would generally be covered by the definition of the term subsidy in Article 1 of the Agreement. In addition, certain kinds of indirect investment incentives, such as the provision of land and infrastructure at less than commercial prices, would also meet this definition. To the extent that investment incentives that are covered by the definition of the term subsidy are specific to certain enterprises or industries within the meaning of Article 2 of the Agreement, they are subject to the substantive disciplines of the Agreement. However, the effectiveness of these disciplines as applied to investment incentives is somewhat limited due to the fact that these disciplines are concerned with the effects of subsidies on trade. For example, because the granting of investment in-

---

29 See the Panel Report in *Indonesia – Certain Measures Affecting the Automobile Industry* WT/DS54/R, 2 July 1998, adopted 23 July 1998, para. 14.73.

centives generally predates production and trade, provisions of the Agreement that require an after-the-fact assessment of adverse trade effects of such incentives may not provide for meaningful disciplines over the provision of investment incentives.[30]

## 4 THE WORKING GROUP ON THE RELATIONSHIP BETWEEN TRADE AND INVESTMENT AND THE THIRD WTO MINISTERIAL MEETING

The 1995-1996 period witnessed a growing interest on the part of a number of WTO Members to examine the relationship between trade and investment as one of the principal new subjects of the WTO's post-Uruguay Round agenda.[31] This included both developed-country Members, notably Canada, Japan, the European Union, and developing-country Members such as Chile, Costa Rica and Peru. The proponents of work on investment in the WTO pointed to the increasing importance of foreign investment in the process of global economic integration, the growing complementarity of trade and investment, the changing geographic pattern of foreign direct investment flows, the increasing competition among governments to attract foreign investment, the lack of coherence of existing international arrangements on foreign investment, and the need to address foreign investment issues in a global forum in order to avoid a confrontation along North-South lines. The proposals put forward during this period on trade and investment as a subject for consideration in the WTO generally envisaged the establishment of a working group to conduct analytical work as the first step in a process of consensus building on the desirability of the creation of multilateral investment disciplines in the WTO.

The suggestion to undertake a comprehensive examination of foreign investment in the WTO was strongly contested by a number of developing-country Members. A general argument advanced by opponents to discussions on investment in the WTO was that priority should be given to addressing problems of implementation of the Uruguay Round agreements and that the introduction of new issues would overload the WTO system. A more specific argument was that there was still an insufficient understanding of the linkages between investment, trade and development, of the costs and benefits of foreign investment, and of the possible implications of a multilateral set of rules on investment for the ability of governments to regulate foreign investment in accordance with their development objectives. It was stressed that the focus of attention should be on the development implications of foreign investment and that the relationship of investment to trade was only one aspect of this development dimension.

---

30 See WTO, *supra* note 17, p. 72.
31 See, e.g., European Commission, Directorate General For External Economic Relations, *Trade and Investment* (1995), Discussion Paper.

An important aspect of the controversy on the proposal for the launch of work on foreign investment in the WTO concerned the relationship between possible future work on foreign investment in the WTO and ongoing activities in other international institutions, notably UNCTAD and the OECD. Those developing-country Members that opposed the inclusion of investment as an issue for consideration in the WTO took the view that, because of the nature of the WTO as an organization aimed at negotiating legal commitments, UNCTAD rather than the WTO was the appropriate forum for analytical work. It was pointed out in this respect that at the UNCTAD Midrand Conference held in 1996 UNCTAD had been mandated to analyze the development aspects of a possible multilateral framework for investment. The opposition of some developing-country Members to work on foreign investment in the WTO was also motivated by a fear that this would eventually lead to the incorporation of the MAI into the WTO framework. In contrast, other developing-country Members supported the initiation of discussions on foreign investment in the WTO because of a concern that without an initiative in the WTO developing countries might one day be faced with a *fait accompli* in the form of a MAI negotiated in the OECD without their involvement. The relationship between the MAI negotiations and possible work on foreign investment in the WTO also generated controversy among the participants in the MAI negotiations. While some of these participants, notably Canada and the European Commission, favoured an approach involving simultaneous negotiations on the MAI in the OECD and exploratory discussions on investment in the WTO, the United States was concerned that an initiative on investment in the framework of the WTO might undermine the prospects of the MAI negotiations.[32]

In light of these divergent views, the issue of possible future work on foreign investment in the WTO remained unresolved prior to the first WTO Ministerial Meeting held in December 1996. At a late stage during that meeting, a compromise was reached to establish a WTO Working Group on the Relationship between Trade and Investment on the understanding that the creation of this Working Group was without prejudice to the issue of whether multilateral disciplines on investment should be established within the WTO framework and that any decision to launch negotiations on investment disciplines in the WTO would require an explicit consensus.[33] The decision establishing the Working Group also emphasized the relationship between the work of this Working Group and the work of another newly created working group on the interaction between trade and competition policy. The decision welcomed the ongoing work on investment in UNCTAD and provided for cooperation between the Working Group and UNCTAD and other appropriate

---

32 See E. Smythe, 'Your Place or Mine? States, International Organizations and the Negotiation of International Investment Rules', 7 *Transnational Corporations* (1998), pp. 85-120.
33 Singapore Ministerial Declaration, adopted on 13 December 1996, *WTO Doc.* WT/MIN(96)/DEC (18 December 1996), para. 20.

international organizations in order to make the best possible use of available expertise and to take account of the development dimension. It was provided that after an initial period of two years the WTO General Council would review the work of the Working Group and decide how the work should proceed.

The decision establishing the Working Group stated that the Working Group's mandate was "to examine the relationship between trade and investment" and did not provide guidance as to what specific subjects should be examined by the Working Group. In June 1997, the Working Group adopted a detailed substantive agenda for its work in the form of a Checklist of Issues Suggested for Study that was based on proposals submitted by Members. This Checklist comprises four main themes:

a) the implications of the relationship between trade and investment for development and growth;
b) the economic relationship between trade and investment;
c) taking stock and analysing the existing international agreements on investment; and
d) a number of questions relevant to assessing the advantages of a possible initiative in the WTO to establish a set of multilateral rules on investment.

In December 1998, the Working Group submitted a report to the General Council, which provided a comprehensive description of the work done in 1997-1998.[34] As recommended in this report, the General Council decided that the Working Group should continue its educational process on the basis of the same Checklist of Issues Suggested for Study.[35]

In addition to analytical work on economic aspects of foreign investment, notably the relationship of foreign investment to economic development and international trade, questions relating to the desirability, scope and content of possible multilateral investment rules in the WTO have figured prominently in the activities of the Working Group. The discussions on these matters have shown that, although there is widespread acceptance among WTO Members of the important role played by international, treaty-based rules on foreign investment, views differ as to whether or not it is necessary to go beyond the existing framework of bilateral and regional investment agreements to establish a multilateral set of investment rules in the WTO. The principal arguments

---

34 Report (1998) of the Working Group on the Relationship between Trade and Investment to the General Council, WTO Doc. WT/WGTI/2 (8 December 1998).
35 A report on the activities of the Working Group in 1999 is contained in Report (1999) of the Working Group on the Relationship between Trade and Investment to the General Council, WTO Doc. WT/WGTI/3 (22 October 1999).

advanced in this connection can be briefly summarized in the following points.[36]

In support of the creation of a multilateral framework of rules on investment in the WTO it has been argued that multilateral rules would be more effective than the existing bilateral and regional agreements on foreign investment in enhancing the predictability and transparency of the legal environment facing foreign investors, thereby promoting investment flows to developing countries. In this connection, the view has often been expressed that commitments made in the framework of the WTO would be more credible in the eyes of foreign investors than commitments made in the context of bilateral and regional arrangements. A related argument is that multilateral rules on investment in the WTO would enshrine the principle of non-discrimination in international investment relations and would contribute to ensuring greater coherence in international trade and investment relations. One aspect of policy coherence that has often been emphasized as a reason for multilateral investment rules in the WTO concerns the limited scope of existing WTO provisions relevant to foreign investment and their lack of symmetry between services and goods. Because of the growing economic complementarity of trade and foreign investment, the lack of comprehensive investment rules in the WTO has been seen to undermine the effectiveness of existing WTO provisions on trade. For example, investment incentives are only to a limited extent addressed by WTO rules on subsidies and countervailing measures. In regard to this need for the WTO to reflect the increasing integration of trade and investment, it has been argued that the incorporation of investment disciplines in the WTO can build on a well established body of basic WTO principles of non-discrimination and transparency and dispute settlement procedures that in principle are applicable to a wide range of international economic transactions. Another dimension of international policy coherence that has been mentioned in support of multilateral investment rules in the WTO concerns the complexity, possible inconsistencies and investment-distorting effects of the existing framework of bilateral and regional investment arrangements. Finally, the argument has been advanced that in view of the WTO's wide membership and its practice of decision-making by consensus, the interests of developing countries are likely to be better protected in a multilateral negotiation on investment in the WTO than in negotiations on bilateral and regional investment arrangements.

Scepticism regarding the desirability of multilateral investment rules in the WTO has been motivated by a concern that such rules would likely entail significant costs for governments in terms of reduced policy flexibility and that it has not been demonstrated how such costs would be outweighed by benefits. It has been argued, in this connection, that a multilateral set of invest-

---

36 A full account of the Working Group's discussions on the possible merits of multilateral investment rules is contained in *WTO Docs.* WT/WGTI/2, paras. 147-160 and 186-219 and WT/WGTI/3, paras. 71-85.

ment rules, especially rules that would contain obligations regarding rights of establishment of foreign investors, would be inherently incompatible with the need for developing countries to enjoy policy flexibility in order to regulate foreign investment in accordance with their national development priorities. There has also been criticism, in this regard, of suggestions that a multilateral framework on investment should contain disciplines on the use of investment incentives and performance requirements. While it has been acknowledged that predictability and transparency of laws and regulations of host countries may be important for attracting foreign investment, doubts have been expressed as to whether multilateral investment rules would be more effective in ensuring such predictability and transparency than the existing bilateral and regional investment arrangements. The view has also been expressed that there is no evidence that multilateral investment rules would result in benefits for host countries, especially developing countries, in the form of increased inflows of foreign investment or enhanced transfer of technology. Related to this, opponents of multilateral investment negotiations in the WTO have more generally questioned the significance of international investment agreements as determinants of foreign investment. The sceptics have also argued that from a development perspective bilateral investment treaties are preferable to multilateral rules in that bilateral treaties can be tailored to the individual needs and priorities of individual countries and typically do not limit the ability of host countries to regulate the admission of foreign investment. In addition, it has been argued that because of significant conceptual differences between trade and foreign investment the applicability to foreign investment of basic WTO provisions in the field of trade is questionable. Finally, the need for further analysis of a range of issues relating to the impact of foreign direct investment on development, for example the role of foreign investment in the technological development of host countries, has also been mentioned as an argument against the launching of investment negotiations in the WTO.

In addition to this debate on the desirability of multilateral rules on investment in the WTO, there has also been extensive discussion of a number of more specific substantive elements of possible future investment rules. One such specific theme concerns the implications of multilateral rules on investment for the regulatory sovereignty of individual host countries, in particular as regards the pursuit of economic development objectives. A key subject of debate in this regard has been the issue of the nature of obligations with respect to the admission of foreign investment. Thus, as noted above, concerns raised by some developing-country Members stem from the perception that WTO negotiations on a multilateral framework of rules on investment would be aimed at obliging host countries to accord an unqualified right of establishment to foreign investors. In response to these concerns, it has been argued that the concept of a right of establishment is not relevant to the debate on the content of possible multilateral investment rules in the WTO as international investment agreements seldom provide for an unconditional right of entry of foreign investment and in most cases are limited to a requirement to accord non-discriminatory treatment to the admission of foreign investment, subject to general exceptions and country-specific reservations. Closely related to this, the Working Group has debated the relative merits of positive list and negative list approaches to the question of the admission of foreign investment. Various possible approaches have been considered with respect to the question of how the development dimension could be addressed in international investment rules, in which connection the Working Group has taken into account the work done on this subject in UNCTAD.

Another specific theme that has received considerable attention is the question of the appropriate definition of the term investment in international investment agreements. Divergent views have been expressed on the advantages of a broad, asset-based definition of investment that includes both direct and indirect foreign investment and that is used in most bilateral investment treaties and regional agreements such as the NAFTA, as compared with a narrow, enterprise-based definition that only comprises direct foreign investment. It has also been argued that, while for purposes of investment protection obligations a broad definition of investment might be appropriate, a narrow definition should be applied in connection with obligations pertaining to the entry of foreign investment. In addition, some Members have taken the view that the Working Group was established on the understanding that its work would be limited to foreign direct investment.

Many WTO Members view the increasing competition among countries to attract foreign direct investment through the granting of investment incentives as a major factor warranting the establishment of multilateral investment disciplines in the WTO. It has been suggested that, in analogy with WTO rules on subsidies, multilateral disciplines on investment incentives should strike a balance between the recognition of the domestic policy objectives served by incentives and the need to restrain their distorting effects. At the same time, the discussions in the Working Group have revealed rather strong differences of opinion on the costs and benefits of investment incentives and on the desirability and feasibility of multilateral rules in this area.

The concept of a balance of rights and obligations between host countries and home countries and between foreign investors and host country governments has been the subject of some debate in the Working Group. The Working Group has considered the OECD Guidelines for Multinational Enterprises, the draft United Nations Code of Conduct for Transnational Corporations and recent developments regarding voluntary corporate codes of conduct. A number of WTO Members have stressed the interrelationship between WTO work on foreign investment and WTO work on competition policy.

In the second half of 1999, the focus of discussions on investment in the WTO shifted from the Working Group on the Relationship between Trade and Investment to the WTO General Council's preparatory deliberations for the third WTO Ministerial Meeting (Seattle, 30 November to 3 December 1999). In the context of this preparatory process, Japan, the European Communities, Switzerland, Korea, Hong Kong China, Poland and Costa Rica submitted concrete proposals for the launching of WTO negotiations on investment in July and August 1999.[37] Many of these proposals reflected an attempt to take account of concerns that had been raised in the Working Group on the Relationship between Trade and Investment by Members opposed to multilateral investment negotiations. Thus, the multilateral framework envisaged in these proposals differed significantly from the MAI in several key areas.[38]

Specifically, the proposals submitted by Japan, the European Communities, Korea and Hong Kong China explicitly limited the scope of the proposed WTO negotiations on multilateral investment rules to foreign *direct* investment, as distinguished from the asset-based definition of the term investment that had been contemplated in the context of the MAI negotiations. The proposals suggested that the core elements of the envisaged multilateral framework should consist of rules concerning the transparency of relevant domestic laws and regulations and the non-discriminatory treatment of foreign investment. In the latter regard, it was proposed that the framework provide for a progressive, positive list approach in respect of the application of national treatment to the entry of foreign investment. The proposals by Japan and Korea included investment protection as a subject to be covered, but the submission by the European Communities stated that this matter required further reflection in light of the controversy generated by investment protection rules contained in some existing international agreements.[39] In this connection, the European Communities and Korea stressed the need for multilateral investment rules to preserve the ability of host governments to regulate the exercise of economic activity on their territories. Japan, Hong Kong China and Costa Rica also included performance requirements and investment incentives as subjects for negotiation but underlined the need to take into account the importance of such practices for development. Regarding dispute settlement procedures under future WTO rules on investment, the proposals suggested that the existing WTO Dispute Settlement Understanding be applied, in which connection Japan and Korea explicitly excluded the introduction of provisions enabling foreign investors to initiate arbitration proceedings against governments. All proposals stressed the need for the future multilateral framework on investment to provide for adequate flexibility to accommodate the special needs of develop-

---

37  See WTO Docs. WT/GC/W/239, 245, 263, 267, 268, 277 and 280.
38  The proposal submitted by Japan stated explicitly that "[a] future WTO agreement on investment rules needs to reflect the interests of all Members; thus, a clear distinction must be made between the forthcoming investment negotiations in the WTO and those carried out in other fora having a different membership." Agreement on Investment – Communication from Japan, WTO Doc. WT/GC/W/239 (6 July 1999).
39  Presumably this was a reference to proceedings pursuant to the investor-to-state arbitration provisions of the NAFTA in which foreign investors have challenged certain environmental regulations as a form of expropriation of foreign investment.

ing countries. Finally, a number of the proposals stressed the need to take into account existing WTO provisions in the negotiation of the envisaged multilateral framework.

In subsequent discussions prior to the Seattle Ministerial Meeting these proposals received support from a significant number of WTO Members but also encountered strong opposition. A number of developing-country Members, notably the Latin American countries, in principle agreed to the launching of investment negotiations in the WTO, subject to them being satisfied with the overall package of decisions at the Seattle Ministerial Meeting, and offered suggestions regarding particular elements of the mandate for such negotiations. Some other developing-country Members as a matter of principle remained opposed to the proposal to start investment negotiations in the WTO. There were also divergent views among the developed-country Members. In particular, the United States did not support the proposal for a decision to start investment negotiations at the Seattle Ministerial Meeting. It would appear that this position of the United States was due to a concern that investment was too controversial a subject to be part of a new round of negotiations, which it was hoped could be concluded within three years. In addition, the United States was critical of the suggestions to confine the negotiations to foreign direct investment and to use a positive list approach with regard to obligations concerning the admission of foreign investment. The position of the United States was probably also the result of a realization of the difficulty of accommodating in the WTO the concerns expressed by non-governmental organizations in the United States regarding the implications of multilateral investment rules for environmental and labour matters.

Discussions in October and November 1999 proceeded on the basis of draft texts of a Ministerial Declaration that contained two main options for a possible decision on investment at the Seattle Ministerial Meeting. One option set forth a draft decision to launch negotiations on investment and specified the mandate for such negotiations. The level of detail of this draft text[40] is explained

---

40 The text provided: "Taking into account the work already undertaken in the WTO Working Group on the Relationship between Trade and Investment, negotiations shall aim to establish a multilateral framework of rules on foreign direct investment, to further the aims of the WTO and to complement its rules, with the objectives of enhancing the contribution of international trade and investment as instruments of economic growth and development, and helping create a stable and predictable climate for the treatment of foreign direct investment world-wide. The framework should:
  · be based on WTO principles of non-discrimination, while accepting the right of host governments to regulate investors' activity in their respective territories;
  · ensure transparency, stability and predictability of domestic investment regimes and the dissemination of information in this respect;
  · address as an integral part of the framework the special needs of developing and least-developed country participants, recognizing the need to enhance the contribution of foreign direct investment to their development and economic growth;

by the fact that it was generally understood that agreement on the launch of investment negotiations would only be possible on the basis of a very carefully balanced definition of the scope, limits and guiding principles of such negotiations. An alternative text provided for the continuation of work of an analytical nature in the Working Group on the Relationship between Trade and Investment. During the Seattle Ministerial Meeting the possibility of a compromise was explored which would have provided for a detailed programme for further analytical work aimed at enabling WTO Members to decide at their next Ministerial Meeting whether or not to launch investment negotiations.[41] It is unclear whether WTO Members would have been able to reach consensus on the basis of this proposal.

At the time of writing (April 2000), there remains considerable uncertainty regarding the prospects for the launching of a new round of trade negotiations in the WTO in respect of subjects other than those covered by the WTO's built-in agenda. A widely held view among WTO Members and commentators is that agreement to launch such comprehensive negotiations is unlikely to be reached

---

· provide for negotiated, positive commitments by participants regarding access to investment opportunities in their territories through a progressive approach;
· address investment-distorting and trade-distorting policies and practices, both with respect to the conduct of investors and of host states, while respecting the ability of host governments to pursue their development objectives;
· take account of, and ensure consistency with, relevant WTO provisions related to investment; and
· provide for the applicability of the WTO disputes settlement mechanism to resolve disputes between governments. The framework shall not provide for international means for the settlement of disputes between investors and governments.
· Consideration shall be given to the possible need for provisions on the protection of investment and investors' responsibilities *vis-à-vis* the host country. Negotiations shall clarify the relationship between the envisaged rules and other relevant international rules and agreements on investment."

41  A non-paper dated 3 December 1999 prepared in consultations with a limited number of delegations provided: 'We agree to undertake further educational and analytical work on foreign direct investment (FDI), based on proposals by Members, and including consideration of:
 · the need to preserve the ability of host governments to regulate the activity of investors in their respective territories;
 · the transparency, stability and predictability of domestic investment regimes;
 · the positive list approach to access to investment opportunities in Members' territories;
 · dispute settlement provisions which exclude investor-state dispute resolution;
 · the specific needs of developing countries;
 · and the relationship between multilateral, plurilateral and bilateral rules and agreements on investment.
This work shall be purposeful and focused, and aim to assist all Members to prepare for, and adequately assess the possible outcomes and implications of, negotiations on this issue. A report on this work shall be presented to the Fourth Ministerial Conference, which shall decide whether specific guidance is needed for any negotiation to be launched at that time under the single undertaking." See 'New Green Room Draft on Trade and Investment', *Inside U.S. Trade*, 3 December 1999.

until 2001. The question of whether multilateral rules on investment should be part of the agenda of such negotiations will likely remain a very contentious issue in this regard. In addition to further discussion as to whether investment should be part of the agenda of a new round of negotiations, there are two other avenues for consideration of foreign investment issues in the WTO in the immediate future. First, the Working Group on the Relationship between Trade and Investment will continue its analytical work. The existence of this Working Group and its mandate are not affected by the outcome of the Seattle Ministerial Meeting. Second, as noted previously, existing WTO provisions relevant to investment contain a built-in agenda including further negotiations on progressive liberalization under the GATS and a review of the TRIMs Agreement, which review will include a consideration of whether that Agreement should be complemented with provisions on competition policy and investment policy. In connection with this built-in agenda, an interesting question is whether, in light of the outcome of the Seattle Ministerial Meeting, support will grow for the view that, instead of attempting to create a comprehensive set of investment rules in the WTO, future work on investment in the WTO should seek to expand and strengthen the investment-related provisions of the GATS and the TRIMs Agreement.[42]

5   CONCLUSION

The wide-ranging debate that has taken place in the WTO since 1995 on the relationship between trade and foreign investment has demonstrated that there remain divergent views on the question of whether foreign investment should be addressed more comprehensively in the WTO than is the case under current WTO rules through the creation of a multilateral framework. Although the timing of this debate was probably influenced by the launching of the negotiations on the MAI, it should be emphasized that the view that the WTO would simply be a conduit for the multilateralization of the MAI has been proved to be ill founded. Rather, the recent discussions in the WTO have shown that negotiations on the establishment of multilateral investment rules in the WTO will only be possible if a genuine consensus can be achieved among WTO Members regarding the rationale, objectives and subject matter of such rules. Given the complexity and sensitivity of the subject, the fact that such a consensus has not yet materialized is perhaps less remarkable than the fact that a substantial number of WTO Members at different levels of economic development have expressed support for such negotiations.

---

42   See, e.g., 'USCIB Calls for WTO Rules on Investment on a Limited Basis', 17 *Inside U.S. Trade* (1999), no. 40, and P. Sauvé and C. Wilkie, *Exploring Approaches to Investment Liberalization in the GATS*, Paper prepared for a conference on 'Services 2000 – New Dimensions In Services Trade Liberalization', University Club, Washington, D.C., 1-2 June 1999.

In comparison with previous discussions on foreign investment in multilateral fora, including in the GATT before and during the Uruguay Round negotiations, the diversity of views expressed in the recent work on trade and investment in the WTO suggests that the division between developed and developing countries has become less pronounced. For some developing countries, the concept of multilateral rules on investment in the WTO is not objectionable as a matter of principle and is seen as preferable to existing bilateral and regional agreements on investment because of the potential discriminatory and investment-distorting effects of such agreements. In contrast, for other developing countries there remains an important distinction between bilateral and regional agreements, which they believe provide them with greater flexibility to pursue their development objectives, and a possible multilateral framework on investment in the WTO, which is seen as detrimental to their ability to define the terms and conditions for allowing entry to foreign investment.

Similarly, among the developed countries, disagreement on the inclusion of multilateral investment rules as a subject for a new round of trade negotiations exists in particular between the United States, on the one hand, and the European Communities and Japan, on the other. Canada was an active proponent of the initiation of discussions on trade and investment in the WTO in 1995-1996 but has recently become more cautious in the wake of the collapse of the MAI negotiations.

The possibility of reaching a consensus on the launching of investment negotiations in the WTO will obviously depend upon political considerations relating to other aspects of the WTO's work programme. For example, it is clear that many developing countries remain sceptical regarding the launching of negotiations on new subjects, especially in the absence of a satisfactory solution to the problems they face regarding the implementation of certain WTO agreements. It should be acknowledged, however, that for many WTO Members the issue of investment negotiations in the WTO raises basic substantive and political concerns that cannot be accommodated through trade-offs with other issue areas. In this regard, it remains to be seen whether the proposals submitted in 1999 by the European Communities, Japan, Korea, Hong Kong China and several other WTO Members can eventually provide a viable basis for a compromise among WTO Members on a mandate for negotiations on investment rules. Such a compromise would need to accommodate the concerns raised by a number of developing-country Members with respect to the costs and benefits of multilateral investment rules from a developmental perspective, while at the same time meeting the concerns of the United States regarding the substantive quality of such rules. Another important question is whether and how it will be possible to address certain concerns that have come to the fore in some developed countries in respect of the implications of multilateral investment rules. Thus, any negotiations on investment rules in the WTO will need to be sensitive to the mounting public concern that international agreements on trade and investment place undue emphasis on the protection of private interests as compared to broader public interests. While there is likely to be wide support among WTO Members for the idea that multilateral investment rules should not undermine the capacity of governments to regulate the exercise of economic activity to attain public policy objectives, including for example social and environmental objectives, attempts to incorporate into WTO rules on investment provisions that would commit Members to the observance of certain standards in areas like labour and environmental policies are bound to encounter strong resistance from developing countries.

More specifically, it is obvious that a number of themes require further reflection in respect of the rationale for, and subject matter of, possible negotiations in the WTO on multilateral investment rules. Foremost is the need to demonstrate the benefits to be derived for the collective Membership of the WTO from the incorporation of multilateral investment rules into the WTO in terms of how such rules would contribute to enhancing the trade opportunities of WTO Members and to improving the functioning of the multilateral trading system. This requires a further elaboration of the contribution that multilateral investment rules in the WTO would make towards helping to exploit the positive synergy between trade and investment and between open trade policies and open investment policies.[43]

With respect to the subject matter of possible multilateral rules on foreign investment in the WTO an important lesson learnt from recent international investment negotiations and from the debate in the WTO is that a WTO multilateral framework of rules on investment cannot simply be conceived as a consolidation of provisions typically contained in regional and bilateral investment agreements. For example, the negotiations on the MAI have shown that the attempt to apply traditional investment protection standards to the mutual relations between developed countries has encountered unexpected difficulties. These negotiations have tended to highlight certain differences between the practices of individual developed countries regarding the investment protection standards contained in their bilateral investment treaties with developing countries. Moreover, the experience with the MAI also suggests that the legitimacy of traditional investment protection rules has become subject to serious questioning by a part of public opinion in the developed countries as the broad scope of these investment protection rules has engendered controversy with regard to their implications for the ability of governments to regulate economic activity in their territories in the pursuit of non-economic objectives. A prominent example is the debate on the scope of rules on expropriation and equivalent measures.

---

43  See R. Eglin, 'Making the Case for Multilateral Rules on Foreign Investment', Paper presented at a Pre-UNCTAD X Seminar, 11-12 January 2000.

Finally, a number of more specific themes have been raised but not yet sufficiently explored in the recent discussions in the WTO on foreign investment. These include:

a) the desired scope of the definition of the term investment;
b) the nature of possible disciplines with respect to the entry of foreign investment;
c) the possible need for, and nature of, provisions on investment incentives and performance requirements;
d) provisions to ensure transparency and predictability of domestic laws and regulations relevant to foreign investment;
e) the development dimension of multilateral investment rules; and
f) the possible relationship of such rules to international instruments that contain norms for corporate conduct.[44]

Questions also remain to be addressed regarding the relationship of future multilateral investment rules in the WTO to existing WTO provisions relevant to foreign investment and to other international agreements on investment concluded outside the WTO framework.

---

44 In regard to many of these themes, future work in the WTO is likely to benefit from the analytical work carried out by other international organizations, notably UNCTAD. E.g., as part of its work programme on international investment agreements, UNCTAD recently published a new series of papers on key concepts and issues in international investment agreements. In January 2000, such papers had been published or were in the process of being published on the following subjects: foreign direct investment and development; scope and definition; admission and establishment; investment-related trade measures; most-favoured-nation treatment; transfer pricing; national treatment; fair and equitable treatment; trends in international investment agreements; lessons from the MAI; taking of property; flexibility in international investment agreements; taxation; employment; host country operational measures; and environment.

# Appendix

## The Multilateral Agreement on Investment
## The MAI Negotiating Text (excerpts)[1]
## (as of 24 April 1998)

This document consolidates the text of the agreement considered in the course of the MAI negotiations so far. The texts reproduced here result mainly from the work of expert groups and have not yet been adopted by the MAI Negotiating Group. They are presented with footnotes and proposals that are still under consideration. The final text will be accompanied by country specific exceptions which will form an integral part of the agreement. The Commentary to this text will be issued separately.

DIRECTORATE FOR FINANCIAL, FISCAL AND ENTERPRISE AFFAIRS

TABLE OF CONTENTS

| | |
|---|---|
| I. GENERAL PROVISIONS | 7 |
| *Preamble* | 7 |
| II. SCOPE AND APPLICATION | 11 |
| *Definitions* | 11 |
| Geographical Scope of Application | 12 |
| Application to Overseas Territories | 12 |
| III. TREATMENT OF INVESTORS AND INVESTMENTS | 13 |
| National Treatment and Most Favoured Nation Treatment | 13 |
| Transparency | 13 |
| Temporary entry, stay and work of Investors and Key Personnel | 14 |
| Nationality Requirements for Executives, Managers and Members of Boards of Directors | 16 |
| Employment Requirements | 17 |
| *Performance Requirements* | 18 |
| Privatisation | 27 |
| Monopolies/State Enterprises/Concessions | 31 |
| Entities with Delegated Governmental Authority | 45 |
| Investment Incentives | 46 |
| Recognition Arrangements | 49 |
| Authorisation Procedures | 49 |
| Membership of Self-Regulatory Bodies | 49 |
| Intellectual Property | 50 |
| Public Debt | 53 |
| Corporate Practices | 53 |
| Technology R&D | 53 |

---

1 (Sub-)headings in italics are (partly) reproduced in this Appendix. Copyright OECD, 1998. Document available at http://www.oecd.org/daf/investment/fdi/mai/maitext.pdf

Not Lowering Standards ... 54
Additional Clause on Labour and Environment ... 55

IV. INVESTMENT PROTECTION ... 57
General Treatment ... 57
Expropriation and Compensation ... 57
Protection from Strife ... 58
Transfers ... 59
Information Transfer and Data Processing ... 61
Subrogation ... 61
Protecting Existing Investments ... 62

*V. DISPUTE SETTLEMENT* ... 63
*State-State Procedures* ... 63
*Investor-State Procedures* ... 70

*VI. EXCEPTIONS AND SAFEGUARDS* ... 77
*General Exceptions* ... 77
*Transactions in Pursuit of Monetary and Exchange Rate Policies* ... 78
*Temporary Safeguard* ... 79

VII. FINANCIAL SERVICES ... 81
Prudential Measures ... 81
Recognition Arrangements ... 81
Authorisation Procedures ... 82
Transparency ... 82
Information Transfer and Data Processing ... 83
Membership of Self-regulatory Bodies and Associations ... 83
Payments and Clearing Systems/Lender of Last Resort ... 84
Dispute Settlement ... 84
Definition of Financial Services ... 85

VIII. TAXATION ... 87
IX. COUNTRY SPECIFIC EXCEPTIONS ... 90
Lodging of Country Specific Exceptions ... 90

X. RELATIONSHIP TO OTHER INTERNATIONAL AGREEMENTS ... 96
Obligations under the Articles of Agreement of the International Monetary Fund ... 96
The OECD Guidelines for Multinational Enterprises ... 96

XI. IMPLEMENTATION AND OPERATION ... 98
The Preparatory Group ... 98
The Parties Group ... 100

XII. FINAL PROVISIONS ... 102
Signature ... 102
Acceptance and Entry Into Force ... 102
Accession ... 103
Non-Applicability ... 103
Review ... 103
Amendment ... 104
Revisions to the OECD Guidelines for Multinational Enterprises ... 104

| | |
|---|---|
| Withdrawal | 105 |
| Depositary | 105 |
| Status of Annexes | 105 |
| Authentic Texts | 105 |
| Denial of Benefits | 106 |

ANNEX 1
COUNTRY SPECIFIC PROPOSALS FOR DRAFT TEXTS

| | |
|---|---|
| Scope | 108 |
| Geographical Scope | 109 |
| Application to Overseas Territories and Non-applicability | 111 |
| Scope of Application | 112 |
| Government Procurement of Services | 115 |
| Substantive Approach to the Respect Clause | 116 |
| Respect Clause | 117 |
| Regional Economic Integration Organisations | 118 |
| Regional Economic Integration Organisations | 119 |
| Additional Environmental Proposals | 120 |
| Conflicting Requirements | 122 |
| Secondary Investment Boycotts | 126 |
| Culture | 128 |
| Subnational measures | 129 |
| The Svalbard Treaty | 130 |
| Labour Market Integration Agreements | 131 |
| Sami People | 133 |
| Dispute Settlement | 134 |
| Dispute Settlement | 135 |
| Dispute Settlement: Response to Non-compliance | 136 |
| Maintaining the Overall Level of Liberalisation | 138 |

ANNEX 2
CHAIRMAN'S PROPOSALS ON ENVIRONMENT AND RELATED
MATTERS AND ON LABOUR                                            140

## I. GENERAL PROVISIONS

*PREAMBLE*

The Contracting Parties to this Agreement,[1] [2] [3]

Desiring to strengthen their ties of friendship and to promote greater economic co-operation between them;

Considering that international investment has assumed great importance in the world economy and has considerably contributed to the development of their countries;

Recognising that agreement upon the treatment to be accorded to investors and their investments will contribute to the efficient utilisation of economic resources, the creation of employment opportunities and the improvement of living standards;

Emphasising that fair, transparent and predictable investment regimes complement and benefit the world trading system;[4]

[Wishing that this Agreement enhances international co-operation with respect to investment and the development of world-wide rules on foreign direct investment in the framework of the world trading system as embodied in the World Trade Organization;][5]

Wishing to establish a broad multilateral framework for international investment with high standards for the liberalisation of investment regimes and investment protection and with effective dispute settlement procedures;

[Recognising that investment, as an engine of economic growth, can play a key role in ensuring that economic growth is sustainable, when accompanied by appropriate environmental policies to ensure it takes place in an environmentally sound manner]

---

1 One delegation, with the support of another delegation, proposes that the Preamble include the following language on natural resources: "Reaffirming the sovereignty and overeign rights of States over natural resources within the limits of national jurisdiction".

2 Three delegations continue to oppose any reference to labour in the Preamble. One delegation is willing to consider preambular language on the environment as part of the entire package on labour and environment. Another delegation also opposes any reference to the environment unless its concerns are met.

3 It is the strong feeling of many delegations that preambular reference to the environment be limited to one paragraph and that it be as short as possible. Similarly, it was the feeling of many delegations that preambular reference to labour be limited to one paragraph and that it be as short as possible.

4 Some delegations propose an explicit reference to the World Trade Organisation. One delegation proposes the addition immediately after the words "world trading system" of: "encompassing multilateral and bilateral investment instruments as well as agreements of the World Trade Organisation". This proposal would need some refinement to ensure that it does not limit the scope of the phrase "world trading system" by excluding, for example, regional agreements.

5 One delegation proposes this language. Some delegations oppose the inclusion of such language because they believe that it would prejudge, and be prejudicial to, future work on investment in the World Trade Organisation.

*Appendix*

[Recognising that appropriate environmental policies can play a key role in ensuring that economic development, to which investment contributes, is sustainable,[6] and resolving to desiring to[7] implement this agreement in accordance with international environmental law and[8] in a manner consistent with sustainable development, as reflected in the Rio Declaration on Environment and Development and Agenda 21, [including the protection and preservation of the environment and principles of the polluter pays and the precautionary approach];[9] [10] [11] [12]

---

6   There is about even support for each "recognising" formulation.
7   Four delegations object to "resolving to" and would prefer "desiring to".
8   This phrase raises the questions whether the MAI intends to set a presumption that multilateral environmental agreements have precedence and over it, and, if so, whether a preambular reference establishes that presumption. One delegation is strongly opposed to the inclusion of this phrase because it is impossible to define precisely.
9   While a majority favour explicit mention of these two principles, a number of delegations prefer a more general reference to Rio Declaration and Agenda 21 principles without specifics. One delegation would explicitly mention two additional principles: "public participation and the right of communities to have access to information, and the avoidance of relocation and transfer of activities causing severe environmental degradation or found to be harmful to human health".
10  One delegation proposes additional language: "and recognising that such environmental policies shall not constitute a means of disguised restriction on international trade and investment;". Some delegations support this proposal in concept but wonder if it belonged in the Preamble or in a more general anti-abuse clause in the MAI.
11  One delegation, supported by another delegation, would insert four additional tirets from its alternative for the Preamble:
    Convinced of the need for optimal use of the world's resources in accordance with the objective of sustainable development;
    Recognising that investment can result in changes in the scale and structure of economic activity within countries, with potential effects on health and the environment;
    Recognising the interdependent nature of their environments;
    Encouraging the protection, conservation, preservation and enhancement of the environment;
12  One delegation believes that the proposal for two paragraphs of preambular language on the environment as set out in the report by DG3 reflected broadly shared ideas of substance and was prepared to continue work on the basis of that text. Bracketed text in that proposal related primarily to nuance. The paragraph now contained in the text has lost or weakened at least two concepts that had been broadly shared by the group. This delegation would like to know why a number of delegations appear to find it a preferred basis on which to continue work. The two key concepts that have been lost and the substance of this elegation's concern are set out below:
    1. The commitment (or desire) of Parties to implement the agreement in a manner consistent with environmental protection and conservation has been omitted. In the current text this idea is expressed only as a subsidiary notion to the Rio declaration when in fact environmental protection and conservation should be a generally affirmed principle that is not limited to the provisions of Rio.
    2. A clear statement of reaffirmation of commitment to the Rio Declaration, writ large, is not clearly made. In the current text, parties resolve to implement the agreement in a manner consistent only with specific ideals (sustainable development and/or international environmental law) as reflected in the Rio Declaration; they do not reaffirm a commitment to the Rio Declaration as a whole. Furthermore, the new text adds the idea of implementing the agreement in accordance with the specified concepts of Rio; this is an idea that has not been explicitly discussed by the group.

Renewing their commitment to the Copenhagen Declaration of the World Summit on Social Development[13] and to observance of internationally recognised core labour standards, i.e. freedom of association, the right to organise and bargain collectively, prohibition of forced labour, the elimination of exploitative forms of child labour, and non-discrimination in employment, and noting that the International Labour Organisation is the competent body to set and deal with core labour standards world-wide.[14] [15]

Affirming their decision to create a free-standing Agreement open to accession by all countries;[16]

[Noting] [Affirming their support for] the OECD Guidelines for Multinational Enterprises and emphasising that implementation of the Guidelines, which are non-binding and which are observed on a voluntary basis, will promote mutual confidence between enterprises and host countries and contribute to a favourable climate for investment;[17]

---

Therefore, based on the report by DG3, and in addition to the position set out in footnote 8 above, the proposal of this delegation is:
Resolving to implement this agreement in a manner consistent with environmental protection and conservation;
Reaffirming their commitment to the RIO Declaration on Environment and Development and Agenda 21, including to sustainable development as reflected therein, and recognising that investment, as an engine of economic growth, can play a key role in ensuring that growth is sustainable, when accompanied by appropriate environmental policies to ensure it takes place in an environmental sound manner;
Noting that the Rio Declaration principles of relevance to investment include, *inter alia*, the polluter pays, the precautionary approach, public participation and the right of communities to have access to information, and the avoidance of relocation and transfer of activities causing severe environmental degradation or found to be harmful to human health;

13 A number of delegations maintain a scrutiny reserve to consider whether there should also be explicitmention of the Singapore WTO Ministerial.
14 One delegation could not support a reference to labour in the preamble if it included explicit statement of basic principles of core labour standards.
15 One delegations would insert three additional tirets from its alternative for the Preamble:
Recognising that development of economic and business ties can promote respect for core labour standards;
Resolved to foster investment with due regard for the importance of labour laws and core labour standards;
Noting that, as members of the International Labour Organisation, they have endorsed the Tripartite Declaration of Principles concerning Multilateral Enterprises and Social Policy, and agreeing to renew their support for that voluntary instrument.
16 Some delegations propose that the statement that the Agreement is open to accession by all countries be strengthened.
17 One delegation proposes that the Preamble state that the Guidelines include, in particular, recommendations on employment and industrial relations and environmental protection; other delegations are of the view that the text introducing the Guidelines as an annex should specify the eight subject areas, including those just mentioned, on which the Guidelines make recommendations (see Section III below). In addition, one delegation would like to add words to the effect that the Contracting Parties consider the Guidelines to be "a valuable part of the framework for the consideration of issues of investment and multilateral enterprises."

*Appendix*

HAVE AGREED AS FOLLOWS:

II. SCOPE AND APPLICATION
*DEFINITIONS*

*1. Investor means:*
(i) a natural person having the nationality of, or who is permanently residing in, a Contracting Party in accordance with its applicable law; or
(ii) a legal person or any other entity constituted or organised under the applicable law of a Contracting Party, whether or not for profit, and whether private or government owned or controlled, and includes a corporation, trust, partnership, sole proprietorship, joint venture, association or organisation.

*2. Investment means:*
Every kind of asset owned or controlled, directly or indirectly, by an investor, including:[18] [19]
(i) an enterprise (being a legal person or any other entity constituted or organised under the applicable law of the Contracting Party, whether or not for profit, and whether private or government owned or controlled, and includes a corporation, trust, partnership, sole proprietorship, branch, joint venture, association or organisation);
(ii) shares, stocks or other forms of equity participation in an enterprise, and rights derived therefrom;
(iii) bonds, debentures, loans and other forms of debt, and rights derived therefrom;
(iv) rights under contracts, including turnkey, construction, management, production or revenue-sharing contracts;
(v) claims to money and claims to performance;
(vi) intellectual property rights;
(vii) rights conferred pursuant to law or contract such as concessions, licenses, authorisations, and permits;
(viii) any other tangible and intangible, movable and immovable property, and any related property rights, such as leases, mortgages, liens and pledges.

(...)

---

18   The Negotiating Group agrees that this broad definition of investment calls for further work on appropriate safeguard provisions. In addition, the following issues require further work to determine their appropriate treatment in the MAI: indirect investment, intellectual property, concessions, public debt and real estate.
19   For greater certainty, an interpretative note will be required to indicate that, in order to qualify as an investment under the MAI, an asset must have the characteristics of an investment, such as the commitment of capital or other resources, the expectation of gain or profit, or the assumption of risk.

## III. TREATMENT OF INVESTORS AND INVESTMENTS
*NATIONAL TREATMENT AND MOST FAVOURED NATION TREATMENT*

1. Each Contracting Party shall accord to investors of another Contracting Party and to their investments, treatment no less favourable than the treatment it accords [in like circumstances] to its own investors and their investments with respect to the establishment, acquisition, expansion, operation, management, maintenance, use, enjoyment and sale or other disposition of investments.

2. Each Contracting Party shall accord to investors of another Contracting Party and to their investments, treatment no less favourable than the treatment it accords [in like circumstances] to investors of any other Contracting Party or of a non-Contracting Party, and to the investments of investors of any other Contracting Party or of a non-Contracting Party, with respect to the establishment, acquisition, expansion, operation, management, maintenance, use, enjoyment, and sale or other disposition of investments.

3. Each Contracting Party shall accord to investors of another Contracting Party and to their investments the better of the treatment required by Articles 1.1 and 1.2, whichever is the more favourable to those investors or investments.

*TRANSPARENCY*

1. Each Contracting Party shall promptly publish, or otherwise make publicly available, its laws, regulations, procedures and administrative rulings and judicial decisions of general application as well as international agreements which may affect the operation of the Agreement. Where a Contracting Party establishes policies which are not expressed in laws or regulations or by other means listed in this paragraph but which may affect the operation of the Agreement, that Contracting Party shall promptly publish them or otherwise make them publicly available.[20]

2. Each Contracting Party shall promptly respond to specific questions and provide, upon request, information to other Contracting Parties on matters referred to in Article 2.1.

3. Nothing in this Agreement shall prevent a Contracting Party from requiring an investor of another Contracting Party, or its investment, to provide routine information concerning that investment solely for information or statistical purposes. Nothing in this Agreement requires a Contracting Party to furnish or allow access to:
a) information related to the financial affairs and accounts of individual customers of particular investors or investments, or
b) any confidential or proprietary information, including information concerning particular investors or investments, the disclosure of which would impede law enforce-

---

20 The Chairman of the Negotiating Group proposes to keep this sentence without brackets, noting that several delegations could go along with this proposal provided that there was a satisfactory explanatory statement in the commentary.

*Appendix* 213

ment or be contrary to its laws[21] protecting confidentiality or prejudice legitimate commercial interests of particular enterprises.

(...)

PERFORMANCE REQUIREMENTS[22] [23]
1. A Contracting Party shall not, in connection with the establishment, acquisition, expansion, management, operation, maintenance, use, enjoyment, sale or other dis-

---

21  Two delegations propose to insert after "laws", the terms "policies, or practices". One delegation can only support the proposed text for paragraph 3 of the Transparency article if these terms are inserted.
22  One delegation reserves its position on all obligations on performance requirements that go beyond those in the TRIMs Agreement and the Energy Charter Treaty. Another delegation maintains a reserve on the prohibition of requirements listed in paragraph 1(a) through (e), when linked to an advantage. Another delegation maintains a reserve on the scope of the article. One delegation reserves its position on the scope of paragraphs 3 to 5 of this article.
23  At the February 1998 consultations, One delegation proposed the following interpretative note to paragraph 1 of the Performance Requirements article as a possible solution to the concerns raised in footnotes 26,27, 29-32 and 37-39. This interpretative note could do away with the need for paragraphs 4 and 5(c) (both alternatives) and lead to the deletion of footnotes 26, 29-32 and 37-39. This proposal reads:
"The Contracting Parties agree that the Performance Requirements Article relates to requirements, undertakings and commitments which are directly imposed on or made by investors and/or their investments in connection with the investment. It does not intend to cover provisions applicable as the general law of the land governing in particular customs, trade or environment matters such as duties (including anti-dumping duties, preferential rates, origin rules) quantitative restrictions, safeguard measures, trade sanctions, measures necessary to protect human, animal or plant life or health or the conservation of living or non-living exhaustible natural resources.
The Article is without prejudice to the rights and obligations of Contracting Parties under the WTO rules".
Delegations agree to consider this proposal further. Some delegations expressed concern that use of the terms "in particular" and "such as" could result in an uncertain and overbroad carve out, which would undermine the article's coverage, perhaps even exempting any law of general application. Several delegations state their preference for recording this understanding in the form of an interpretative note rather than in a separate article since, in their view, an interpretative note would be more enlightening for arbitrators about the real intentions of negotiators. It would be very difficult, on the other hand, to draft an article that would translate faithfully this intention into legal text. A number of delegations wonder whether "environment matters" and *"measures necessary to protect human, animal or plant life or health or the conservation of living or non-living exhaustible natural resources"* should be covered by this note. This also relates to how these subjects would be treated elsewhere under the MAI (see also footnote 29). Some delegations propose the deletion of the phrase "intend to" at the beginning of the second sentence of this delegation's text to give greater precision to the proposed interpretative note.
One delegation restates its position that the Performance Requirements article should not apply to conditions imposed on an investment which are linked to cross-border trade (such as refunds, preferential rates, rules of origin, and anti-dumping duties). This could be made it clear in a separate indent to paragraph 2 (see footnote 27).

position[24] of an investment in its territory of an investor of a Contracting Party or of a non-Contracting Party, impose, enforce or maintain[25] any of the following requirements, or enforce any commitment or undertaking:[26]

(a) to export a given level or percentage of goods or services;
(b) to achieve a given level or percentage of domestic content;
(c) to purchase, use or accord a preference to goods produced or services[27] provided in its territory, or to purchase goods or services from persons in its territory;

---

24 A large majority of delegations consider that the enumeration of activities in the chapeau should closely follow the list of activities in the National Treatment/MFN articles to avoid any confusion over the meaning of any differences in the lists. They consider furthermore that there are no substantive grounds for the deletion of the terms "maintenance, use, enjoyment" since the implications for intellectual property rights are taken care of by the proposed carve-out in paragraph 1(f) and the consequences of keeping them as regards land assets are immaterial. It is noted that these are also arguments for not mentioning these terms in the chapeau. One delegation favours the deletion of these terms. Two delegations question the relevancy of the terms "sale or other disposition".

25 One delegation reserves its position on the inclusion of the word "maintain". This delegation suggests that the use of this word could oblige Contracting Parties to undertake the burdensome task of having to expunge all possible non-conforming requirements from existing laws, regulations, contracts, etc. It should be sufficient, and less burdensome, for a Contracting Party to be obliged not to "impose" and "enforce" such requirements.

26 One delegation presented an explanatory note on the formulation of NAFTA article 1106 which, in its view, is significantly clearer than the proposed MAI article on Performance Requirements. In order to improve on the MAI articles, this delegation proposes that the following phrase be added at the end of the chapeau of this paragraph: "or condition the receipt or continued receipt of an advantage on compliance with any of the following requirements". This addition is intended to make clear that the performance requirements article applies in two basic circumstances: *i)* when linked to the establishment, expansion, etc. of an investment; and *ii)* when linked to the granting of an advantage.

According to this delegation, unless expressly stated (as proposed) in paragraph 1, there may always be some uncertainty as to whether the article would apply in cases of granting an advantage. This delegation considers this addition necessary to provide greater certainty. As was the intention in the development of a "one list" approach in the MAI article, the proposed addition would, in the second case (linked to an advantage), limit prohibitions to "requirements" imposed by governments. Extending the prohibitions to only certain (but not all) "commitments and undertakings" would, according to this delegation, unduly interfere with government practices regarding "voluntary" commitments in exchange for an advantage and could result in a significant burden on Contracting Parties on lodging reservations for government-firm agreements containing "prohibited" voluntary undertakings.

The other delegations feel, however, that there is no need to modify the structure of the Article.

27 It is understood that item (c) is not meant to cover the provision of cross-border services as defined under the GATS. It is felt that this understanding could be recorded by using the following language: *"This provision does not obligate a Contracting Party to permit cross-border trade in services beyond the obligations it has undertaken pursuant to GATS."* This understanding could also be part of a general provision in the Agreement concerning the relationship between the MAI and the GATS. One delegation reserves its position on the inclusion of "services" in 1(c) with respect to requirements associated with the granting of an advantage. It is noted that the relationship between the MAI and the GATS is an issue that could be addressed in a number of ways, including by way of individual footnotes.

(d) to relate in any way the volume or value of imports to the volume or value of exports or to the amount of foreign exchange inflows associated with such investment;
(e) to restrict sales of goods or services in its territory that such investment produces or provides by relating such sales to the volume or value of its exports or foreign exchange earnings;
(f) to transfer technology, a production process or other proprietary knowledge to a natural or legal person in its territory, except when the requirement
– is imposed or the commitment or undertaking is enforced by a court, administrative tribunal or competition authority to remedy an alleged violation of competition laws, or
– concerns the transfer of intellectual property and is undertaken in a manner not inconsistent with the TRIPS Agreement;[28]
(g) to locate its headquarters for a specific region or the world market in the territory of that Contracting Party;[29]
(h) to supply one or more of the goods that it produces or the services that it provides to a specific region or the world market exclusively from the territory of that Contracting Party;
(i) to achieve a given level or value of research and development in its territory;[30]
(j) to hire a given level of nationals;[31]

---

28  The wording of this tiret is being elaborated in consultations with intellectual property experts. These experts have not agreed whether the current wording covers future IPRs and moral rights. It remains to be seen how the article will relate to other agreements such as the Rome and Berne Conventions. Paragraphs 1(b) and 1(c) may also have implications for IPRs. Some delegations note that a general provision for interpreting MAI obligations in a manner consistent with other obligations under international agreements would avoid the need for specific language for IPRs. It is understood that the concept of "proprietary knowledge" has a broader coverage than that of "trade secrets" or "undisclosed information" (see TRIPS Article 39) and can include information collected by an investor from publicly available sources by "the sweat of the brow".
29  One delegation reserves its position on paragraph (g) and notes that the inclusion of (g) may inadvertently oblige Contracting Parties to lodge reservations in respect of basic business incorporation laws in so far as such laws oblige the establishment and/or maintenance of representative or head offices for legal purposes. It is noted that the prohibition is intended to apply to head offices or headquarters and not to the establishment of other offices.
30  Two delegations maintain a scrutiny reserve on this paragraph while two other delegations maintain the view that paragraph (i) should be deleted.
31  There is wide agreement to retain paragraph (j) with the inclusion of the following footnote with the same legal standing as the paragraph itself:
*"Nothing in this paragraph shall be construed as interfering with programmes targeted at disadvantaged regions/persons or other equally legitimate employment policy programmes. It is also understood that permanent residency requirements are not inconsistent with this paragraph."*
It is confirmed that this provision will not overlap with the MAI article on Employment Requirements since it is meant to cover specific performance requirements expressed in terms of given numbers or percentages of employees while the article on employment requirements addresses problems of discrimination among natural persons holding a valid permit of sejour and work in a given Contracting Party.
Two delegations continue to favour the deletion of paragraph (j).

(k) to establish a joint venture with domestic participation;[32] or
(l) to achieve a minimum level of domestic equity participation other than nominal qualifying shares for directors or incorporators of corporations.[33]

2. A Contracting Party is not precluded by paragraph 1 from conditioning the receipt or continued receipt of an advantage, in connection with an investment in its territory of a Contracting Party or of a non-Contracting Party, on compliance with any of the requirements, commitments or undertakings set forth in paragraphs 1(f) through 1(l).[34][35]

---

32  Paragraph (k) includes joint ventures even if not covered by paragraph 1(l) because they do not involve equity participation. It allows, however, joint venture requirements, not involving a requirement of domestic participation, which may be motivated by an economic concern to spread risk.
   Some delegations, maintain a scrutiny reserve on paragraph (k) and (l) on the basis that they are covered by the National Treatment provision of the MAI.
   Some delegations point out to the difficulty of defining "joint-ventures". It is agreed to clarify in an interpretative note that *"Paragraphs 1(k) and (l) do not prevent a Contracting Party from establishing a joint venture in which it is the domestic participant itself"*. One delegation points outs out it is most unlikely that the Contracting Party would be the participant in a joint venture and proposes the phrase *"a Contracting Party, a state agency or a state enterprise"*. It is also noted that Paragraph 2 of the Privatisation article states that "Nothing in this Agreement" shall be construed as imposing an obligation to privatise.
33  The phrase "other than nominal qualifying shares for directors or incorporators of corporations" clarifies that this performance requirement will not be breached merely because members of boards of directors and those who establish a corporation (incorporators) may be required by domestic law, as a condition of that position, to hold a small equity participation in the corporation.
34  It is understood that the receipt or continued receipt of an advantage with respect to paragraphs (k) and (l) will need to be granted on a non-discriminatory basis (provided that no country reservation has been lodged).
   Several delegations consider that the concerns that paragraph 5(abis) intends to cover in respect of rights and obligations under the WTO agreements would better be addressed by the reinsertion of paragraph 1(a) in paragraph 2. This would avoid, in particular, confusion and overlap with respect to the dispute settlement provision of the MAI and the WTO. In that regard, some delegations note, in particular, a concern that if the extent of paragraph 1(a)'s disciplines were defined, ?as proposed in one of the alternatives to paragraph, 5(a bis) (see footnote 34)?, by reference to WTO Disciplines, then if paragraph 1(a) were to become a subject of MAI dispute settlement, the MAI arbital panel would have to determine whether a WTO violation had occurred, which would be an inappropriate role for it to undertake. Two delegations would also support a reference to paragraphs 1(b) and 1(c) in paragraph 2 to exclude the coverage of advantages associated with services from paragraph 1. Some delegations view adding paragraphs 1(b) and 1(c) to paragraph 2 as an undesirable "TRIMs-minus" solution because TRIMs covers paragraphs 1(b) and 1(c) with respect to goods in all circumstances. Other delegations consider that the reinsertion of any of these items would result in too much of a carve-out from paragraph 1 because this carve-out would apply across the board to all sectors or economic activities and not limited to the exclusions allowed under the WTO provisions. They favour instead a solution in the context of paragraph 5(a bis).
   At the February 1998 consultations, a majority of delegations reiterated their preference for a solution along the more limited parameters of paragraph 5(a bis).

3. [ ][36]

4.[37] [Provided that such measures are not applied in an arbitrary or unjustifiable manner, or do not constitute a disguised restriction on investment, nothing in paragraphs 1(b) and 1(c) shall be construed to prevent any Contracting Party from adopting or maintaining measures, including environmental measures:

(a) necessary to secure compliance with laws and regulations that are not inconsistent with the provisions of this Agreement;

(b) necessary to protect human, animal or plant life or health;

(c) necessary for the conservation of living or non-living exhaustible natural resources.][38] [39]

---

35  In February 1998, one delegation considered that the concerns with respect to paragraphs 4 and 5 could better be addressed by the addition of a second indent to paragraph 2. This indent could read:
" Requirements or obligations expressed in laws, regulations and other government measures of a general application concerning conditions of, or incentives linked to, cross-border trade on goods or services are not covered by paragraph 1. "
This provision could also be relevant for the understanding recorded in footnote 19 about the coverage of paragraph 1(c). Several delegations reserved their judgement on this proposal. It was recognised, however, that it could provide a way to avoid a problematic overlap between the dispute settlement procedures of the MAI and WTO which has been associated with an earlier proposal outlined in footnote 35. On the other hand, this would still constitute a limitation to investor-to-state dispute settlement.

36  It is agreed to transform the previous paragraph 3 in the special topics report into an interpretative footnote to paragraph 1 with the same legal standing and which reads:
*"For the avoidance of doubt, nothing in paragraph 1(a), 1(b), 1(c), 1(d) and 1(e) shall be construed to prevent a Contracting Party from conditioning the receipt or continued receipt of an advantage, in connection with an investment in its territory of an investor of a Contracting Party or of a non-Contracting Party, on compliance with a requirement, commitment or undertaking to locate production, provide particular services, train or employ personnel, construct or expand particular facilities, or carry out research and development in its territory."*
One delegation notes that the question of the status of footnotes and interpretative notes for the MAI remains to be determined.

37  A majority of delegations see no need for paragraph 4. They consider that the proposed text is too broad, especially that of paragraph 4(a). Some delegations also wonder whether there is a need for an interpretative note. If there is such a need, a majority of delegations consider that it should be along the line proposed by one delegation which reads as follows:
"Provided that such measures are not applied in an arbitrary or unjustifiable manner, or do not constitute a disguised restriction on investment, nothing in paragraphs 1(b) and 1(c) shall be construed to prevent any Contracting Party from adopting or maintaining measures necessary to secure compliance with environmental laws and regulations [that are not otherwise inconsistent with the provisions of this Agreement and] that are necessary for the conservation of living or non-living resources, [or that are necessary to protect human, animal or plant life or health.]"
It is recognised that the Negotiating Group's general deliberations on environmental issues would provide guidance with regard to a solution regarding this paragraph. The retention of this paragraph may also depend on the final position of delegations concerning the proposals by two delegations outlined in footnotes 16 and 28 respectively.

38  One delegation would like the words "within its jurisdiction" to be added to paragraph 4(c) to make it clear that this provision has no extra-territorial ramifications.

5.[40] (a) Paragraphs 1(a), 1(b), and 1(c) do not apply to qualification requirements for goods or services with respect to export promotion[41] and foreign aid programmes; [(a *bis*) Paragraph 1(a), 1(b), and 1(c) do not apply to:[42]

---

39   One delegation believes that paragraph 4 is properly framed and that its scope should not be limited to environmental measures, which would be the consequence of another delegation's proposal. It suggests replacing the words "necessary for" by "relating to", which are used in article XX of GATT 1994. One delegation has withdrawn the example it provided in footnote 29 in the special topics report; the example did not describe a situation that would be disciplined by this article.
One delegation favours the retention of paragraph 4.
It is confirmed that no other general exceptions covered by Article XX of GATT 1994 would need to be covered by the proposed paragraph 4. The same confirmation is given with respect to Article XI of GATT 1994 on the General Elimination of Quantitative Restrictions.
40   Prior to the submission of its proposal in footnote 15, one delegation favoured the inclusion of the following header to paragraph 5: "Without prejudice to rights and obligations under the WTO" to ensure that the WTO obligations are not modified by the provision.
41   One delegation suggests adding the word "and investment" after the word "export". It also suggests clarifying by means of an interpretative note the meaning of "promotion" for the purposes of this article.
42   The obligations of the Performance Requirements article relate to requirements, undertakings and commitments that are directly imposed on or made by investors and their investments. In addition, they are not intended to discipline "advantages" as such. It is recognised that the performance requirements article raises questions about the relationship with the WTO Agreements, notably relating to agriculture, services and government procurement.
In this connection, it is agreed that the performance requirements article should not undo or undermine the Contracting Parties obligations under any WTO Agreements. It is also generally recognised that this article should not interfere with WTO rights and obligations in the agricultural sector. Some delegations consider in addition that the MAI should not attempt to discipline subsidies relating to services since this matter is presently being addressed in the WTO.
Paragraph 5(a bis) has been proposed as a way of addressing these concerns. Discussions on this proposal focused on: a) the need of specific reference to measures covered by WTO Agreements; b) the coverage of such a reference; and c) whether it could be a viable alternative to the inclusion of a reference of paragraph 1(a), and possibly paragraphs 1(b) and 1(c) in paragraph 2.
One delegation questions the need for subparagraph (5 abis) since the underlying problems could be addressed in country specific exceptions. One delegation questions the exclusion of the agriculture sector with respect to export performance requirements not linked to an advantage. It also wonders whether paragraph 5(a bis) would provide an exception for duty drawback programs outside the agriculture sector (e.g., chemicals).
Two delegations have proposed the following language as a possible alternative to paragraph 5(a bis):
"*Paragraphs 1(a), 1(b) and 1(c) do not apply to measures consistent with rights and obligations under the WTO Agreements.*" One delegation also proposes to limit the scope of this wording by adding the phrase "*if linked to an advantage*" at the end of this sentence.
While some delegations recognise that the proposals by these two delegations presented above could provide a technical solution, several delegations remain concerned about the reference to WTO disciplines which, as noted in footnote 27, could lead a MAI panel to pass judgement on WTO provisions. There is general agreement that a MAI panel should not be put in a situation of interpreting WTO disciplines. One delegation notes that under the safeguard provisions of the MAI, the IMF would be consulted in any MAI dispute settlement case involving a measure that the IMF approved or found to be consistent with the MAI.

– [measures] advantages related to the production, processing and trade of agricultural and processed agricultural products;[43]
– advantages related to trade[44] in services;]
b) Paragraphs 1(b), 1(c), 1(f), and 1(h) do not apply to procurement by a Contracting Party or an entity that is owned or controlled by a Contracting Party;[45]
[c) paragraphs 1(b) and 1(c) do not apply to requirements imposed by an importing Party relating to the content of goods necessary to qualify for preferential tariffs or preferential quotas.[46]]

---

This delegation suggests that a similar solution could be found in the dispute settlement provisions of the MAI where it could be stated that WTO provisions can only be interpreted by WTO.
The following examples were provided to focus discussion on which cases should or should not be covered by the Performance Requirements article, so that the article's exclusions (paragraph 2) and exceptions (paragraph 5) can be drafted appropriately.
1. A Contracting Party screens investments:
(a) In connection with the establishment of a widget manufacturing plant, a Contracting Party imposes a requirement that the investor export 100 percent of the widgets produced.
(b) Same as 1(a), but the investor receives an advantage: no customs duties are imposed on manufacturing equipment or materials.
2. A Contracting Party allows any investor to establish a widget manufacturing plant:
(a) Any widget manufacturer may operate in an "export processing zone" but if it does so, it is required to export 100 per cent of the widgets produced in the zone. No customs duties are imposed on manufacturing equipment or materials that enter the zone.
(b) Any widget manufacturer may operate in an "export processing zone". No customs duties are imposed on manufacturing equipment or materials that enter the zone. Customs duties are imposed on any products produced in the zone that are sold within a Contracting Party's territory.

43 A number of delegations would prefer the use of the more general term "measures" while other delegations would prefer the term "advantages" which is also used in the TRIMs Agreement. Two delegations question the need to extend the coverage of this indent to the production and processing of agricultural products and to processed agricultural products. One delegation proposes, on the other hand, that the indent also should be extended to apply to fisheries products including processed ones.
44 One delegation suggests that the second indent of subparagraph 5(a bis) should apply as well to advantages linked to the provision of services and proposes the insertion of the words "the provision and" before the word "trade".
45 It is agreed to add the following interpretative note:
"The Performance Requirements article does not affect any obligations that may exist under the WTO Government Procurement Agreement."
Two delegations consider that a reference to paragraph 1(i) may be needed if that paragraph is retained.
46 One delegation provided the following example to illustrate the need for subparagraph (c).
"A French manufacturer of textiles located in the US manufactures and cuts cloth for garments in the US, sends it to a country eligible for the special programme (e.g., Jamaica), to be assembled into finished garments, and then re-imports the garments into the US for retail sale. The tariff rate on the re-imported garments is lower than on garments from other countries. Without the subparagraph 5(c) exception, subparagraphs 1(b) and 1(c) would prevent the US from offering the special access programme, which is consistent with existing international obligations. Many MAI countries have similar programmes."

[c) Paragraphs 1(a), 1(b), 1(c) and 1(d) do not apply to customs duties, exemptions from such duties and preferential tariffs or to any trade measure regulating imports and exports provided that such measures are not applied in an arbitrary or unjustified manner, and do not constitute a disguised restriction on investment.[47]]

(...)

## V. DISPUTE SETTLEMENT[48]

*STATE-STATE PROCEDURES*
*A. GENERAL PROVISIONS*
1. The rules and procedures set out in Articles A-C shall apply to the avoidance of conflicts and the resolution of disputes between Contracting Parties regarding the interpretation or application of the Agreement unless the disputing parties agree to apply other rules or procedures. However, the disputing parties may not depart from any obligation regarding notification of the Parties Group and the right of Parties to present views, under Article B, paragraphs 1.a and 4.c, and Article C, paragraphs 1.a, 4, and 6.e.
2. Contracting Parties and other participants in proceedings shall protect any confidential or proprietary information which may be revealed in the course of proceedings under Articles B and C and which is designated as such by the Party providing the information. Contracting Parties and other participants in the proceedings may not reveal such information without written authorisation from the Party which provided it.
3. [EC or Contracting Party REIO text being developed for possible inclusion]

*B. CONSULTATION, CONCILIATION AND MEDIATION*

*1. Consultations*
a. One or more Contracting Parties may request any other Contracting Party to enter into consultations regarding any dispute between them about the interpretation or application of the Agreement. The request shall be submitted in writing and shall provide sufficient information to understand the basis for the request, including identification of any actions at issue. The requested Party shall enter into consultations within thirty days of receipt of the request. The requesting Contracting Party shall provide the Parties Group with a copy of the request for consultation, at the time it submits the request to the other Contracting Party.

---

Several other delegations believe that customs tariff issues fall outside the scope of this article and thus there is no need for the proposed general carve-out in subparagraph 5(c). There may also be a link with the issues raised with respect to paragraph (a).

47 As indicated in footnote 15, one delegation considers that the Performance Requirements article should not apply to the general law of the land governing customs and trade.

48 Note: It is understood that for a number of delegations further work is needed on dispute settlement. In particular, different options remain in the field of multilateral consultations and scope of dispute settlement. The present text has been prepared by the Chairman of the Expert Group on Dispute Settlement on the basis of the discussions in the Group. It is under consideration by the Negotiating Group.

b. A Contracting Party may not initiate arbitration against another Contracting Party under Article C of this Agreement unless the former Contracting Party has requested consultation and has afforded that other Contracting Party a consultation period of no less than 60 days after the date of the receipt of the request.

## 2. Multilateral Consultations

a. In the event that consultations under paragraph 1 of this Article have failed to resolve the dispute within 60 days after the date of receipt of the request for those consultations, the Contracting Parties in dispute may, by agreement, request the Parties Group to consider the matter.
b. Such request shall be submitted in writing and shall give the reason for it, including identification of any actions at issue, and shall indicate the legal basis for the complaint.
c. The Parties Group may make recommendations to the Contracting Parties in dispute. The Parties Group shall conclude its deliberations within 60 days after the date of receipt of the request

## 3. Mediation or Conciliation

If the Parties are unable to reach a mutually satisfactory resolution of a matter through consultations, they may have recourse to good offices or to mediation or conciliation under such rules and procedures as they may agree.

## 4. Confidentiality of Proceedings, Notification of Results

a. Proceedings involving consultations, mediation or conciliation shall be confidential.
b. No Contracting Party may, in any binding legal proceedings, invoke or rely upon any statement made or position taken by another Contracting Party in consultations, conciliation or mediation proceedings initiated under this Agreement, with the exception of factual representations.
c. The Parties to consultations, mediation, or conciliation under this Agreement shall inform the Parties Group of any mutually agreed solution.

## C. ARBITRATION

## 1. Scope and Initiation of Proceedings

a. Any dispute between Contracting Parties as to whether one of them has acted in contravention of this Agreement shall, at the request of any Contracting Party that is a party to the dispute and has complied with the consultations requirements of Article B, be submitted to an arbitral tribunal for decision. A request, identifying the matters in dispute, shall be delivered to the other Party through diplomatic channels, unless that Contracting Party has designated another channel for receipt of notification and so notified the Depositary, and a copy of the request shall be delivered to the Parties Group.
b. A Contracting Party may not initiate proceedings under this Article for a dispute which its investor has submitted, or consented to submit, to arbitration under Article D, unless the other Contracting Party has failed to abide by and comply with the award rendered in that dispute or those proceedings have terminated without resolution by an arbitral tribunal of the investor's claim.
c. If a dispute arises between Contracting Parties as to whether one of them has acted in contravention of a substantially similar obligation of that Contracting Party under

this Agreement and another agreement to which both are party, the complaining Contracting Party may submit it for decision under the agreement of its choice. In doing so, it waives its right to submit the matter for decision under the agreement not chosen.

*2. Formation of the Tribunal*
a. Within 30 days after receipt of a request for arbitration, the Parties to the dispute shall appoint by agreement three members of the tribunal and designate one of them as Chairman. Except for compelling reasons, the members shall be persons proposed by the Secretary General ICSID. At the option of either party or, where there is more than one Party on the same side of the dispute, either side, two additional members may be appointed, one by each party or side.
b. If the necessary appointments have not been made within the periods specified in subparagraph a, above, either Party or side to the dispute may, in the absence of any other agreement, invite the Secretary General of the Centre for the Settlement of Investment Disputes to make the necessary appointments. The Secretary-General shall do so, to the extent feasible, in consultations with the Parties to the dispute and within thirty days after receipt of the request.
c. Parties and the Secretary-General should consider appointment to the tribunal of members of the roster maintained pursuant to subparagraph f, below. If arbitration of a dispute is considered by either Contracting Party to the dispute or the Secretary-General to require special expertise on the tribunal, rather than solely through expert advice under the rules governing the arbitration, the appointment of individuals possessing expertise not found on the roster should be considered.
d. Members of a particular arbitral tribunal shall be independent and impartial.
e. Any vacancies which may arise in a tribunal shall be filled by the procedure by which the original appointment had been made.
f. The Parties Group shall maintain a roster of highly qualified individuals willing and able to serve on arbitral tribunals under this Agreement. Each Contracting Party may nominate up to four persons who shall be included as members of the roster. Nominations are valid for five year terms. At the end of a term, the Contracting Party which nominated a member may renew the nomination or nominate a new member of the roster. A member shall withdraw from the roster if no longer willing or able to serve and the Contracting Party which nominated that member may nominate another member for a full term.

*3. Consolidation*
a. Contracting Parties in dispute with the same Contracting Party over the same matter should act together as far as practicable for purposes of dispute settlement under this Article. Where more than one Contracting Party requests the submission to an arbitral tribunal of a dispute with the same Contracting Party relating to the same question, a single arbitral tribunal should be established to consider such disputes whenever feasible.
b. To the extent feasible, if more than one arbitral tribunal is formed, the same persons shall be appointed as members of both and the timetables of the proceedings shall be harmonised.

*4. Third Parties*
Any Contracting Party wishing to do so shall be given an opportunity to present its views orally or in writing to the arbitral tribunal on the issues of a legal nature in dispute. Such a Contracting Party shall be given access to the documents of the proceedings, other than confidential or proprietary information designated under Article A, paragraph 2. The tribunal shall establish the deadlines for such submissions in light of the schedule of the proceedings and shall notify such deadlines, at least thirty days in advance thereof, to the Parties Group.

*5. Scientific and Technical Expertise*
a. On request of a disputing Contracting Party or, unless the disputing Contracting Parties disapprove, on its own initiative, the tribunal may request a written report of a scientific or technical review board, or expert, on any factual issue concerning environmental, health, safety or other scientific or technical matters raised by a disputing Contracting Party in a proceeding, subject to such terms and conditions as such Parties may agree.
b. The board, or expert, shall be selected by the tribunal from among highly qualified, independent experts in the scientific or technical matters, after consultations with the disputing Parties and the scientific or technical bodies identified by those Parties.
c. The disputing Contracting Parties shall be provided:
i. advance notice of, and an opportunity to provide comments to the tribunal on the proposed factual issues to be referred to the board, or expert; and
ii. a copy of the board's, or expert's, report and an opportunity to provide comments on the report to the tribunal.
d. The tribunal shall take the report and any comments by the disputing Contracting Parties on the report into account in the preparation of its award.

*6. Proceedings and Awards*
a. The tribunal shall decide disputes in accordance with this Agreement, interpreted and applied in accordance with the applicable rules of international law.
b. The tribunal may, at the request of a Party, recommend provisional measures which either Party should take to avoid serious prejudice to the other pending its final award.
c. The tribunal, in its award, shall set out its findings of law and fact, together with the reasons therefore, and may, at the request of a Party, award the following forms of relief:
i. a declaration that an action of a Party is in contravention of its obligations under this Agreement;
ii. a recommendation that a Party bring its actions into conformity with its obligations under the Agreement;
iii. pecuniary compensation for any loss or damage to the requesting Party's investor or its investment; and
iv. any other form of relief to which the Party against whom the award is made consents, including restitution in kind to an investor.
d. The tribunal shall draft its award consistently with the requirement of confidentiality set out in Article A, paragraph 2. It shall issue its award in provisional form to the Parties to the dispute on a confidential basis, as a general rule within 180 days after the date of formation of the tribunal. The parties to the dispute may, within 30 days thereafter, submit written comment upon any portion of it. The tribunal shall consider

such submissions, may solicit additional written comments of the parties, and shall issue its final award within 15 days after closure of the comment period.

e. The tribunal shall promptly transmit a copy of its final award to the Parties Group, which shall make it publicly available.

f. Tribunal awards shall be final and binding between the parties to the dispute, subject to paragraph 7 below.

g. Each party shall pay the cost of its representation in the proceedings. The costs of the tribunal shall be paid for equally by the Parties unless the tribunal directs that they be shared differently. Fees and expenses payable to tribunal members will be subject to schedules established by the Parties Group and in force at the time of the constitution of the tribunal.

*7. Nullification*

a. Either party to the dispute may request the annulment of an award, in whole or in part, on one or more of the following grounds, that:

i. the Tribunal was not properly constituted;

ii. the Tribunal has manifestly exceeded its powers;

iii. there was corruption on the part of a member of the Tribunal or on the part of a person providing decisive expertise or evidence;

iv. there has been a serious departure from a fundamental rule of procedure; or

v. the award has failed to state the reasons on which it is based.

b. The request shall be submitted for decision by a tribunal which shall be constituted and operate under the rules applicable to a dispute submitted under paragraph 1 of this article .

c. Such a request must be submitted within 120 days after the date on which the award was rendered or after the discovery of the facts relevant to nullification on the grounds of corruption, whichever is later and, in any event, within five years after the date on which the award was rendered.

d. The tribunal may nullify the award in whole or in part. If the award is nullified, the fact of nullification shall be communicated to the Parties Group. In such a case, the dispute may be submitted for decision to a new tribunal constituted under this Article or to any other available forum, notwithstanding the Contracting Parties waiver under paragraph 1.c. of this article.

*8. Default Rules*

The PCA Optional Rules for Arbitrating Disputes between Two States shall apply to supplement provisions of these Articles. The Parties Group may adopt supplemental provisions to ensure the smooth functioning of these rules, in particular to clarify the inter-relationship between these rules and the PCA Optional Rules.

*9. Response to Non-compliance*[49]

a. If a Contracting Party fails within a reasonable period of time to comply with its obligations as determined in the award, such Contracting Party shall, at the request of any Contracting Party in whose favour the award was rendered, enter into consulta-

---

49   Note: The text in paragraph 9 has been circulated separately. The Commentary indicates the general state of development on this issue in informal consultations at expert level.

tions with a view to reaching a mutually acceptable solution. If no satisfactory solution has been agreed within thirty days after the date of the request for consultations, any Contracting Party in whose favour the award was rendered, shall notify the other Contracting Party and the Parties Group if it intends to [take measures in response] [suspend the application to the other Contracting Party of obligations under this agreement].

b. The effect of any such [responsive measures][suspension] must be proportionate to the effect of the other Party's non-compliance.[50]
Such measures may not include suspension of the application of Article[s _ (General Treatment) and] _ (Expropriation) [and should not include denial of other protections to established investment].

c. At the request of any Party to the award upon conclusion of the thirty day period for consultation, the Parties Group shall consider the matter. [Until twenty days after the receipt by the Parties Group Secretariat of the request, responsive measures shall not be taken.] The Parties Group may:
i. make recommendations, by consensus minus the disputing Contracting Parties;
ii. suspend the non-complying Party's right to participate in decisions of the Parties Group, by consensus minus the non-complying Contracting Party; and
iii. [by consensus minus the Contracting Party which had intended to take responsive measures, decide that some or all of the responsive measures shall not be taken. The Contracting Party shall comply with that decision.]

d. Any dispute concerning the alleged failure of a Contracting Party to comply with its obligations as determined in an award or the lawfulness of any responsive measures shall, at the request of any Contracting Party that is party to the dispute, be submitted for decision to the arbitral tribunal which rendered the award or, if the original tribunal is unavailable, to a single member or three member arbitral tribunal designated by the Secretary-General. The request shall be submitted in the same fashion, and the proceedings carried out in accordance with the same rules as are applicable to a request made under paragraph 1.a of this Article, with such modifications as the tribunal deems appropriate, and the final award shall be issued no later than 60 days after the date of the request, in case of the original tribunal, or after the date of its formation, in the case of a new tribunal. [No responsive measures may be taken from the time of submission of a dispute unless authorised by the tribunal as an interim measure or found lawful.]

## INVESTOR-STATE PROCEDURES
## D. DISPUTES BETWEEN AN INVESTOR AND A CONTRACTING PARTY

### 1. Scope and Standing

a. This article applies to disputes between a Contracting Party and an investor of another Contracting Party concerning an alleged breach of an obligation of the former under this Agreement which causes loss or damage to the investor or its investment.

---

50 As variant of this approach, one delegation suggests utilizing language based on the WTO agreements:
"The level of the suspension of benefits ... shall be equivalent to the level of the nullification or impairment of benefits, which the aggrieved Party reasonably expected to accrue to it, resulting from the non-compliance."

b. An investor of another Contracting Party may also submit to arbitration under this article any investment dispute concerning any obligation which the Contracting Party has entered into with regard to a specific investment of the investor through:
i. An investment authorisation granted by its competent authorities specifically to the investor or investment,
ii. a written agreement granting rights with respect to [categories of subject matters] on which the investor has relied in establishing acquiring, or significantly expanding an investment.

*2. Means of Settlement*
Such a dispute should, if possible, be settled by negotiation or consultation. If it is not so settled, the investor may choose to submit it for resolution:
a. to any competent courts or administrative tribunals of the Contracting Party to the dispute;
b. in accordance with any dispute settlement procedure agreed upon prior to the dispute arising; or
c. by arbitration in accordance with this Article under:
i. the Convention on the Settlement of Investment Disputes between States and Nationals of other States (the "ICSID Convention"), if the ICSID Convention is available;
ii. the Additional Facility Rules of the Centre for Settlement of Investment Disputes ("ICSID Additional Facility"), if the ICSID Additional Facility is available;
iii. the Arbitration Rules of the United Nations Commission on International Trade Law ("UNCITRAL"); or
iv. the Rules of Arbitration of the International Chamber of Commerce ("ICC").

*3. Contracting Party Consent*
a. Subject only to paragraph 3.b, each Contracting Party hereby gives its unconditional consent to the submission of a dispute to international arbitration in accordance with the provisions of this Article.
b. A Contracting Party may, by notifying the Depositary upon deposit of its instrument of ratification or accession, provide that its consent given under paragraph 3.a only applies on the condition that the investor and the investment waive in writing the right to initiate any other dispute settlement procedure with respect to the same dispute and withdraw from any such procedure in progress before its conclusion. A Contracting Party may, at any time, reduce the scope of that limitation by notifying the Depositary.

*4. Time periods and notification*
An investor may submit a dispute for resolution pursuant to paragraph 2.c of this Article after sixty days following the date on which notice of intent to do so was received by the Contracting Party in dispute, but no later than five years from the date the investor first acquired or should have acquired knowledge of the events which gave rise to the dispute. Notice of intent, a copy of which shall be delivered to the Parties Group, shall specify:
a. the name and address of the disputing investor;
b. the name and address, if any, of the investment;
c. the provisions of this Agreement alleged to have been breached and any other relevant provisions;

d. the issues and the factual basis for the claim; and
e. the relief sought, including the approximate amount of any damages claimed.

5. *Written Agreement of the Parties*
The consent given by a Contracting Party in subparagraph 3.a, together with either the written submission of the dispute to resolution by the investor pursuant to subparagraph 2.c or the investor's advance written consent to such submission, shall constitute the written consent and the written agreement of the parties to the dispute to its submission for settlement for the purposes of Chapter II of the ICSID Convention, the ICSID Additional Facility Rules, Article 1 of the UNCITRAL Arbitration Rules, the Rules of Arbitration of the ICC, and Article II of the United Nations Convention on the Recognition and Enforcement of Foreign Arbitral Awards (the "New York Convention"). Neither party may withdraw its consent unilaterally, except as provided in paragraph 9.e of this Article.

6. *[EC or Contracting Party REIO text being developed, for possible inclusion]*

7. *Appointments to Arbitral Tribunals*
a. Unless the parties to the dispute otherwise agree, the tribunal shall comprise three arbitrators, one appointed by each of the disputing parties and the third, who shall be the presiding arbitrator, appointed by agreement of the disputing parties.
b. If a tribunal has not been constituted within 90 days after the date that a claim is submitted to arbitration, the arbitrator or arbitrators not yet appointed shall, on the request of either disputing party, be appointed by the appointing authority. For arbitration under paragraph 2, subparagraphs c.i, c.ii and c.iii, and paragraph 9, the appointing authority shall be the Secretary-General of ICSID. For arbitration under paragraph 2, subparagraph c.iv, the appointing authority shall be the International Court of Arbitration of the ICC.
c. The parties to a dispute submitted to arbitration under this article and the appointing authority should consider the appointment of:
i. members of the roster maintained by the Contracting Parties pursuant to Article C, paragraph 2.f; and
ii. individuals possessing expertise not found on the roster, if arbitration of a dispute requires special expertise on the Tribunal, rather than solely through expert advice under the rules governing the arbitration.
d. The appointing authority shall, as far as possible, carry out its function in consultation with the parties to the dispute.
e. In order to facilitate the appointment of arbitrators of the parties' nationality on three member ICSID tribunals under Article 39 of the ICSID Convention and Article 7 of Schedule C of the ICSID Additional Facility Rules, and without prejudice to each party's right independently to select an individual for appointment as arbitrator or to object to an arbitrator on grounds other than nationality:
i. the disputing Contracting Party agrees to the appointment of each individual member of a tribunal under paragraph 2.c.i or ii of this Article; and
ii. a disputing investor may initiate or continue a proceeding under paragraph 2.c.i or ii only on condition that the investor agrees in writing to the appointment of each individual member of the tribunal.

*8. Standing of the Investment*

An enterprise constituted or organised under the law of a Contracting Party but which, from the time of the events giving rise to the dispute until its submission for resolution under paragraph 2.c, was an investment of an investor of another Contracting Party, shall, for purposes of disputes concerning that investment, be considered "an investor of another Contracting Party" under this article and "a national of another Contracting State" for purposes of Article 25(2)(b) of the ICSID Convention regarding a dispute not submitted for resolution by the investor which owns or controls it.

*9. Consolidation of Multiple Proceedings*

a. In the event that two or more disputes submitted to arbitration with a Contracting Party under paragraph 2.c have a question of law or fact in common, the Contracting Party may submit to a separate arbitral tribunal, established under this paragraph, a request for the consolidated consideration of all or part of them. The request shall stipulate:

i. the names and addresses of the parties to the proceedings sought to be consolidated,

ii. the scope of the consolidation sought, and

iii. the grounds for the request.

The Contracting Party shall deliver the request to each investor party to the proceedings sought to be consolidated and a copy of the request to the Parties Group.

b. The request for consolidated consideration shall be submitted to arbitration under the rules chosen by agreement of the investor parties from the list contained in paragraph 2.c. The investor parties shall act as one side for the purpose of the formation of the tribunal.

c. If the investor parties have not agreed upon a means of arbitration and the nomination of an arbitrator within 30 days after the date of receipt of the request for consolidated consideration by the last investor to receive it:

i. the request shall be submitted to arbitration in accordance with this article under the UNCITRAL rules, and

ii. the appointing authority shall appoint the entire arbitral tribunal, in accordance with paragraph 7.

d. The arbitral tribunal shall assume jurisdiction over all or part of the disputes and the other arbitral proceedings shall be stayed or adjourned, as appropriate if, after considering the views of the parties, it decides that to do so would best serve the interest of fair and efficient resolution of the disputes and that the disputes fall within the scope of this paragraph.

e. An investor may withdraw the dispute from arbitration under this paragraph 9 and such dispute may not be resubmitted to arbitration under paragraph 2.c. If it does so no later than 15 days after receipt of notice of consolidation, its earlier submission of the dispute to that arbitration shall be without prejudice to the investor's recourse to dispute settlement other than under paragraph 2.c.

f. At the request of the Contracting Party, the arbitral tribunal established under this paragraph may decide, on the same basis and with the same effect as under paragraph 9.d, whether to assume jurisdiction over all or part of a dispute falling with the scope of paragraph 9.a which is submitted to arbitration after the initiation of consolidation proceedings.

## 10. Preliminary Objections

a. Any objection to the jurisdiction of the tribunal or to the admissibility of the application shall be raised no later than in the statement of defence.

b. Upon receipt of such an objection, the tribunal may suspend the proceedings on the merits.

c. After hearing the parties, the tribunal should give its decision, by which it shall either uphold the objection or reject it, within 60 days after the date on which the objection was made.

## 11. Indemnification

A Contracting Party shall not assert as a defence, counter-claim, right of set-off or for any other reason, that indemnification or other compensation for all or part of the alleged damages has been received or will be received pursuant to an indemnity, guarantee or insurance contract.[51]

## 12. Third Party Rights

The arbitral tribunal shall notify the Parties Group of its formation. Taking into account the views of the parties, it may give to any Contracting Party requesting it an opportunity to submit written views on the legal issues in dispute, provided that the proceedings are not unduly delayed thereby. Any Contracting Party requesting it within thirty days after receipt by the Parties Group of the notification of the tribunal's formation shall be given an opportunity to present its views on issues in dispute in which it has a legal interest.

## 13. Scientific and Technical Expertise

a. On request of a disputing Contracting Party or, unless the disputing Contracting Parties disapprove, on its own initiative, the tribunal may request a written report of a scientific or technical review board, or expert, on any factual issue concerning environmental, health, safety or other scientific or technical matters raised by a disputing Contracting Party in a proceeding, subject to such terms and conditions as such Parties may agree.

b. The board, or expert, shall be selected by the tribunal from among highly qualified, independent experts in the scientific or technical matters, after consultations with the disputing Parties and the scientific or technical bodies identified by those Parties.

c. The disputing Contracting Parties shall be provided:

i. advance notice of, and an opportunity to provide comments to the tribunal on, the proposed factual issues to be referred to the board, or expert; and

ii. a copy of the board's, or expert's, report and an opportunity to provide comments on the report to the tribunal.

d. The tribunal shall take the report and any comments by the disputing Contracting Parties on the report into account in the preparation of its award.

---

51   This subparagraph does not bar as a defence, counter-claim, right of set-off or for any other reason, that the Contracting Party has already paid indemnification or other compensation to the subrogee or assignee of the investor's rights in the matter.

## 14. Applicable law

a. Issues in dispute under paragraph 1.a. of this article shall be decided in accordance with this Agreement, interpreted and applied in accordance with the applicable rules of international law.

b. Issues in dispute under paragraph 1.b. of this article shall be decided in accordance with such rules of law as may be agreed by the parties to the dispute. In the absence of such agreement, such issues shall be decided in accordance with the law of the Contracting Party to the dispute (including its rules on the conflict of laws), the law governing the authorisation or agreement and such rules of international law as may be applicable.

## 15. Interim measures of relief

a. An arbitral tribunal established under this Article may recommend an interim measure of protection to preserve the rights of a disputing Contracting Party or to ensure that the Tribunal's jurisdiction is made fully effective.

b. The seeking of interim relief not involving the payment of damages, from judicial or administrative tribunals, by a party to a dispute submitted to arbitration under this article, for the preservation of its rights and interests pending resolution of the dispute, is not deemed a submission of the dispute for resolution for purposes of a Contracting Party's limitation of consent under paragraph 3.b, and is permissible in arbitration under any of the provisions of paragraph 2.c.

## 16. Final awards

a. The arbitral tribunal, in its award shall set out its findings of law and fact, together with the reasons therefor and may, at the request of a Party, provide the following forms of relief:

i. a declaration that the Contracting Party has failed to comply with its obligations under the this Agreement;

ii. pecuniary compensation, which shall include interest from the time the loss or damage was incurred until time of payment;

iii. restitution in kind in appropriate cases, provided that the Contracting Party may pay pecuniary compensation in lieu thereof where restitution is not practicable; and

iv. with the Agreement of the parties to the dispute, any other form of relief.

b. In appropriate cases where the loss or damage was incurred by an investment which remains a going concern, the tribunal may direct that the compensation or restitution be made to the investment.

c. An arbitration award shall be final and binding between the parties to the dispute and shall be carried out without delay by the party against whom it is issued, subject to its post-award rights under the arbitral systems utilised.

d. The award shall be drafted consistently with the requirements of paragraph 17 and shall be a publicly available document. A copy of the award shall be delivered to the Parties Group by the Secretary-General of ICSID, for an award under the ICSID Convention or the Rules of the ICSID Additional Facility; by the Secretary-General of the ICC International Court of Arbitration, for an award under its rules; and by the tribunal, for an award under the UNCITRAL rules.

## 17. Confidential and Proprietary Information
Parties and other participants in proceedings shall protect any confidential or proprietary information which may be revealed in the course of the proceedings and which is designated as such by the party providing the information. They shall not reveal such information without written authorisation from the party which provided it.

## 18. Place of Arbitration and Enforceability
Any arbitration under this article shall be held in a state that is party to the New York Convention. Claims submitted to arbitration under this article shall be considered to arise out of a commercial relationship or transaction for purposes of Article 1 of that Convention. Each Contracting Party shall provide for the enforcement of the pecuniary obligations imposed by an award rendered pursuant to this Article D.

## 19. Tribunal member fees
Fees and expenses payable to a member of an arbitral tribunal established under these Articles will be subject to schedules established by the Parties Group and in force at the time of the constitution of the tribunal.

## 20. Supplemental Provisions
The Parties Group may adopt supplemental provisions to ensure the smooth functioning of these rules, in particular to clarify the inter-relationship between these rules and the rules of arbitration available under paragraph 2.c of this article D.

(...)


VI. EXCEPTIONS AND SAFEGUARDS
GENERAL EXCEPTIONS[52]

1. This Article shall not apply to Article IV, 2 and 3 (Expropriation and compensation and protection from strife).
2. Nothing in this Agreement shall be construed:
a. to prevent any Contracting Party from taking any action which it considers necessary for the protection of its essential security interests:
(i) taken in time of war, or armed conflict, or other emergency in international relations;
(ii) relating to the implementation of national policies or international agreements respecting the non-proliferation of weapons of mass destruction;
(iii) relating to the production of arms and ammunition;
b. to require any Contracting Party to furnish or allow access to any information the disclosure of which it considers contrary to its essential security interests;
c. to prevent any Contracting Party from taking any action in pursuance of its obligations under the United Nations Charter for the maintenance of international peace and security.

---

52  This text was proposed for discussion by the Chairman. It is under consideration by the Negotiating Group.

3. Subject to the requirement that such measures are not applied in a manner which would constitute a means of arbitrary or unjustifiable discrimination between Contracting Parties, or a disguised investment restriction, nothing in this Agreement shall be construed to prevent any Contracting Party from taking any measure necessary for the maintenance of public order.[53]

4. Actions or measures taken pursuant to this Article shall be notified to the Parties Group.

5. If a Contracting Party (the "requesting Party") has reason to believe that actions or measures taken by another Contracting Party (the "other Party") under this article have been taken solely for economic reasons, or that such actions or measures are not in proportion to the interest being protected, it may request consultations with that other Party in accordance with Article V, B.1 (State-State Consultation Procedures). That other Party shall provide information to the requesting Party regarding the actions or measures taken and the reasons therefor.

*TRANSACTIONS IN PURSUIT OF MONETARY AND EXCHANGE RATE POLICIES[54]*
3

1. Articles XX (National Treatment), YY (Most Favoured Nation Treatment) and ZZ (Transparency) do not apply to transactions carried out in pursuit of monetary or exchange rate policies by a central bank or monetary authority of a Contracting Party.

2. Where such transactions do not conform with Articles XX (National Treatment), YY (Most Favoured Nation Treatment) and ZZ (Transparency), they shall not be used as a means of avoiding the Contracting Party's commitments or obligations under the Agreement.

*TEMPORARY SAFEGUARD*

1. A Contracting Party may adopt or maintain measures inconsistent with its obligations under:
· Article xx (Transfers);
· Article yy, paragraph 1.1 (National Treatment) relating to cross-border capital transactions[55]
(a) in the event of serious balance-of-payments and external financial difficulties or threat thereof; or
(b) where, in exceptional circumstances, movements of capital cause, or threaten to cause, serious difficulties for macroeconomic management, in particular monetary and

---

53 The public order exception may be invoked only where a genuine and sufficiently serious threat is posed to one of the fundamental interests of society.

54 While one delegation questions the need for any specific provisions carving out transactions by a central bank or monetary authority in pursuit of monetary and exchange rate policies, most delegations can support adoption of this text.

55 It is understood that such measures may not discriminate between resident entities owned or controlled by investors of other Contracting Parties and resident entities controlled by local investors. Some delegations question whether this bullet is necessary, but would like to consider the IMF arguments in this respect. See Commentary.

exchange rate policies.[56]

2. Measures referred to in paragraph 1:

(a) shall be consistent with the Articles of Agreement of the International Monetary Fund;

(b) shall not exceed those necessary to deal with the circumstances described in paragraph 1;[57]

(c) shall be temporary and shall be eliminated as soon as conditions permit.

3. (a) Measures referred to in paragraph 1 shall be promptly notified to the Parties Group and to the International Monetary Fund, including any changes in such measures.

(b) Measures referred to in paragraph 1 and any changes therein shall be subject to review and approval or disapproval within six months of their adoption and every six months thereafter until their elimination.

(c) These reviews shall address the compliance of any measure with paragraph 2, in particular the elimination of measures in accordance with paragraph 2 (c).

4. Measures referred to in paragraph 1 and any changes therein that are approved by theInternational Monetary Fund in the exercise of its jurisdiction shall be considered as consistent with this Article.

5. With regard to measures referred to in paragraph 1, and any changes therein, not falling within paragraph 4:

(a) The Parties Group shall consider the implications of the measures adopted under this Article for the obligations of the Contracting Party concerned under this Agreement.

(b) The Parties Group shall request an assessment by the International Monetary Fund of the conditions mentioned under paragraph 1 and of the consistency of any measures with paragraph 2. Any such assessment by the International Monetary Fund shall be accepted by the Parties Group.

(c) Unless the International Monetary Fund determines that the measure is either consistent or inconsistent with the provisions of this Article, the Parties Group may either approve or disapprove the measure. The Parties Group shall establish procedures for this purpose.

6. The Contracting Parties shall seek agreement with the International Monetary Fund regarding the role of the International Monetary Fund in the review procedures established under this Article.

7. Measures referred to in paragraph 1 and any changes therein that are approved by the International Monetary Fund in the exercise of its jurisdiction or determined to

---

56 Several delegations feel that the reference to "macroeconomic management" is too broad. They could accept paragraph 1 (b) if "macroeconomic management, in particular monetary and exchange rate policies" were replaced with "the operation of monetary or exchange rate policies". Some delegations question whether paragraph 1 (b) was necessary. On the other hand, other delegations would have preferred a provision in which restrictions could be taken in cases of serious difficulties for "the operation of economic, monetary or exchange rate policies".

57 One delegation suggests adding: "and shall provide for the least disruptive effect to the functioning of the Agreement". Reference is also made in this context to the language in paragraph 2. (c) of Article XII of the GATS: "shall avoid unnecessary damage to the commercial, economic and financial interest of any other Member".

be consistent with this Article by the International Monetary Fund or the Parties Group cannot be subject to dispute settlement.[58]

Additional Article

If a dispute arises under this Article or under Article ... (obligations under the Articles of Agreement of the Fund), a Dispute Settlement Panel shall request an assessment by the International Monetary Fund of the consistency of the measures with its Articles of Agreement, of the conditions mentioned under paragraph 1 and of the consistency of any measures as applied with paragraph 2. Any such assessment by the International Monetary Fund shall be accepted by the Panel.[59]

(…)

---

58 The dispute settlement provisions would apply if the measure as actually applied differed from that approved or determined to be consistent with this Article.
59 Text proposed by the IMF and supported by most delegations. Placement of this proposed text in the Agreement may need to be considered further. Four delegations oppose the proposal that assessments by the IMF shall be accepted by the Panel and expressed concern that, as drafted, this text leaves no room for the Panel to assess compliance with the MAI Safeguard provision.

# About the authors

MARCEL BRUS is Senior Lecturer in the Department of Public International Law at Leiden University. His research and teaching concentrates on the interaction between international politics and international law, with special emphasis on the development of dispute settlement mechanisms in international law, and on international environmental law. At the time this book was prepared he was Research Coordinator in the E.M. Meijers Institute for Legal Research of the Leiden Law Faculty, and Director of the Ph.D. Programme of the Leiden Law Faculty. He has held a part-time position as senior teaching fellow at the Law Faculty of the University of Oxford since September 1997.

HUIPING CHEN is Lecturer in Law at Xiamen University Law since 1995. She studied international economic law at Xiamen University from where she graduated in 1990. Between 1990 and 1994 she studied civil and commercial law. From 1994 until 1999 she worked on her Ph.D. in international economic law. She is author of several publications on multilateral investment law and related subjects.

VALPY FITZGERALD is Reader in International Economics and Finance at the University of Oxford, and Professorial Fellow of St Antony's College, Oxford. He is Director of the Finance and Trade Policy Research Centre at Oxford, and Extraordinary Professor of Development Economics at the Institute of Social Studies at The Hague. Professor FitzGerald has acted as an advisor to a number of developing countries and international organizations and is presently a consultant to the UK Department for International Development on multilateral investment negotiations and a member of the UNCTAD expert group on international capital flows. His current research interests include the effect of global financial instability on vulnerable economies, the links between banks and productive investment in industrializing countries, and the economic consequences of conflict in poor societies.

MARK KOULEN is Counsellor in the Trade and Finance Division of the Secretariat of the World Trade Organization.

PETER MALANCZUK is Director (and founder) of the GLODIS-Institute, Institute of Globalization, International Economic Law and Dispute Settlement. He is Head of the Department of International Law of the Law Faculty, Erasmus University Rotterdam. He is Honorary Professor at Peking University, at Nankai University, Tianjin, and at the China University of Political Science and Law, Beijing. He is also Chairman of the International Law Association (ILA) Study Group on State

Responsibility. Furthermore, he is Counsel of the international law firm Lalive& Partners, Geneva, and Arbitrator of the China International Economic and Trade Arbitration Commission (CIETAC).

Previously he was Professor of International Law at the University of Amsterdam and the legal assistant of the President of the Iran-United States Claims Tribunal in the Hague. He has also held positions at the Max-Planck-Institute for Comparative Public Law and International Law in Heidelberg and the Universities of Exeter, England and Giessen, Germany. He has been visiting Professor at Michigan Law School, Moscow State University, Peking University, and other universities.

His more than 130 publications include the 7$^{th}$ revised edition (1997) of the widely used textbook *Akehurst's Modern Introduction to International Law*, which has been translated into Japanese and Lithuanian. He is the Series Editor of the book series *Studies and Materials on the Settlement of International Disputes* (Kluwer Law International), has been a General Editor of *The Netherlands Yearbook of International Law* and is on the advisory boards of a number of other international journals.

EVA NIEUWENHUYS studied international law at the University of Amsterdam from where she was graduated in 1985. She worked as researcher at the Netherlands Institute for Social and Economic Law at Utrecht University until 1992 when she joined Leiden University as lecturer at the Law Faculty, Department *Metajuridica*. In 1995 she obtained her doctorate with a thesis on the regulation of foreign investment in Indonesia and China. She is author of several publications on the Chinese and Indonesian investment laws, on transnational enterprises and human rights, and on the MAI.

NICO SCHRIJVER is Professor of International Law at the Free University of Amsterdam and the Institute of Social Studies, The Hague. He is also Visiting Professor Europe and North-South relations at the *Université libre de Bruxelles* and serves on various advisory committees of the Netherlands Government on foreign policy, international development co-operation and international law as well as ad hoc advisory bodies of the United Nations. Professor Schrijver is the General Rapporteur of the Committee on Legal Aspects of Sustainable Development of the International Law Association and the Chairman of the Academic Council on the United Nations System. His book *Sovereignty over Natural Resources: Balancing Rights and Duties*, Cambridge University Press, 1997, includes an extensive chapter on 'International Investment Law: from nationalism to pragmatism'.

MARINUS SIKKEL is Head of the Investment Policy and International Organisations Division of the Netherlands Ministry of Economic Affairs. He is responsible for international Agreements relating to investment, commodity Agreements and Unctad-matters. He was head of the Netherlands delegation in the MAI negotiations and chaired drafting group 3 of the MAI. Since 1998 he is the chairman of the Working Party on the Guidelines for Multinational Enterprises of the OECD. He studied Law and Economics at the Erasmus University of Rotterdam, which awarded him a Masters' Degree in Economics in 1976.

## About the Authors

SAMAN ZIA-ZARIFI is Associate Counsel and Director, Program on Academic Freedom, at Human Rights Watch. At the time he wrote his article for this book he was senior research fellow at Erasmus University, Rotterdam, Department of International Law, where he conducted a project on the legal status of multinational corporations. He is co-editor, along with Prof. Menno Kamminga, of Liability of Multinational Corporations Under International law. He has written extensively on the human rights impact of multinational corporations and international economic law. He received his B.A. and Juris Doctor degrees from Cornell University and an LL.M. in Public International Law from New York University School of Law.

# Index

## A
Agreement on Arab Investment 26
Agreement on the Application of Sanitary and Phytosanitary Measures 129, 133
Amnesty International 132
Annan, K. 131
Arab Investment Court 26
Argentina 80
assets
 · intangible 8
 · tangible 8
Association of Petroleum Exporting Countries (APEC), Non-Binding Investment Principles 76, 82, 139
Association of South-East Asian Nations, Agreement for the Promotion and Protection of Investments 26, 138
awards, arbitral 4, 28

## B
balance of payments 43
bargaining
 · positions 40, 64
 · power 58
barriers
 · import 56
 · trade 116
bilateral investment treaties (BITs) 4, 10, 17, 25, 27, 38, 64, 69, 73, 80, 82, 131, 138, 157, 161, 181, 188, 190, 195, 196, 202
 · legal status of 26
Brazil 56, 58, 84, 157
Bretton Woods 18
Bulgaria 80

## C
Calvo doctrine 74, 79
Canada 11, 31, 79, 131, 161, 164, 170, 171, 185, 191, 192, 201
Canada Foreign Investment Review Act 184
capital
 · foreign 8
 · free movement of 60
 · flight 58, 62, 63
 · flows 49-51, 56-57
 · flows, management of 53-56
 · surges 51-53
Cartagena Free Trade Agreement 139
Chile 52, 58, 84, 191
China 45, 45, 67, 84
 · national treatment and 86-87
Convention Establishing the Multilateral Investment Guarantee Agency (MIGA Convention) 24
Convention for the Elimination of All Forms of Discrimination Against Women (CEDAW) 105
Convention for the Elimination of Racial Discrimination (CERD) 105
corporate conduct 203
Costa Rica 191, 196, 197
criminal acts 112

## D
decolonization 21
deregulation 1, 8
developing countries, distinct interests between 40-42
development, social and economic 1, 28
development, sustainable 2, 3, 27, 28, 44, 45, 48, 54, 111
discrimination against foreign nationals 53, 72, 80, 186
dispute settlement 8, 10, 64, 85, 128, 194
 · arbitration 15, 140, 150-155
 · consultation, conciliation and mediation 141
 · interim measures 154

- international investments and 4, 17, 58, 140, 148-155
- investor-to-state procedures 148, 154
- methods of 149-150
- non-compliance and countermeasures 146-148

distribution of risks 149
double taxation treaties (DTTs) 61, 62
Draft Convention on Investments Abroad (Abs-Schawcross Convention) 22

### E
East Asian crisis 50, 51, 101, 124
Egypt 80
ELSI (Elettronica Sicula S.p.A.) Case 143
Energy Charter Treaty (ECT) 26, 29, 73, 76, 81, 82, 139
enterprises, national 8
entry, unqualified right of 10
environment 3, 15, 33, 48-49, 65, 101, 128-129, 165, 167
European Commission 192
European Community (EC) 151, 196, 197, 201
European Convention on Human Rights (ECHR) 169
European Energy Charter 43
European Union (EU) 4, 25, 35, 60, 61, 75, 78, 175, 191
expropriation 10, 20, 124, 125, 157, 168, 187, 202
extraterritoriality 165

### F
financial services sector 55
*Financial Times* 163
foreign direct investment (FDI) 17-19, 24, 36, 44-45, 52, 62, 102, 110, 111, 116, 112, 124, 127-128, 161, 195, 196
France 12, 25, 31, 52, 79, 138, 166, 171, 172, 175
free admission and free establishment 91-95, 194, 195
Friendship, Commerce and Navigation (FCN) Treaties 25

### G
General Agreement on Tariffs and Trade (GATT) 18, 25, 66, 116, 127, 129, 130, 147, 182, 183-184, 185, 189, 200

- Resolution on International Investment for Economic Development 183

Germany 25
global financial markets, volatility of 37, 51
globalization 1, 12, 161, 166-167, 172-174, 179
- and loss of local culture 168

### H
home state 5, 11, 27
Hong Kong China 196, 197, 201
host state 5, 64, 99
human rights 3, 8, 9, 33
- and economic development 103
- and political constituencies 116
- internationally-prohibited acts 9
- labour rights 9, 15, 48-49, 65, 101, 106-107
- linking with international investment 10, 101, 117, 130, 133
- questions of primacy of vis-à-vis international economic law 104
- significance of economic policy to 8, 103-109
- social rights 9, 105-106
Human Rights Watch 132

### I
immigration laws 85
import substitution 65
Inter-Arab Investment Protection Treaty 26
International Center for the Settlement of Investment Disputes (ICSID) 143-144, 150-152
International Chamber of Commerce (ICC) 150, 178
- 1972 Guidelines for International Investment 4, 27, 32
- International Court of Arbitration 151
international code of conduct 2
International Court of Justice (ICJ) 143
International Covenant on Civil and Political Rights (ICCPR) 103
International Covenant on Economic, Social and Cultural Rights (ICESCR) 103
international economic institutions
- increasingly political tone of 134

· public demonstrations and 103
· reluctance to address social issues 118
international financial architecture, reform of 50-51
international governmental organizations 1
international insurance facility 23
International investment agreements
· developing countries and 38-40
· sources of international law and 181
international investment community
· lack of interaction with international human rights community 130
international investment flows 35
international investment regulation 17, 39, 42, 52, 83, 181
International Labour Organization (ILO) 107, 119, 132, 133, 174
· Codes of Conduct for Multinational Enterprises 30
· Declaration on Core Labour Standards 33, 171
· Tripartite Declaration of Principles Concerning Multinational Enterprises and Social Policy 19
International Law Commission (ILC) 147
International Monetary Fund (IMF) 1, 51, 131, 158
· Interim Committee 52
International Trade Organization (ITO) 183, 185
· Havana Charter for Trade and Employment 18, 21
internationally-recognized prohibited acts 108
internet 172, 177
intervention 52
investment 2, 7, 10, 15, 124, 203
· and multilateral trading system 181, 191, 193
· conditions of 2
· domestic 5, 47
· expatriate 5
· foreign 4, 6, 7, 18, 187, 192, 193, 194, 203
· importance of to poor countries 36-38
· international regulatory framework for 5, 43-44, 82, 90, 194
· promotion of 27
investment incentive 67, 190

investment protection 4, 13, 25, 29, 33, 42, 55, 64, 125, 202
investments, phases of 73
investors 2, 15
· domestic 70
· foreign 5, 6, 10, 70, 79
· rights and responsibilities of 32, 33
Iran-United States Claims Tribunal 140
Iraq 108
Italy 52, 143

*J*
Japan 191, 196, 197, 201
Jospin, L. 166

*K*
Kellogg-Briand pact 118

*L*
League of Nations 61
legal person 8
liberalization of foreign investment 7, 31, 45-46, 49, 64, 65, 67-68, 79, 112, 165, 200
· social instability 114
· impacts on developing countries 84-87, 123
local remedies rule 142-143
Lomé Conventions (Convention of Cotounou) 26

*M*
Maghreb Union Treaty 26
Malaysia 52, 58
market access 175
· asymmetric 56-58
· concessions for 59
markets, heterogeneity of 95
MERCOSUR, Colonia and Buenos Aires Investment Protocols 139
Mexico 115, 161
money laundering 61
Multilateral Agreement on Investment (MAI) of the OECD 2, 29, 47, 69, 115, 127, 130-131, 163, 182
· failure of 11, 29, 102, 117, 137, 162, 172-176
· lessons learned from failure 176-177
· national treatment obligations as "hard law" 72
· politicization of 164-165, 175
Multilateral Investment Convention 27

Multilateral Investment Guarantee Agency (MIGA) 4, 162
multilateral investment guarantee facilities 17
multilateral investment rules 195-202, 203
multilateral investment treaties (MITs) 4, 10, 80
- human rights linkages and 101, 109-121, 129, 130
- implementation of 123-130
- minimum standards of behaviour and 121
- objectives of 28, 121-122
- strengthening institutions of 132-133
multilateral tax agreement 61
Multinational Arab Guarantee Agency 23
multinational corporations (MNCs) 3, , 46, 47, 48, 108

## N
national security 64
National Treatment Instrument 162
nationalization 19
negotiations 6, 58, 198-199
- assistance and reciprocity with developing countries 58-60
Netherlands' Credit Corporation (NCM) 23
Netherlands, the 163, 171
- pig farming and 168-169
New International Economic Order (NIEO) 19, 117
New York Convention on the Recognition and Enforcement of Foreign Arbitral Awards 150, 155
non-governmental organizations (NGOs) 11, 30, 59, 65, 89, 106, 119, 131, 132, 133, 137, 164-165, 170-171, 172-173, 175-176, 177, 178, 179
North American Free Trade Agreement (NAFTA) 4, 26, 29, 42, 43, 49, 69, 81, 82, 83, 103, 116, 125, 128, 138, 161, 164, 171, 190, 196
- Ethyl Case 156, 169-170
not-lowering-standards clause 11
Nuremberg trials 108

## O
offshore companies 54
Organization for Economic Cooperation and Development (OECD) 2, 60, 78, 101, 103, 107, 111, 120, 162, 175, 192
- Business and Industry Advisory Committee (BIAC) 178
- Codes on the Liberalization of Current Invisible Operations and on the Liberalization of Capital Movements 22, 161, 162
- commitment to Copenhagen Declaration 112
- Draft Taxation Convention/Model Tax Conventions 61
- Guidelines for Multinational Enterprises 11, 19, 32, 49, 114, 132, 158, 176, 196
Organization of the Islamic Conference, 1981 Investment Agreement 138

## P
parent company 92
performance requirements 10, 44-48, 67, 91, 92, 190, 203
Permanent Court of Arbitration (PCA), Optional Rules for Arbitrating Disputes between Two States 145
Peru 191
Philippines, the 80
Poland 196
privitization 1, 8, 31, 54, 65, 67
property rights 15, 22
prosperity-protection 7
protectionism 9

## R
Reformulated Gasoline dispute 119
Regional Economic Integration Organization (REIO) 75
reserve requirements 53
Ricardo, D. 106, 110
Rio Declaration of Principles on Environment and Development 33, 48
risk assessment 50
Rostow, W. 18
Ruggie, J. 110
Russia 56, 69

## S

services 79
Shihata, I. 24
social responsibility 9
societal organization 113
soft law 4
South Africa 108
South Korea 56, 58, 115, 196, 197, 201
sovereignty
- cultural 31-32
- economic 7, 65, 82
- permanent 4, 21
- state 6, 30, 82, 85, 158, 195

Spain 52
standstill principle 91
state responsibility, international law of 147
states 1, 20-23, 73
- industrialized 4

subsidies 127
Switzerland 196

## T

Taiwan 58
tariffs 18
tax cooperation, international 60-63
tax haven 61
taxation 6, 60
- corporate 60
- domestic 55

technology transfer 46, 47, 190
Tokyo Round of Multilateral Trade Negotiations 186
trade and investment 13, 191-200
trade unions 178
transfer pricing 63
transnational enterprises 1, 8, 89
- business strategies under multilateral investment system 91-98
- opportunities for investment 95-96
- social responsibility of 2
- treatment of 90-91

transparency 10, 67, 71, 75, 130, 177, 194, 197, 203
secrecy in MAI negotiations 173
treatment
- most-favoured-nation 7, 42, 67, 126, 139, 157, 187
- national 7, 31, 40, 42, 64, 68-76, 79, 80, 97, 126, 139, 157, 187
- national and most-favoured nation rules, exceptions to 76-79
- national and most-favoured nation rules, liberalization and 81-84
- of foreign investors 6, 15, 22, 26, 31, 38, 65, 68-76, 185
- principle of equitable and non-discriminatory 7, 10, 49, 68, 91, 126, 194, 197

## U

UNCITRAL rules 150
United Kingdom 86
United Nations 117
- Charter 77, 106
- Conference on Trade and Development (UNCTAD)19, 59, 111, 120, 122, 131, 133, 192, 196
- Conference on Trade and Development (UNCTAD), Midrand Conference 192
- Development Programme (UNDP)111
- Development Programme (UNDP) Human Development Report 1
- Draft Code of Conduct on Transnational Enterprises 4, 28, 32, 117, 196
- Economic and Social Council (ECOSOC) 118, 133
- General Assembly (UNGA) Commission on Transnational Corporations 20
- Industrial Development Organization (UNIDO)19
- Model Double Taxation Convention between Developed and Developing Countries 62
- Sub-Commission on Prevention of Discrimination and Protection of Minorities 133
- Special Fund 18

United States of America 11, 30, 35, 56, 69, 73, 81, 82, 108, 119, 130, 143, 161, 162, 175, 176, 184, 192, 198, 201
Universal Declaration of Human Rights (UDHR)103, 106
Uruguay Round 30, 34, 43, 59, 66, 183, 184, 191, 200
US Overseas Private Investment Corporation 23

**V**
Venezuela 119

**W**
*Wall Street Journal* 163
wealth, just distribution of 99
wealthy countries, benefits from liberal worldwide investment system 96-97
wider-investment instrument 11
World Bank 130, 131
- Convention on the Settlement of Investment Disputes between States and Nationals of other States (ICSID) 22-23, 150-152, 155, 157
- Guidelines on the Treatment of Foreign Investment 4, 28, 29, 139
- Inspection Panel 10, 133
- International Finance Corporation (IFC) 18

World Economic Forum 89
World Summit on Social Development 1, 33
World Trade Organization (WTO) 2, 43, 61, 66, 111, 117, 130, 131, 132, 138, 147, 178, 192, 196, 203
- Agreement on Government Procurement 185, 186
- Agreement on Subsidies and Countervailing Measures 185, 190-191
- Agreement on Trade Related Aspects of Intellectual Property Rights (TRIPS) 13, 139, 161, 185, 188-189
- Agreement on Trade Related Investment Measures (TRIMS) 13, 66, 123, 127, 139, 161, 185, 189-190, 200
- Appellate Dispute Settlement Body 147
- Dispute Settlement Understanding (DSU) 43, 197
- General Agreement on Trade in Services (GATS) 12, 30, 42, 43, 75, 82, 83-84, 139, 147, 161, 185, 186-188, 200
- Ministerial Meeting, Seattle, November-December 1999 14, 34, 89, 182, 196, 198, 199
- Multilateral Agreements on Trade in Goods 185
- Telecommunications Agreement 43
- Working Group on the Relationship of Trade and Investment 12, 13, 30, 182, 192-193, 196, 197, 199, 200